THE ART OF SOUTHEAST ASIA

LOUIS FRÉDÉRIC

THE ART OF
SOUTHEAST ASIA

TEMPLES AND SCULPTURE

FOREWORD BY

JEANNINE AUBOYER

Curator of the Musée Guimet, Paris

HARRY N. ABRAMS, INC., NEW YORK

To Her Royal Highness

Princess Pantip Chumbhot of Nagara Svarga

and

Her Most Serene Highness

Princess Marsi Paribatra

Translated from the French by Arnold Rosin

Gravure plates printed in France

Text printed in Holland. Bound in West-Germany

CONTENTS

FOREWORD

THIS IS THE SECOND BOOK that Louis Frédéric has devoted to the art and architecture of Southeast Asia, completing the excellent material he published in his book on Indian art. Thanks to these two works, we now have the essential information to help us to appreciate the beauty of these styles, to study their relationships or dissimilarities, and, if necessary, to refer to a known or unpublished work of art. Collected and selected with conscientiousness and integrity, the material reflects the author's enthusiasm and interest in Southeast Asian civilizations.

The material shows India's cultural role in these areas immediately following contact established by sea or land. It also stresses the various contributions, the variation of certain themes and their local distortions, and the original qualities of each civilization represented.

The best known of these civilizations already proved the importance and extent of Indian influence. Scholarship makes it easier to analyze the degrees of this influence, to understand its detailed aspects elsewhere, to appreciate the nuances of reaction it encountered or caused, to stress what really belongs to it, and is the result of the genius of each civilization influenced by India. This influence was effected without haste or violence, and the situation is so rare that it is worth emphasizing. India herself does not seem to have preserved the memory of her historical past, and not until contemporary research was done did she become aware of it. Such pacific influencing, well within the tradition of nonviolence proper to Indian civilization, was promulgated by bold merchants, travelers, and missionaries stimulated by the desire to spread their faith. Except in unusual circumstances, India never interfered in these *manu militari* countries. Her own traditions, whose force and perpetuity are familiar, found a soil suitable for implantation among less cultured peoples, who were predisposed to adopt ideas in accordance with their political and social structure.

This Indian impulse took different forms. A careful study reveals constant laws and local interpretations which often bordered on genius. This was the case with the Khmers, the most gifted in the field of artistic creation, who developed beautiful architectural forms based on Indian ones without copying them, yet giving them a new accent. The result was a paradox— Indian architectural symbolism, even within India itself, was never interpreted with more precision than in the Khmer Empire, nor elsewhere related so closely to the idea of royalty. It is even thought that their artistic production soon became one of the essential means whereby Khmer royalty affirmed its omnipotence and its belonging to a divine world, and asserted its authority for undeniable political and social pre-eminence. It was in such an ambitious perspective that the famous Angkor mountain temples were built.

Without entering into detail, it is undeniable that the results of Indian influence in Southeast Asia acquired in other regions certain aspects which at least were equally original to those in the Khmer Empire, if not similar. The famous Borobudur Stupa in Java, for example, which is so impregnated with Indian influence that it is considered the very expression of this hybrid civilization—once qualified as Indo-Javanese—is its most characteristic representative. Without

7

citing the complex symbolism which seems to have prevailed at its conception and whose source lies in Indian art, the iconography and style of the Borobudur reliefs justify its being regarded as one of the greatest achievements of Asiatic art.

It may be possible to imagine that Southeast Asia would never have enjoyed such a great artistic period without having benefited from India's influence, but it is only fair to mention the Chinese influence, which although late was felt in many of these countries. It resulted in a great variety of expression and an exchange of new formulas or, rather, of decorative combinations.

For an art historian it is fascinating to discover the role each country played in the development of a cultural past. But it is often a delicate task, all the more so where there is a close and scarcely glimpsed mingling of aboriginal elements, where successive contributions persist for several centuries, and where the progressive resurgence of primitive material is evident.

However, such comparisons will help us to understand the analogies, divergencies, contaminations, and vigor of ingenious creations. These comparisons are all the more striking because of the limited number of examples shown in this book. Styles were created and differentiated from one another, affinities were established, and similarities—often misleading—seem obvious. An almost inextricable intermingling of ideas several centuries old overlaps and becomes rigid. In short, we enter a particular world where we must be wary of hasty conclusions, easy solutions, and even theories.

As always, we must turn to historical facts which confirm a change in iconography or decoration. Many civilizations here represented have a chronology corroborated by inscriptions on stone or dependable chronicles. In spite of obscure periods where only conjecture is possible, the main development of these civilizations can now be studied even in detail. Thus the material in this book is not only interesting for itself but also forms a logical complement to the author's first work, *The Art of India*.

In every architectural form, we shall easily find an Indian formula often simplified or transformed, but in any case adapted to the needs and technical means of the Indianized kingdoms of Southeast Asia. The traditional symbolic importance given to the roof in India will appear more systematic and stylized here, but it would seem meaningless if we were not familiar with their prototypes. The curvilinear roof of the *sikharas* (best represented at Bhuvaneshvara in Orissa and Khajuraho in Bundelkhand, and used as far as the environs of Madras) was adopted in Burma, where it was combined with other Indian elements, such as the stupa. The recessed pyramidal roof, with its "reduced edifices" and acroteria, or accent pieces, retains its symbolism everywhere; it inspired many variations, a careful study of which will lead to the prototype or intermediary, both originating in India.

This origin is more evident in sculpture and iconography. In studying them, we find verification of both the existence of an initial Indian influence that was constantly renewed during the course of centuries, and the vigor of aboriginal beliefs which modified or altered Indian motifs while still becoming generally Indianized.

The progressive renewal of Indian motifs by aboriginal elements, so evident in Eastern Java, doubtless led to a desire for artistic liberation on the traditional plane—but the result was the flowering of different styles gradually breaking away from the past.

All this has been taken into consideration by Louis Frédéric, whose fine choice of illustrations represents considerable effort, for almost all the photographs were taken by the author and reflect his good taste and sensitivity.

This homage to Asiatic civilizations is a great credit to the major project launched by UNESCO for a better mutual understanding of East and West.

JEANNINE AUBOYER
Curator of the Musée Guimet, Paris
Member of the French National
Commission for UNESCO

PREFACE

THIS BOOK was completed as a result of a six months' journey of study made under the auspices of the United Nations Educational, Scientific, and Cultural Organization. The author, presented to this organization by the French National Committee of UNESCO, received a fellowship in the East-West Major Project. During the course of his journey to Burma, Thailand, Laos, Cambodia, South Vietnam, and Indonesia, he was constantly aided by the national commissions of the countries in question and their governments, thanks to which he was able to obtain the necessary documentation to accomplish this work.

The author would very much like to thank them all and dedicate this book to them, which he hopes will be able, in its own modest way, to participate in the campaign of better understanding between the countries of Asia and Europe organized by the East-West Major Project of the UNESCO programs.

This work was the logical outcome of a book written by the author in 1959 and issued by the present publishers under the title, *The Art of India.*

The author would also like to thank the individuals who aided him by their encouragement, advice, and collaboration:

In France:

His publisher, M. O'Meara
M. Y. Brunswick, of the French National Commission of UNESCO
M. G.-H. Rivière, President of the International Council of Museums
M. F. Trapero, of UNESCO
M. Vadime Elisséeff, Secretary of the East-West Committee and Curator of the Musée Cernuschi, Paris
Mlle. Jeannine Auboyer, Curator of the Musée Guimet, Paris

In Burma:

U Twe Sein, Assistant Engineer, Archaeology Dept., Pagan
U Aung Thaw, Director, Archaeological Survey, Rangoon
Sein Maung U, Officer-in-Charge, Archaeological Survey, Mandalay
U Tin Aye, National Commission for UNESCO, Rangoon
M. Jean Perrin, Secretary of the French Embassy, Rangoon
U Thant Thut and U Daw Nyunt Han, Museum Directors, Rangoon
M. Percy, Officer-in-Charge, Archaeology Dept., Hmawza, Prome

In Thailand:

H.R.H. Prince Subhadradis Diskul, Chief Curator, Archaeological Services, National Museum, Bangkok

H.R.H. Princess Pantip Chumbhot of Nagara Svarga, Bangkok
M. Thanit Yupho, Director, Fine Arts Dept., Bangkok
M. M. Jhumsai, of UNESCO, Bangkok
M. Thep Sukhratni, Director, Fine Arts Dept., Ayuthia Branch
M. Charles Archaimbault, Representative of the Ecole française d'Extrême-Orient, Bangkok
M. Banchob Thiamthat, Chief of Excavation and Restoration Service, National Museum, Bangkok

In Laos:
M. Raymond Eches, of UNESCO, Vientiane
M. Padoux, Cultural Attaché of the French Embassy, Vientiane
M. Galetti, Director of the United Nations Office, Vientiane

In Cambodia:
M. Ken Tiourn, UNESCO delegate, Phnom Penh
M. Deselys-Longchamps, United Nations Technical Board, Phnom Penh
M. Claude Jacques, of the Ecole française d'Extrême-Orient, Phnom Penh
M. Bernard-Philippe Groslier, Curator of the Angkor Monuments and Director of Archaeological Research in Cambodia
M. Claude Guioneaud, pilot and photographer

In South Vietnam:
M. Declerck, of UNESCO, Saigon
M. P. B. Lafont, of the Ecole française d'Extrême-Orient

In Indonesia:
Dr. Soekmono, Director of Archaeological Services, Djakarta
Prof. Amir Sutaarga, Director of the National Museum, Djakarta
M. and Mme. Louis-Charles Damais, of the Ecole française d'Extrême-Orient, Djakarta–Paris
M. The Yang Lok, of UNESCO, Djakarta
Mlle. Irawati, Assistant, UNESCO, Djakarta
MM. Samingoen and Sujono, Archaeological Dept., Prambanan, Java
M. Soevarsono, Chief of Conservation, Borobudur-Dieng, Java
Dr. Soejono, Director of Archaeological Services, Bali
M. J. Made Sutaba, Assistant, Archaeological Services, Bali
Tjokorda Putera Dharma Jhuda, Ubud, Bali

The author would also like to say how much he appreciated the presence of Mme. Sooky Maniquant, who aided him in his task during this journey, and also that of Yvan Butler, photographer and cinematographer, who was a constant friend in Laos and Cambodia. Lastly, he would like to thank François Duffort and his assistants for the extreme care they took in developing films and enlarging the photographs used in this book.

If I have failed to mention anyone deserving my gratitude, I hope I shall be forgiven. If all the names are sometimes difficult to remember, kindness is never forgotten.

LOUIS FRÉDÉRIC

I. INTRODUCTION

SOUTHEAST ASIA comprises the countries on the Indochinese Peninsula: Burma, Thailand, Laos, Cambodia, and Vietnam; the Malay Peninsula; the string of islands forming the present Republic of Indonesia: Java, Sumatra, Bali, Borneo, the Sunda Isles, and Celebes; and the Philippines. Geographically an extremely varied group concentrated around the waters of the Sunda Isles and the South China Sea, Southeast Asia forms a bridge between two great Oriental civilizations, China and India. Although Southeast Asia has been a crossroads of peoples and ideas, a passage between the Indian Ocean and the Pacific, a transition between continental and oceanic powers, it has never formed a political or ethnic unity.

China and India have often confronted one another, sometimes even blending, the one contributing ethnic and political elements, the other the religious and civilizing factor. Southeast Asia is rich in tropical resources: its huge alluvial plains covered with rice fields, its great forests full of rare natural resources, its rich mountain slopes suitable for growing tea, tobacco, rubber, and those spice plants which were once so highly prized that the islands and coastal mainlands were given such wonderful names as the Spice Islands and the Gold Coast.

However, in all this we must differentiate two distinct geographical groups which played an important role in the division of the peoples and their history. The first group, which is still part of the continent, consists of an alternation of mountain chains, almost all of them running north-south, and such rivers as: the Irrawaddy and its tributary, the Chindwin; the Sittang; the Salween; the Chao Phraya; and the hydrographic network of the Mekong—all flowing north to south. These rivers empty into the Bay of Bengal, the Gulf of Siam, and the South China Sea. Fluvial access is difficult from east to west but easy from China toward the ocean. The climate is tropical. The second geographical group comprises islands, has few and short rivers, and consists of high volcanic regions which are continually watered by equatorial rains. This group acts as a transition toward the Melanesian and Polynesian civilizations of the Pacific Ocean.

If the ocean, whose depth never exceeds about 650 feet, could recede slightly, it would be seen that these two groups would form a single, massive stretch of continental land.

The geographic outline of Southeast Asia, its strategic position, and its wealth of natural resources will help us to understand how peoples settled there. The development has been traced to man's earliest beginnings, especially at Java, from those of the *Meganthropus* giant (Von Koenigswald's *Meganthropus paleojavanicus*) to the *Homo sapiens* of Wadjak, Java, with, in the intermediary phase, the *Pithecanthropus robustus*, Dubois' *Pithecanthropus erectus*, and the *Homo soloensis*. Consequently, we can only surmise the rest, for the study of Southeast Asian prehistory is still in its infancy. The *Homo sapiens* of Java seemingly did not develop as rapidly as his counterparts in Europe. A civilization developed with its center probably at Hoa Binh, in Annam. About 4000 B.C. it was taken over by members of the Bacsonian civilization who began to use polished stone implements and seem to have been the first in Southeast Asia to practice elementary agriculture. These Bacsonians, who lived in caves beyond the danger of tidal inundation or at the edge of marshlands, were familiar with pottery and polished axes. They were a proto-Indochinese type with long skulls, and they interbred with the indigenous groups who were probably Melanesian. They were replaced by populations of harvesters, farmers who turned to *ladang* (nonirrigated rice planting). These Dongsonians (of Dong-son in Thanh Hoa) belonged to the Paleolithic, Neolithic, Bronze, and Iron ages, and used not only chipped and polished stone but metals as well. They planted rice and raised oxen. Rice cultivation by means of irrigation and corn growing were probably introduced by hordes of invaders who came from the northwest during the first thousand years before Christ. These invaders were most likely the small clans known as Mon-Khmers, who left traces of their passage in southern India (the Santalis speaking a Munda dialect) and who spread out in Burma, Siam, and Cambodia, becoming part of the indigenous setting and not distinguishable until later. Almost at the same

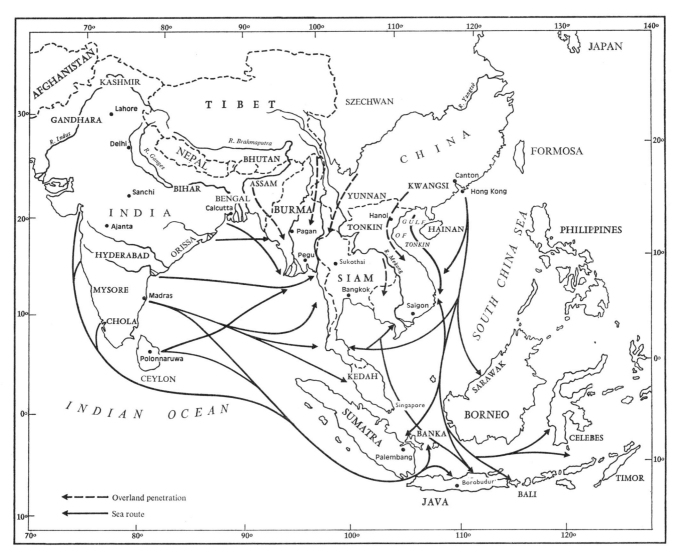

FIG. I. COMMUNICATIONS BETWEEN INDIA AND SOUTHEAST ASIA IN ANCIENT TIMES

time, peoples who originated in South China probably arrived, scattering in groups in the plains and mountains of eastern Indochina and the Malay Peninsula, then swarmed across the Sunda Isles. These proto-Indochinese and Melanesians became more or less part of the peoples who had settled in the plains, sometimes isolating themselves in the mountains or the islands (the Moi of Annam and Dyaks of Borneo). The imprint they left on Southeast Asia is not to be found elsewhere: houses built on piles, dugout canoes with outriggers, characteristically prepared fish (*nuoc-mam*), magic rites (the use of a rain-making bronze drum which is found from Nan Ch'iao

12

in South China to Bali) which they have preserved to the present day in spite of the influence of the Indians who came by sea or land, or the Burmese, Thai, or Vietnamese who entered from the north following river valleys or the coast.

About the beginning of the Christian Era, Indian influence began to be felt in Southeast Asia. The most ancient Indian inscription known in Southeast Asia is that of Vo-Canh, near Nha Trang (South Vietnam), and dates from about the third century after Christ. During that period, however, Indian penetration seems to have been very strong. Chinese chronicles already mention its influence at Champa (Annam, now central Vietnam) and Funan (south Cambodia and Cochin China, now the southern tip of Vietnam) about the second century. The first Indian travelers and colonists probably arrived before the Chinese in Indochina, where they established trading centers about the close of the third century B.C. Explorers, merchants, and missionaries settled peacefully at Champa, engaged in trade, and evangelized. They introduced many civilizing elements such as language, writing, political techniques, religions, and art styles, and the indigenous populations soon took advantage of them. Coming from different parts of India, they formed separate groups. The Mon peoples (or Talaings) of Burma are said to have come from the Telingana coast (Madras region); others left the Coromandel area and through trading settled thickly along the coast.

South India was at that time in full political and religious development. Buddhism, which had made great progress, flourished there equally with Hinduism. Zealous and determined Buddhist missionary endeavor contributed to the spread of "The Doctrine." Buddhist monks, who did not hesitate to undertake long and hazardous journeys in order to bring the teaching of The Enlightened (Gautama Buddha) to other countries, left to convert the people of the Himalayan borders and redescended to Burma. By sea they spread Buddha's Law among the Mon populations of the deltas of the Irrawaddy, the Salween, and Chao Phraya rivers, and along the coastal plains of south Cambodia. The Hindus soon followed their example. Until the end of the Srivijaya Empire, at the height of the Chola Kingdom's maritime power, India continued to contribute to the lands of Farther India and the "Indian Islands."

In the third century, under the impulse of the great Emperor Ashoka, Buddhist missionaries sailed from the ports of southern India and the east coast to preach Buddha's Law in Ceylon (where the earliest Buddhist tradition continuing today, Theravada—the Teaching of the Elders —Buddhism, has remained intact), whereas the countries of Southeast Asia were to fall under the influence of the Mahayana philosophy. About the second and third centuries a flourishing center of Buddhism existed at Amaravati and Nagarjunakonda, on the Kistna River. This resulted in a new missionary zeal. Finally in the fifth century numerous proselytes departed from Kanchipuram. Meanwhile the Brahmanic faith had also made conquests, establishing itself firmly among the peoples of the Annam coast, in southern Cambodia, and in the Malay Peninsula, and its doctrine began to spread in Sumatra and Java. Buddhists had founded prosperous establishments near the mouth of the Salween in Burma, at Phra Pathom and Pong Tuk in Siam on the territory which became the Mon-Dvaravati Empire, at Oc Eo in Funan on the lower Mekong, at the Lin Pi of the Chinese, and at Champa on the Annam coast. It was not long before they settled in the Indian Archipelago. After Sumatra and Java, they exported their bronze images and architectural methods as far as Kalimantan in Borneo and Sulawesi (Celebes).

Once in power, Indian colonists began to modify the political and religious regime of the countries in which they had settled; they established the political framework of the Buddhist kingdoms of the Mon-Dvaravati and the Funan empires. They greatly contributed to the foundation of the Cham kingships and supported the Srivijaya Empire. In the seventh century, Hindu kingdoms were founded on the high plateaus of Central Java, especially at Dieng.

But while Buddhism remained active—despite several vagaries in doctrine—in the territories of what is now Burma and Thailand, it was gradually replaced by Hinduism in Cambodia and Annam. It is very probable that the peoples of these regions retained a kind of primitive Buddhism, associated, as it still is today, with many ancient animistic practices, and that only the ruling castes adopted Hinduism, enabling them to practice a politico-religious philosophy to serve their own aims. In both cases this resulted in a kind of religious syncretism in which the greatest tolerance—or indifference— was practiced. Consequently, Hindu kingdoms were created in Java in conjunction with the establishment of Buddhist communities. In the early fifth century the Buddhist pilgrim Fa Hsien stayed at a Buddhist community in Java. About 710 another Chinese pilgrim, Yi Tsing, visited Sumatra. After a Buddhist flowering in Java in the eighth century, Hinduism gained the upper hand. In the fifteenth century, despite the introduction of Islamic ideas, principally by Moslems from Gujarat, the Hindu spirit on the island of Bali remained almost untouched (and has remained so down to this day). In Cambodia, Hinduism soon replaced Buddhism by introducing from Java the cult of the god-king. Although there was a late return to this doctrine in the thirteenth century, priests and brahmans nevertheless remained at the Javanese royal court. On the other hand, the Brahmanic cult never implanted itself in Burma and Thailand, for the people remained faithful—at least in principle—to the Theravada Doctrine, which may have been introduced from Ceylon as early as the third century. In the early fifth century, Funan was the most important Indianized political power in Southeast Asia. Buddhist, Shivaist, and Vishnuist cults were active there and art followed the canon clearly inspired by that of south India. In the sixth century, under the impulse of Chen La, Funan freed itself, to the benefit of the Khmers, who soon established a reputation as excellent builders. The kings were under complete Brahmanic obedience and the cult of the lingam-king was honored. It was not until the close of the twelfth century under the impulse of a remarkable ruler, Jayavarman VII, that Buddhism replaced Hinduism. At the close of the seventh century, Champa witnessed the predominance of Hinduism.

Naturally, India continued to exercise an enormous influence on the "Indianized" countries. Ceylon, Bengal, and Lamaist Tibet made their contribution to Burma, which in turn influenced north Siam. Gupta sculpture followed by the Pala and Sena styles of Bengal were imitated everywhere. But under the influence of the Burmese who came from the Tibetan borders, the Thai who had been turned back from Nan Ch'iao, the Khmers who had descended from the plateaus of Laos, and the Vietnamese who had conquered Champa, the types were modified and achieved truly "national" styles in which the inspiration of religious themes determined by iconography alone were recognized. On the other hand, as Theravada Buddhism permitted no other divine representation than that of Buddha, it authorized in Burma and Siam the flowering of original ornamental and architectural themes which had been borrowed from various folklores. Furthermore, as Hinduism had furnished inexhaustible iconographic themes of such great Indian epic poems as *The Mahabharata* and *The Ramayana*, local artists surpassed themselves in representing lively and very animated scenes. Those artists, who were influenced by the Mahayana Doctrine of Buddhism, displayed their excellent talent in the description of the *Jatakas* (episodes) in the life of Shakyamuni (the historic Buddha), and the bodhisattvas' paradises. Their art culminated in the bas-reliefs of the sculptured galleries of Borobudur and Srivijaya.

This was due, on the one hand, to Indian influences of various creeds and, on the other, to the different receptions of these influences because of the different kinds of peoples among whom they were felt. It is not surprising that the development of these influences did not occur in the same manner. It would therefore be very difficult, if not absurd, to draw up a general outline of the arts of Southeast Asia by attempting to establish a chronological parallel between the different styles that were created, that developed and disappeared among different peoples who themselves were often affected by events, and by invasions that sometimes eliminated them from the political scene.

This difficult task could be conceived only by drawing up a chart comparing styles and peoples. Another method adopted by many authors would be to mention the arts only so far as they belong to a specific country. This is how we would have to discuss separately Burma, Siam, Laos, Cambodia, Malaya, and Indonesia. Although empirical, this method has a certain value, but we will not adopt it entirely. For it would mean designating vague limits to the arts and creating arbitrary frontiers which really do not correspond to anything definite. After much thought, the most intelligent procedure seems to be the following: to take as sole divisions those which time and men have assigned to their civilizations in their period, and to arrange these divisions according to the rules of influence. This will make it much easier to follow chronologically the development of societies and their art. The first, then, would be Ceylon, although the description of the monuments does not quite correspond with the geographical area defined by Southeast Asia. Ceylon was a very active center both from the cultural and artistic points of view. We will continue with the Indianized kingdoms of Southeast Asia, containing the real Indian style, whose extensive area included south Burma, present Thailand, Cambodia, and Sumatra. This will lead us to the double impact of the Burmese and the Khmers in about the twelfth century.

We will then take up the art of the Burmese kingdom of Pagan down to the modern aspects of Burma's artistic heritage. In the second part we shall discuss the very special art of Indonesia up to the period when Moslem influence replaced that of Hinduism.

This will help us to study the art of the Khmers and that of the Chams, who owe some of their characteristics to Java. The Khmer-Thailand part, which is known as the Lopburi style, will be discussed in this chapter. We will at last come to Siam, whose art, resulting from the impact of different influences—Dvaravati in the south, Khmer in the east, Thai and Burmese in the north—finally led to a national Thai style. The art of Laos, which is so often questioned and so little known, and strongly related to that of the Thai, will be discussed with the Thai style. We will dismiss the primitive civilizations of the islands and those of the Philippines, where as yet no Indian influence has been found.

We shall then have the following arrangement and chronology:

Ceylon
The Indianized Kingdoms of the West
   The Pyus (to 800)
   The Dvaravati and Thaton Mons (to 1057)
   The Beginnings of Pagan (849–1057)
The Burmese Kingdoms
   Pagan (1057–1287)
   The Burmese Renaissance (1287–1885)
The Island Kingdoms
   Srivijaya (to 1100)
   Java and Bali (seventh–twentieth century)
The Oriental Kingdoms
   Funan (first–seventh century)
   Chen La (sixth century–802)
   The Northern Chams (seventh century–982)
   The Khmers (802–fifteenth century)
   The Southern Chams (982–1471)
The Thai Kingdoms
   Sukhothai (thirteenth–fourteenth century)
   Northern Styles (thirteenth–sixteenth century)
   U Thong and Ayuthia (1350–1785)
   Laos (fifteenth–twentieth century)
   Bangkok Style (1785–twentieth century)

*

This book, which logically follows its predecessor, *The Art of India*, could also be called *The Art of Farther India*, an extensive term which a number of earlier writers applied to the countries of Southeast Asia. We hope that our illustrations will prove useful for a better understanding of India's enormous influence on the civilizations of Southeast Asia, and for an appreciation of the great conflict which arose when India opposed the influence of Chinese culture in the same regions. Although the Chinese, or those races related to them, had politically and militarily invaded a large part of the Indochinese Peninsula, their cultural influence was less important than that of India. Chinese penetration, however massive, did not occur until relatively late, in fact long after Indian ideas had asserted themselves. And yet Chinese influence was very important. The Thai sweep toward the south and that of the Vietnamese against the inhabitants of Champa stemmed from the Chinese. They were the source of many cross-breedings (Siamese, Khmers, Vietnamese, Malays, Burmese, and Javanese, not forgetting the Filipinos and the inhabitants of the coast of Borneo and the Sunda Isles). The Chinese occupied the territories adjoining their own (Tonkin) not only as warriors but also as settlers. Great merchants and travelers, they naturally established themselves where nature and mankind facilitated trade and easily adapted themselves to the ways and customs of the different countries in which they had settled, often marrying local women while retaining their own language and customs. Since the nineteenth century, this commercial colonization seems to be on the increase. In fact, the great cities of Southeast Asia—Bangkok, Cholon, Singapore, Malacca—have almost become Chinese cities.

On the technical level, China introduced the arts of ceramics and bronze, a certain type of plow, farming methods, and, above all, trading principles which contributed to the wealth of the countries in which the Chinese had settled, although profits were enjoyed by them rather than by the natives. Since ancient times, the Chinese had controlled trade in spices, rhinoceros horns (used in Chinese pharmacology), benzoin, swallows' nests (for gastronomic purposes), and silk. We can imagine the keen competition that often occured between these wily merchants and the no less clever Indian traders.

But in the end a partition was made. India benefited from the cultural influence (except in Vietnam, where after the disappearance of the Chams only the Chinese influence remained), and China from the monopoly of trade. Today the contrary is taking place. India has lost her prestige and China is too powerful or dangerous a neighbor to be ignored. As a result, we are witnessing a gradual change in values which this time appears irreversible. However, India has enabled her many, varied peoples to find a solid basis on which to build civilizations whose splendid vestiges remain as outstanding evidence of the intelligence and skill of Asiatic peoples at a period when Europe was still in the throes of barbarism.

We would have liked to show all the art and architecture of Southeast Asia, but unfortunately the size of this volume necessitated making a careful selection from 8000 photographs. This choice was guided by three principles. The first obviously had to be that of the archaeological and historical interest of the monument or work of art. The second was dictated above all by our desire to present together with well-known monuments certain rare works which may never have been reproduced. The beauty of the photograph and its clarity were our final concern. We hope that this concise text and very limited choice of photographs will give the reader a general idea of the arts of Southeast Asia and enable him to appreciate them for their true value. We hope also that this effort (a concentrated synthesis on the subject) will strengthen the cultural bonds which already link East and West.

II. CEYLON

T HE MOUNTAINOUS green island of Ceylon, lying off the southern tip of India, like a pearl in the ear of Asia, does not really belong to India. Constant conflict with her neighbor inspired the great epic poem, *The Ramayana*, which was written by a Hindu. It is mainly the story of the great and just King Rama, whose wife Sita is taken away by force by the king of Ceylon, Ravana, and is later rescued by Rama after defeating Ravana's forces. Some authors have read in this allegory an Indian attempt to appropriate a "fresh field," a pleasant land, basing their claim on the confusion of a vowel in the name Sita. But the legend became so famous that it was the basis of numerous Hindu bas-reliefs and sculptures in such distant countries as Java and Cambodia. It is nevertheless curious that this legend seems to be unknown in Ceylon itself.

Essentially a Buddhist country (since the rise of this religious philosophy on the island dates from the time of the great Emperor Ashoka in the third century B.C.), Ceylon offers a wonderful panorama of the arts from the earliest period of Buddhism in its purest form, the Theravada Doctrine, called by its detractors Hinayana (Lesser Vehicle) in opposition to the Mahayana (Greater Vehicle). But Ceylonese art offers another subject of interest, for it was the source of certain architectural forms which developed in the countries of Southeast Asia. Its monks preached the doctrine of Buddha's Law in every port of this part of the world. They were well received, for the spirit of religious tolerance was deep-rooted in the mind of the Asiatic peoples. Most of the small tribes with whom the monks came in contact adopted their philosophy and manner of living. Ceylon long served as a model for Burmese rulers and others who, not content to turn to the Buddha's precious teaching at the source itself (one Burmese ruler even reintroduced monks into Ceylon at a time when a lack of doctrines was noticed), also went to find sources of inspiration for their commemorative monuments known as stupas. This is why, in spite of few modifications, the very form of Sinhalese *dagobas* (stupas) is found not only in Burma but also in Thailand and more distant countries like Indonesia. Ceylonese art probably influenced that of India, especially Amaravati, where stupas have the characteristics of the Anuradhapura dagobas. Although many monuments erected in this capital (which was founded in the fourth century B.C. and became Buddhist in the middle of the third century B.C.) have been destroyed, we can easily find their description and form, thanks to two architectural treatises, *The Dipavamsa* and *The Mahavamsa*, which were compiled in the fourth and fifth centuries after Christ, respectively. According to tradition, it was one of the sons of the famous Ashoka, Mahinda, and his daughter, Sangamitta, who introduced Buddhism into Ceylon together with a branch of the very holy Bodhi tree beneath which Buddha had attained final Enlightenment.

Anuradhapura remained the capital until the close of the eighth century when the city was abandoned because of continual raids by the Tamils of south India, but many monuments of its splendid period still exist. The second capital, founded in the early twelfth century, inaugurated another splendid period and probably continued to furnish models for architects and sculptors in distant Eastern countries with whom monks and rulers had always remained in close contact.

The most ancient monuments to have survived from this early Buddhist kingdom were stupas, here known as dagobas (from *dhatu-gharba*, which Europeans called "pagoda"). They were probably similar to those used in India about the third century and have completely disappeared, but not without leaving superb successors, especially at Bharhut and Sanchi. The architectural form of these dagobas seems to have been set by early Sinhalese writings in such a manner that no change could be made without the utmost precaution. Foreign architects were so impressed by this constant form that they could not help but export it to their own countries. The dagoba consisted mainly of a square base which often supported a semicircular mass (*anda* or *garba*), topped by a cubic "reliquary casket." A series of parasols, or *chattras*, signs of royalty, surmounted the last section and were supported by a pillar fixed in the center of the *harmika* (reliquary casket).

These monuments were all built of stone and brick. Their decoration was severe, as the

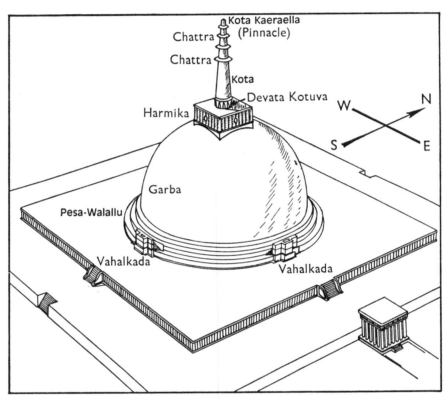

FIG. 2. THE RUVANVELI DAGOBA: AN EXAMPLE OF THE TYPICAL STUPA FOUND IN CEYLON

Theravada Doctrine of Ceylon did not permit any decorative fantasy on themes concerning Buddha himself or the elaboration of secular scenes. It is true that their material scarcely facilitated detailed execution. The Ruvanveli Dagoba, one of the most ancient and among the greatest, begun by King Duthagamini in the second century B.C., is a huge brick mass measuring almost 290 feet high and 328 feet in diameter, resting on a pedestal of stone and clay compressed by the weight of hundreds of elephants brought especially for the purpose, and surrounded by three platforms which were used for the *pradakshina* (the circumambulatory rite of the faithful). A projection on each of the four cardinal points contained the *vahalkadas*, or relic chambers. Low stair risers whose decorative edges were in the form of a semicircle, or "moonstone," led from one gallery to another. Originally the entire structure was coated with plaster or stucco, probably painted or gilded. The Thuparama, erected in the third century, was somewhat smaller, measuring 164 feet in diameter. The tradition continued long after the beginning of the Christian Era and the style of the Indian stupas at Amaravati certainly owes some of its peculiarities to

Sinhalese dagobas. But they were always enormous. The Abhayagiriya, which was built about the year 300, and the fourth-century Jetawana Dagoba both measured almost 328 feet in diameter, representing a volume of brick equal to that of the Pyramid of Mycerinus at Gizeh. These impressive structures were undecorated with the exception of four vahalkadas which were decorated with elephant heads and often a statue of Buddha. On the summit the chattras, typical of Indian stupas, were no longer designed as parasols one above the other but as a kind of mast, perhaps reminiscent of totem poles. These "early" stupas had six shapes: egg, dome, bell, bubble, lotus, and cylinder. But they invariably retained the cubic *kotuva* (base) on the summit, surmounted by the pillar (*kota*) bearing the chattras. Below, the circular platforms, used for the circumambulatory rite, on square bases flanked by stairs in the center of each side, could vary in number: two, three, or five. Many of these forms were exported mainly to Burma, where the "bell" enjoyed the success we are going to discuss and whose shape remains to this day that of the Burmese *zedi*.

These dagobas were not isolated but part of the monasteries (*samgharama*), where many buildings were created for worship and to house monks. Among these we must distinguish the *pilima-ge*, where the image of Buddha was contained, the preaching hall (*bana salava*), where the monks gathered for prayer, and a basin (*pokana*) for ablutions. Like present-day monasteries, these buildings were surrounded by a wall with gates which were often protected by a small building. But what is most impressive—they are still standing—are the concentric rows of monolithic pillars which were probably used to support canopies, during processions, or lamps.

The *prasadas* were generally wooden structures several stories high, supported by a forest of granite pillars. The Lohaprasada of the second century B.C. was built on almost 1600 single-block columns. A faint idea of its superstructure is gained by considering the Dharmaraja Rath of Mahamallapuram which translates into stone an architectural style that was probably very ancient in southern India and Ceylon. The final dome was probably overlayed with gilt bronze. The columns of the base are typical of the style and the order can be considered Sinhalese. Square or octagonal and without a base, these monolithic columns included a capital (*puhul*) with somewhat sculptured, splayed forms toward the top, and were separated from the top of the column, which was surrounded by a garland motif, by an unornamented section. An exception to this style is a capital in the form of a trident, although an unornamented octagonal section separated it from the garland on the top of the column.

DECORATIVE MOTIFS

Numerous steles erected near vahalkadas have ornamental decoration—series of animals and figures arranged in the midst of a floral décor emerging from a vase of abundance, which was often supported by a dwarf (*gana*). Typical examples are the Abhayagiriya Dagoba steles. Like the *lats* (columns) of Ashoka, these steles often support an animal, lion, or elephant. They were often associated with an image of Naga. Others, like the Kantaka Chaitya of Mihintale, had an alternating décor of animals and floral motifs treated as rosettes or palmettes. Ornamental decoration often included figures or animals.

MOONSTONES

Characteristic of Ceylonese art, these stair risers are decorated with a central lotus flower, surrounded by alternating concentric friezes of animals or herbaceous decorations. A running order is given by the following series, beginning from the center: lotus flowers, geese, ornamental motifs, animals (horses, lions, oxen, elephants), and finally a decorative border in the shape of short, stylized flames.

These moonstones are more or less elaborated according to the development of the style; the most ancient are without decoration. A variation of this motif is often found in Javanese and Khmer art.

STAIRS

These have ornamental railings generally representing dragon fish (*makaras*) mounted on a railing and sticking out their long tongues, terminating in a scroll, a motif that was used again, especially in Javanese temples. The outer sides of the railings are often decorated with an animal, usually a very stylized lion. The steps are often sculptured with dwarfs (ganas) and heads of monsters.

VAHALKADAS

The only decorative parts of the dagobas, the vahalkadas, are sculptured with horizontal moldings between which run friezes of dwarfs, lions, or small narrative panels treated in a rather crude but very lively style. Contemporary to the most ancient dagobas, these decorations are the finest examples of Sinhalese art in the first centuries.

Certain sculptured rocks, like those of Isurumunya, reveal a true sense of animal art. They seem to be contemporary with the rock-cut sculptures of Mahamallapuram (seventh-century India) with which they show deep affinities. The sculpture, which also tends to be gigantic, reveals both post-Gupta and Pallava influences. The works are principally representations of Buddha standing, alone or with Avalokiteshvara or Tara, either in bas-relief (Buduruvegala) or sculptured in the round (Avukana). The attitudes are stiff, the faces expressionless, and the proportions often poorly observed. Representations of gatekeepers (*dvarapalas*) generally follow the post-Gupta style. Usually surmounted by a blind arcade, these bas-reliefs could well be taken for Indian works. Toward the close of the period, there appeared "floral altars" which are typical examples of Ceylonese art. They consist of a basin designed as a double lotus and standing on a high pedestal decorated with floral motifs generally treated in a rather baroque style. Certain elements were later used abroad, especially in Java in Majapahit sculptures.

An original type of bas-relief is to be found on a number of urinal bases; these slabs still exist in certain Thailand monasteries.

THE POLONNARUVA STYLE

After the Cholas had forced the Sinhalese to abandon their capital, the Sinhalese soon rallied at Polonnaruva, a less exposed city. Toward the close of the eleventh century they felt it was their duty to rebuild a capital worthy of their kings. But the Chola influence, however short, had been very strong. The buildings followed the style then popular in Dravidian India, but instead of building in stone after the manner of the invaders, the Sinhalese used brick almost exclusively. This technique resulted in the elaboration of very thick walls which hardly lent themselves to an elegant style or to the possibility of decorating the edifices (such as the Thuparama Dagoba). However, toward the close of the twelfth century, Parakrama Bahu the Great (1153–86), after freeing himself from Chola influences, established the grandeur of his capital by inaugurating a building style. The city was enclosed by massive walls forming a quadrangle measuring almost 3¾ miles in circumference and containing every type of monument—palaces, monasteries, stupas, pools. Dagobas were no longer built to worship Buddha but, instead, gigantic effigies were enclosed within huge buildings constructed to their dimensions, high and narrow structures decorated on the exterior with rows of pilasters. The Lankatilaka, which was built of brick and covered with stucco, contained a statue of Buddha measuring over 65 feet high, and also built of brick and stucco (a method later greatly used in Burma). The statue stood in a cella surrounded by a pillared gallery and fronted by a very high and narrow antechamber.

The Sat-Mahal-Prasada is a dagoba in an entirely new form. A massive, seven-story structure built of brick, it resembles a step pyramid. Each story is decorated with stucco statues. A flight of steps leads only to the first story. Built by Nissanka Malla about the close of the twelfth century, this building seems to have been inspired by certain buildings known as late Dvaravati, like that of Vat Kukut of Lampun.

20

The Vatadage, a huge, roofless circular construction surrounded by columns, contains a small dagoba and statues of Buddha. Entrance to this curious edifice is by means of four flights of steps situated at the cardinal points and profusely decorated.

At Polonnaruva there are a few examples of elaborate stone Dravidian architecture which conform to the type of constuction current in southern India at the close of the twelfth century and the beginning of the thirteenth. These are Hindu temples, one of which is dedicated to Shiva and still wonderfully preserved.

Although this is a very brief account, Ceylon not being part of Southeast Asia, we hope nevertheless that it will serve as a logical introduction to the arts of what is known as Farther India, and that it will offer an easier understanding of the origin and development not only in Burma and Java but also in Cambodia and Thailand.

III. THE INDIANIZED KINGDOMS OF THE WEST

1. THE PYUS (Third–Eighth Century)

As the territory of present Burma has scarcely been explored from the archeological point of view, it is difficult to draw conclusions from the few rare architectural vestiges, sculptures, and inscriptions, or achieve absolute certainty about the exact beginnings of the peoples who had inhabited the country before the arrival of the Burmese and Thai. Burmese chronicles, like the *Glass Palace*, scarcely offer precise information. To imagine what ancient Burma was like, we must turn to scarce archaeological evidence and compare it with Chinese chronicles. Before the creation of the Pagan Kingdom, two different cultural centers existed in Burma: middle Burma, the land of the Pyu Kingdom, with Prome as its center, and lower Burma, fief of the Mon peoples, with its two capitals, Thaton and Pegu, sharing the influence. It is difficult to go beyond the fifth century and find evidence to help us state that these two types of culture enjoyed full development before that time. Archaeological work and excavation in Burma still do not enable us to chance some general statement. However, from what has already been accomplished on the principal sites of these cultures, we can conclude that from the beginning of the fifth century until at least the eighth, the Pyu and Mon peoples, each in its own manner, had developed a type of civilization based on that of eastern India. It is very probable that Buddhist monks of the Kanchipuram school and followers of Brahmanic cults were the founders of these kingdoms or, in any case, their religious inspiration.

Long established in middle Burma on the banks of the Irrawaddy, the important Burmese river route, the Pyus (who called themselves "Tirchul" and whom the Chinese named "P'iao") seem to have been a kind of federation of numerous tribes (probably of close Tibetan origin, like their cousins, the Burmese, who later completely absorbed them). Using the river, the Pyus scattered as far as Prome, where they encountered different peoples such as the Mon. From certain archaeological traces and ancient Chinese annals, we know that they were farmers, mainly cultivating rice, and that they founded several cities whose names have come down to us either from their Indian or their Pyu name. Thus it appears that their capital was Thayekhettaya, whose ruins now lie on the site of the village of Hmawza, near the old city of Prome. Its Indian name, Sriksetra, which was also that of the city of Puri on the Orissa Coast, could lead us to imagine that its founders had come from that region of India. At which period? Nothing exists to help us to make such an assumption. Although the name of the city is a Hindu one, the architectural remains and the few sculptures that have been found are mostly of a Buddhist nature. In fact, fragments of Buddhist writing in Pali were discovered among the most ancient vestiges of the cities.

Similarly, somewhat more to the north, near Taungdwingyi on the banks of the Yu Pe River, the Pyu city of Peikthanomyo is known as that of Vishnu. Although we cannot attempt to describe how the people lived nor what were their artistic aspirations, we can, nevertheless, judge something of the achievements of the ruling class. This class, at least at the beginning when cities were founded, was probably of the Indian race or at least of the Hindu religion, initiates perhaps of Brahmanic cults imported from the Orissa Coast. But the people probably had long been converted to Buddhism, imported by monks from Ceylon and southern India. In fact two Buddhist sects have been discovered among the Pyus: Theravada, of Pali tradition, and Mulasarvastivada, of Sanskrit tradition. The kings' names are typically Hindu: Suryavikrama, Harivikrama, Sihavikrama. As little has been found (a few Brahmanic images), and, on the other hand, as evidence of Buddhist religion is relatively frequent, we are led to believe that the sovereigns (or at least the ruling class) had adopted Buddhism as the official religion. Hinduism remained merely the nominal religion of the ruling family (which is now the case in Cambodia, where Brahmans continue to officiate at the royal palace, whereas the entire country has long been converted to Buddhism). This was not at all surprising at a period when dogmas inter-

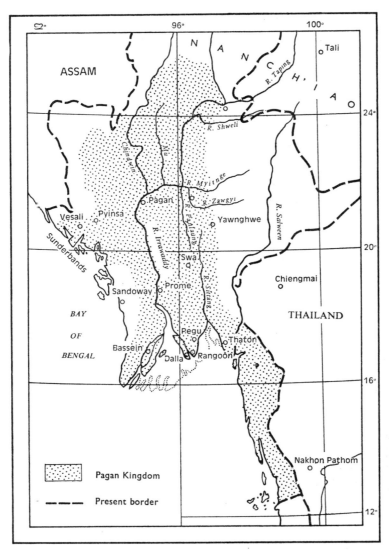

FIG. 3. BURMA IN THE SEVENTH AND EIGHTH CENTURY

mingled easily, becoming a broad-minded syncretism, although the masses nevertheless remained very much attached to nature spirits and primitive agrarian rites. Only the tombs of kings and queens have been found, simple stone urns buried in the ground, each with a lid, and often having an inscription in Sanskrit. These funerary urns, which were scarcely common in India but were, on the other hand, very numerous in Southeast Asian countries—particularly Laos, near Xieng Khouang—are perhaps the vestiges of a custom dating from before Indian influence. As for the

Pyu cities, we are best informed about the capital. Chinese chronicles of the T'ang Dynasty offer a precise description of this powerful city at a period when the Pyus in 802 and 807 exchanged ambassadors with China through the intermediary of the kingdom of Nan Ch'iao who proclaimed himself ruler of the Pyus, probably unduly, in 754. "The city walls, built of brick and covered with green glazed tile, are 160 *li* in length. They are surrounded by moats and have twelve gates and pagodas at each corner. . . . The people are Buddhist and have a hundred monasteries built of green brick, decorated with gold and silver. . . . The floors are painted and covered with carpets. The houses are covered with lead and tin. . . ."

The city walls can still be seen, and appear to cover the length of about 8 miles. The site of a palace, those of several ornamental lakes, and rather unidentifiable outbuildings have been found, to which peasant imagination has given fantastic or legendary names. On each of the four corners of the city walls there stood a stupa; three can still be seen and are remarkable: the Bawbawgyi, the Payagyi, and the Payama. Scattered in the countryside between the villages and among the plantations are a few structures which once were temples. Of Indian inspiration, they nevertheless begin to show an original design enabling us to consider them prototypes of monuments which later determined the Burmese styles of Pagan.

On the site of Peikthanomyo, another city which archaeologists have scarcely cleared away, the archaeologist U Aung Thaw has identified burnt-brick structures (with all the characteristics of lodgings, having a single story, with semicircular door stones similar to those of Ceylonese Amaravati monuments), probably the site of a palace, and the remains of a brick enceinte wall almost $3^3/_4$ miles in length, originally having three entrances on each side. Beyond the walls are numerous low mounds containing funerary urns which were generally "incased" in large geometrical structures measuring about 16 by 9 by $3\frac{1}{8}$ inches. In contrast to the stone funerary urns of the Pyu lords of Hmawza, these were of poor quality red terra cotta, decorated merely with incisions and moldings, different in size and form, and probably reserved for the ashes of not very important people. According to recent research made on the site, it is possible that light structures of wood and plaster, kinds of funerary chapels, may have been built above these urns, perhaps indicating the existence at that time of a cult of the dead, the origin dating from before the introduction of Indian religions. Many pieces of pottery have been found, almost all made by wheel but badly fired and having little decoration. They are rather similar to the type known as Arikamedu, near Pondichéry, which probably indicates an additional link with southern India. Pearl necklaces and ivory sticks reveal little about the coquetry of Pyu women. But certain stone molds show impressions of jewelry, and a Brahmi inscription of the Gupta style dates them from between the fourth and the eighth century.

Numerous Pyu sites remain to be explored and much research is necessary to reveal some of the past of central Burma and define more accurately certain aspects of the civilization which seemed to flourish before what is known as the Burmese historical period. Although no local chronicle can really be taken seriously, certain legends concerning the Pyus seem to contain a germ of truth. The one related in the *Taungdwingyi Tamaing*, a nineteenth-century work, describes the arrival of two blind princes who had come from the north on a raft down the Irrawaddy. After having regained their sight, they each in turn married a hermit's daughter, and one of the brothers founded Thayekhettaya. But an ogress, who had known the brothers, miraculously gave birth to a girl, who after many adventures was recognized by Vishnu as his sister. The city of Peikthanomyo was then given to her. The king of Thayekhettaya declared war, captured her in spite of her magic drum, and married her, thus unifying the Pyus. From such a legend it would be easy to assume that two leaders of related tribes coming from the north had settled in the country and founded families, and that the unity of the Pyus with Thayekhettaya as capital did not occur until after the struggle among the descendants. The queen of Peikthanomyo's magic drum seems similar to the famous Dong-son drum, or rain-maker, that was used among the peoples of Nan Ch'iao and Tonkin and is found as far as Bali. The Pyus still pose many problems which cannot be solved until complete archaeological exploration of Burma is made. Unfortunately, present conditions hardly permit rapid progress in this sector.

The Pyu capital was destroyed about the close of the eighth century by the Mons or Talaings who settled and remained there until Aniruddha's Burmese troops recaptured the city in 1056. The Pyus were absorbed, and history no longer mentions them. Only their monuments remain, and they will help us to understand the development of Burmese architecture.

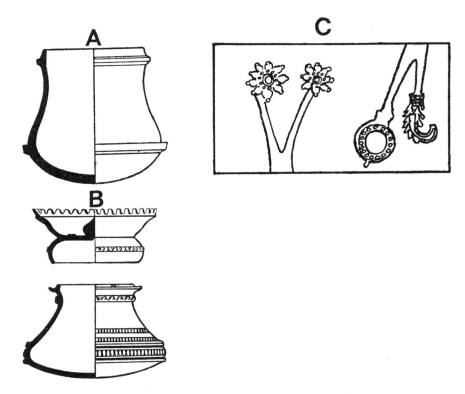

FIG. 4. TYPES OF CERAMIC URNS AND MOLDS FOR CASTING JEWELRY USED BY THE PYUS IN THE EIGHTH CENTURY (*After U Aung Thaw*)

1. BURMA, HMAWZA, BEBE PAYA TEMPLE. A cubic block of brick (about 9½ feet square) surmounted by three stepped terraces and a round sikhara. This curious sanctuary (fifth–eighth century) forms a single room with groined vaulting, at the back of which is a stone plaque carved with a relief of Buddha attended by two divinities. On the side walls are two niches which once contained statues. The sanctuary has a single entrance. The three other outer sides are blind and contain false doors, including an arch supported by pilasters. All the decoration in this sanctuary has disappeared.

2. BURMA, HMAWZA, SANCTUARY OF YA HAN DAR GU. Standing somewhat beyond the limits of the ancient city of Sriksetra, this long, low structure built of brick with corbelled barrel vaulting now stands in the midst of the jungle. One of the inner walls is decorated with two slabs of sandstone measuring 5 feet 6⅞ inches by 2 feet 11½ inches, placed end to end and sculpted with eight seated Buddhas, all identical. Traces of paint indicate that they were

originally polychromed. The purpose and use of such a chapel are still unknown. It may have been built in connection with a cemetery of stone funerary urns known as "The Tomb of Queen Vishnu" which lies in the forest, not far away. Although the date of this monument is unknown, it can nevertheless be placed, like most of the Pyu monuments shown here, between the fifth and the eighth century.

3. BURMA, HMAWZA, PAYATAUNG TEMPLE. Entirely filled in by masses of fallen earth, and difficult to reach, this sanctuary seems to have been built on the same plan as Bebe Paya, but with more impressive dimensions. The sikhara has disappeared. The walls were decorated with a niche per side, surmounted by a *clec* arch (see page 73 for a discussion of this term). This temple is built entirely of brick.

4. BURMA, HMAWZA, ZEGU TEMPLE. This temple is certainly later in date than the others. The roofing

25

and vaulting have completely disappeared. Although built on the same plan, instead of false doors or niches it has fretted windows made of piled bricks. These openings are decorated with projections embellished with pilasters and clecs. The construction appears more skillful. Like the pilasters, the bases of the walls are decorated with moldings.

5. BURMA, HMAWZA, LEMYETHNA TEMPLE. It is difficult to date this temple in relation to the others, yet it appears slightly earlier. There is no bold vaulting but a central pillar, leaving a narrow corridor, between the pillar and the wall, which is reached by means of four barrel-vaulted entrances. The sides of these doors are shored up by brick buttresses. They do not seem to have been decorated with a clec motif but rather by a kind of bracket pagodon (small pagoda) on the top of the arch. The roof is formed of sloping stepped terraces. The final sikhara has disappeared, or perhaps this temple never had one. These four temples were probably built between the fifth and the eighth century. Lemyethna is the oldest, then Bebe Paya and Payataung, and finally Zegu. These structures, the only survivors of the Pyu period of Thayekhettaya (Sriksetra), are perhaps the most ancient examples of solid architecture in Burma, the direct ancestors of Pagan monuments.

6. BURMA, HMAWZA, PAYAMA PAGODA. On the four corners of the Pyu capital stood huge stupas in the form of pointed beehives, typical of those erected in Orissa in India during the same period (fifth-seventh century). The model was probably taken from the city of Pegu, the Pyu name of which (Ussa) indicates that this last city was originally populated, colonized, or evangelized by people from Orissa. The base, still to be cleared away, consisted of three or five terraces. One was restored in 1959. The *hti* (gilt metalwork crown, indicating the sanctity of the edifice) which surmounts the stupa is an addition of the last century.

7. BURMA, HMAWZA, PAYAGYI PAGODA. Of the same style and period as the preceding one. Three ter-

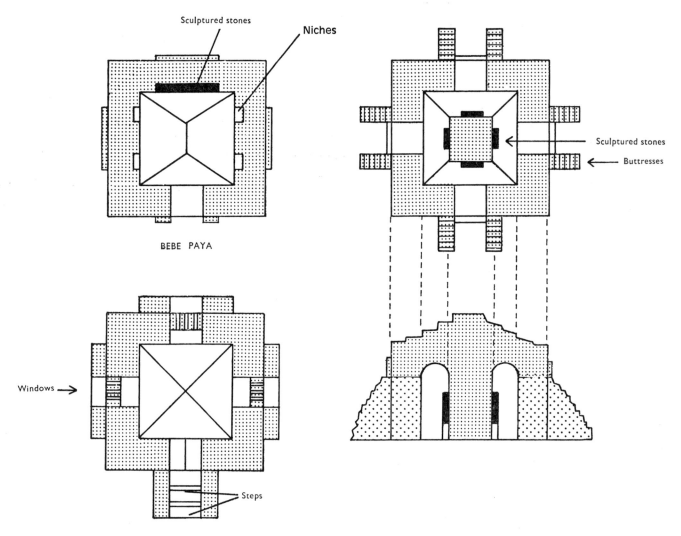

FIG. 5. PLANS OF THREE PYU TEMPLES AT HMAWZA

races of the base have been cleared away to date. Work in progress will restore this pagoda, decorated with a modern hti, to its original aspect. It measures about 160 feet in height.

8. BURMA, HMAWZA, FUNERARY URN (*detail*). Shown is an inscription in Nigari letters indicating the name of the deceased, who was a member of the Vikrama Dynasty. About 2 feet 4 inches high, this urn was hewn from a stone block. The inscription is the sole ornament of this eighth-century funerary urn. *Hmawza Museum.*

9. BURMA, HMAWZA, TERRA-COTTA BAS-RELIEF. Probably once part of a stupa base, it represents Buddha seated in the Western manner on a throne placed above a lion shown full-face and flanked by two standing personages. This very Indian style seems to be an intermediary one between those of Kushan and Gupta, thus enabling us to date this work from about the fourth century. It perhaps reveals a Mon influence of the Dvaravati style, which is not at all surprising since a relationship existed between the two peoples. 18 by 20 inches. *Hmawza Museum.*

10. BURMA, HMAWZA, STATUE OF BUDDHA. Part of a sanctuary that has disappeared, this sculpture of dark sandstone shows how much the artist has taken advantage of a slim stone block. The body, which is treated summarily in a formal attitude of presenting fruit and in which Buddha is touching the earth as witness (right hand), has a remarkably well-defined face carved in a perfect semicircle and bordered by a halo. The rather heavy chin is the prototype of certain Burmese Buddhas. This work seems to be strongly influenced by Mon-Dvaravati art. The very stylized hair has a scarcely visible *ushnisha* (chignon). Eighth century(?). *Hmawza Museum.*

11. BURMA, HMAWZA, TERRA-COTTA BAS-RELIEF. This section of a decorative panel is strikingly realistic. Details have been scratched into the modeled form. This may be the ethnic type of a Pyu. The figure is probably that of an ascetic. Height: 3¾ inches. *Hmawza Museum.*

12. BURMA, HMAWZA, STELE DECORATED WITH A STUPA. This slab of sandstone in very low relief represents an obviously Indian stupa surmounted by five parasols. On the square base are five seated figures meditating—the repetition of Buddha or the evocation of his first five disciples. This type of stupa, which probably existed at Hmawza, is probably earlier in date than the large structures that are still seen there. Related to the Amaravati style, it shows that Buddhism flourished in the Pyu capital perhaps as early as the third century. This stele may date from that period. *Hmawza Museum.*

13. BURMA, HMAWZA, VOTIVE STATUETTES. These are cast in white metal, and represent a dragon (Burmese *chinthe*?) and a worshiper who has brought offerings. They are an example of Pyu folk art. Height: 2¾ inches. *Hmawza Museum.*

14. BURMA, HMAWZA, VOTIVE TABLETS. These terracotta tablets representing Buddha seated on a base of lotus flowers, spread out in two positions accepted by the Pali Canon, were found in great number on the pagoda sites of the city of Thayekhettaya. The central one is 2 inches high. These are only casts. *Hmawza Museum.*

15. BURMA, HMAWZA, STATUETTE OF BUDDHA. A lost-wax bronze figure, typical of Pyu folk art. The style is clumsy and naïve yet quite charming. Treated in the form of a reversed lotus, the hair was once surmounted by an ushnisha. Clothing is indicated by incised lines. Height: 2 inches. *Hmawza Museum.*

3

4

5

9

10

12

13

14

15

2. THE DVARAVATI AND THATON MONS (First–Fourteenth Century)

We have seen that before the Burmese historical period this region comprised not only the Pyu states but also the two Mon kingdoms, whose capitals were Thaton and Pegu. Thaton, an ancient harbor once situated on the Gulf of Martaban, is now inland about 8 miles north of the city of Moulmein. Pegu, another harbor which until the sixteenth century was still connected to the sea by lagoons, is about 55 miles from the modern city of Rangoon. Much evidence, geological as well as archaeological (gradual silting up of the mouths of the Irrawaddy and the Salween, excavations revealing sections of foreign ships, vestiges of chains and anchors), proved that these two sister cities at the time of their foundings—probably before the fifth century for Thaton and the sixth century for Pegu—had active harbors; they conducted continuous trade with foreign countries, principally India and, through her, perhaps even with the Roman Empire. These Mons of proto-Indochinese origin spoke a language similar to that of the Khmers. The Burmese called them Talaings, that is, "people of Telingana," an eastern province of India. The name "Pegu" was in fact "Ussa," a corruption of that of the Indian province of Orissa. But the name Talaing seems better applied to the people of Pegu than to those of Thaton (Ramanadesha), the older of the rival cities. In any case, the Mons, who occupy most of the geographical setting of present Burma, extended over a large part of Thailand, where they had a third capital, Nakhon Pathom (Nagara Pathama), the principal city of the Suvarnabhumi Kingdom (*The Golden Land*), according to legend founded in the time of the Emperor Ashoka. It would not be unusual if it could be actually confirmed that the great emperor had sent missions in every direction—his son to Ceylon and, according to texts, other ambassadors toward the Golden Land. If these envoys did not actually create the city of Nagara Pathama, they at least preached Buddha's Law on its site. The native population did the rest. These Suvarnabhumi Mons, who soon created the powerful Dvaravati Empire, were able to maintain themselves for a long period. Traces of them are found as far as northern Siam, at Lampun, where they erected a stupa which was rebuilt in the thirteenth century by the Thai. Whereas the site of Nakhon Pathom and its surroundings have been very carefully excavated and explored (by Prince Damrong and Pierre Dupont), those of Thaton and Pegu have still to reveal their entire wealth. Prince Damrong thought that the city of Thaton mentioned in Burmese chronicles was really that of Nakhon Pathom. As evidence he offered the facts that gold is not found at Thaton but in Thailand, that coins minted at Nakhon Pathom were found on the site of Pagan, and finally that the lack of vestiges of important monuments at Thaton proved that the latter had never been a capital.

We have few documents to help us understand and visualize the early period of the Mon kingdoms of Thaton and Pegu. On the other hand, the more numerous Dvaravati sites enable us to form some idea of the art which was one of the aspirations of these kingdoms. The people were strictly Hinayanists (Lesser Vehicle), having most probably been converted to the doctrine well before the schism of the Mahayana (Greater Vehicle) by monks from India or even from Ceylon. The sole surviving structure of any importance, which is extremely difficult to date, even approximately (it dates, however, from before the eleventh century), and which stands not far from Thaton, is the octagonal base of the Zokhethok Stupa, known in Burma as the Htsitaung Pagoda. This form is found in several other places—modern forms probably developed from a Mon type, the most famous example being the Sule Pagoda in the center of the city of Rangoon. We will see that at Pagan, in the twelfth century, this special type was to be perpetuated—with certain variations, however. There on Burmese territory we find the most ancient example of the use of laterite—a soft, reddish, very porous stone which in contact with air and light becomes extremely hard through oxidation. Although this laterite hardly lent itself to sculptural decoration, certain rather crude attempts were made in this medium at Zokhethok. Other Mon sculptures found in Burma either on Pegu territory or that of Thaton, still far from being original works, are clumsy copies of Indian works, generally in the Gupta style. They are either terra-cotta slabs or bronzes representing Buddha in one of the four positions accepted by the Theravada Canon.

With respect to the Dvaravati Kingdom, we are infinitely richer, although no architectural structure has survived. There are only a few stupa bases, like that of Phra Pathom Chedi, a few miles from Nakhon Pathom; that of Phra Men, not far away, discovered in 1939 by Pierre Dupont which, unprotected, is completely disappearing beneath rich tropical vegetation; and finally, the group of vestiges of Ban Kou Bua (comprising 44 monuments) about 11 miles south of Ratburi. With bases of laterite, these monuments were decorated with wonderful stucco reliefs, fragments of which are in the Bangkok Museum and in several private collections. From this early period there exists a natural cave decorated with two gigantic Gupta-style Buddhas carved in the wall, one standing and the other seated. The cave is intact. Mon architecture generally consists of a low structure on a laterite base made of large baked bricks assembled (and not cemented) with a kind of vegetable glue. Decoration was usually of terra cotta with stucco coating rather than sculptured stone. The superstructures of light material have perished and we have no idea what they were. Statues of Buddha existed in large numbers, generally of stone, sometimes of bronze, and more often of stucco. They are all derived from the Indian Gupta style. Standing and hieratic, they usually have both hands raised. The left hand is often holding the robe which clings to the body and which does not reveal the slightest muscle. And yet symmetry and crude execution easily distinguish them from their Gupta models. The gestures (*mudras*) are almost always explanations (*vitarka*), with thumb and index finger joined. The head is often splendidly treated yet lacking the delicacy of Indian models. In the seated position, Buddha is represented either in the European manner (at Phra Khas, Ngu Hill, Phra Pathom) or in one of the positions dear to Hinayana iconography: the diamond position, *vajrasana*, also known as the lotus position; that of the hero, *virasana*; or more simply in a "tailor position." The seat is often formed of the bent coils of the serpent Mucilinda, the Naga king. Legend relates how he saved the Buddha from drowning by carrying him off on the coils of his body and protecting him from rain with his hood spread like a parasol. Images of Buddha made of stucco were mainly designed for the decoration of stupa niches. Few complete examples exist, since stucco suffered the same fate as brick; but we can gain some idea of their style from certain fragments and from examining the square stupa reerected in 1218, probably from the same plans, at Lampun (Vat Kukut).

Stone slabs treated as bas-relief also reveal little about Dvaravati stupas. One of their special forms is one derived from the Indian motif of the vase of abundance (*purnaghata*) surmounted by a ringed cone, replacing and recalling the *stambha* and chattras of Indian stupas. The curious Gu Thao of Xieng Mai, the sole example of its type, erected about 1580, may be considered a late reminiscence of this form. We have already mentioned polygonal stupas (Zokhethok), an octagonal one at Lampun, and a quadrangular one at Lampun (Vat Kukut). The latter was probably founded in 755 by King Mahandayok, the son of queen Chamatdevi.

In Thailand, the Mon-Dvaravati Kingdom encountered a powerful rival in the eleventh century; the Khmer Empire had captured Lavo (Lopburi) and advanced toward the west. The Thai soon descended from the north both along the Salween and Chao Phraya valleys. Politically shaken, the Mons survived in isolated minorities or were absorbed by their conquerors. Their art suffered the same fate, but before falling into oblivion, it blended with that of the invaders to form a new aesthetic type which led to outstanding development—namely, Thai art.

16. BURMA, ZOKHETHOK, LATERITE RELIEF (*Thaton district*). This comes from the north side of the Mugalu Hill, near Zokhethok, and probably decorated a frieze on the base of a stupa now in ruins. On the left is a lion and on the right the remains of an elephant. In the center, an attractive decoration consists of three superimposed vases of abundance. These bas-reliefs were originally coated with stucco which has since disappeared. (*Photograph by the Burmese Archaeological Service.*)

17. BURMA, ZOKHETHOK, HTSITAUNG PAGODA (*Thaton district*). An old photograph, showing the octagonal laterite foundation of one of the most ancient Mon pagodas in Burma. The terrace, with its few architectural fragments, was probably decorated with stucco laterite panels. The relatively recent pagoda above this base may, however, have been built according to a traditional type characteristic of the Buddhism of the Thaton Mons who seem to have had a predilection for octagonal monuments. It is difficult, if not impossible, to assign an exact date to this edifice. All we can state is that it dates from the early centuries after Christ. (*Photograph by the Burmese Archaeological Service.*)

18. BURMA, KYONTHU, TERRA-COTTA BAS-RELIEF (*Pegu district*). A small slab, this is part of a pagoda decoration. From the composition of the decoration and its treatment, it appears to have been influenced by the Amaravati style. Child musicians (one is playing the flute, another a tambourine) seem to be enjoying the sight of a bullfight. This lively scene may be the work of Indian artists and would therefore date from the third or fourth century. (*Photograph by the Burmese Archaeological Service.*)

19. BURMA, RANGOON, SULE PAGODA. By its often modified form, this pagoda, which was rebuilt many times, seems, with its octogonal base and main section, to have kept the chief characteristic of Burmese Mon pagodas. If the upper spire, a relatively recent addition, were removed and replaced by parasols, we would perhaps have some idea of Mon pagodas in southern Burma during the early centuries after Christ. This greatly venerated pagoda now stands in the center of the Burmese capital.

20. THAILAND, NAKHON PATHOM, WHEEL OF THE LAW. This Wheel of the Law, made of stone and wonderfully treated, is almost 6 feet in diameter. It was found in the ruins of a sanctuary of Phra Pathom Chedi, one of the most ancient, if not the first, stupas erected at Suvarnabhumi about the close of the fifth century and since rebuilt in its modern form by King Mongkut about 1860. Before the introduction in India of the early images of Buddha (second century), it was customary to represent the Sage in the form of a symbol: throne, lotus, Wheel of the Law. This wheel may date from before the close of the second century. Discovered broken, it has been restored (white parts). The style of its decoration relates it to the early Amaravati style. At its feet, a gazelle of the same period symbolizes the site where for the first time Buddha had turned the Wheel of the Law at Sarnath, near Benares. Sandstone. *National Museum, Bangkok.*

21. THAILAND, AYUTHIA, VAT NANG KUI, BUDDHA. This Dvaravati stele represents Buddha in the usual position of meditation. In addition to the characteristic treatment of the legs, we find a double halo, encircling both body and head (perhaps due to Sinhalese influence), and the fold of the robe with its Indian pleat (itself inspired by the Greek fold typical of Gandharan sculpture). Pilgrims have pasted leaves of gold onto the statue. A beautiful work of the early style. Sixth–seventh century. Sandstone. Height: about 3 feet 3 inches. *Ayuthia Museum.*

22. THAILAND, PRACCHINBURI, FRAGMENT OF A COLUMN. With the exception of stupas (or pagodas or *chedis*), we know practically nothing about the architecture of the Mon-Dvaravati. Palaces, houses, and monasteries during the period when the Dvaravati Empire was being created (fifth–sixth century) were probably built of perishable materials: unbaked brick, wood, plaster, and tile. This column, probably part of a palace, is of utmost interest. Octagonal, of gray sandstone with a gilt-colored patina, it is still entirely Indian, with its decoration of intersecting garlands, and may be of the Gupta style. Height: 2 feet 8¾ inches. Sixth–eleventh century. *National Museum, Bangkok.*

23. THAILAND, THAM RUSI, THE CAVE BUDDHA. An early sanctuary, this cave is known especially for its Buddha seated in the European manner with an inscription (sixth–seventh century) at its feet indicating the donor's name. But the left wall has a very large, sculptured standing Buddha, unfortunately ruined by running water, which is less known. Probably contemporary with the seated Buddha, this image was originally lacquered and gilded. Height: 8 feet 4 inches.

24. THAILAND, AYUTHIA, VAT NA PHRA MERU BUDDHA (*detail and full figure*). This head, with its delicate features, is decorated with an ornamental ogival halo (Gupta influence). It belongs to a large statue 9 feet high, seated in the Western manner on a throne with a decorated back. The hands are resting flat upon the thighs, the feet set on a base in the form of a twin lotus. The hands and the lower parts of the statue have been badly restored. Limestone. Seventh–ninth century.

25. THAILAND, NAKHON PATHOM, MODEL OF A STUPA. Made from a single block of sandstone, this stupa was probably destined for the top of an edifice. Here the anda is in the form of an alms bowl and the harmika that of a drum. The seventeen chattras, or parasols, piled one above the other, lead to the high ringed spire which terminates the Thai *chedis* of later date. Height: about 6 feet. *National Museum, Bangkok.*

26. THAILAND, NAKHON PATHOM, INCISED STONE. Traced with a point on soft limestone and resembling a sketch from life, this amusing graffito was perhaps made for some magic purpose. The figure has long, curled hair, wears large earrings, has jewelry on his arm, and is seated on his right leg. He seems to be contemplating the objects around him: a vase with a narrow neck, a shell, a wheel(?), and a star. A small, charming duck has been added beyond the frame of this delightful work, probably by a monk. Sixth–ninth century. *National Museum, Bangkok.*

27. THAILAND, AYUTHIA, VAT SHIN, BUDDHIST STELE. A beautiful Dvaravati sculpture (sixth–eleventh century) representing the Great Miracle which, according to the Pali legend, Buddha performed near the city of Sravasti. The hierarchy of the figures grouped around that of Buddha seated in the Western manner and the symmetrical balance of the composition make this piece one of the most remarkable and typical works of that style. Buddha wished to confound the Thirthikas (Brahmans opposed to his doctrine) in the presence of King Prasenajit (represented here on the left, legs crossed). After having risen in the air and surrounded his body with flames and running water, Buddha multiplied his image infinitely, in the four positions symbolizing the episodes in his life, amazing the Thirthikas (below, right) by such wonders. Gray-green sandstone with traces of lacquer. Total height: 4 feet 2 inches. *National Museum, Bangkok.*

28. THAILAND, AYUTHIA, VAT SHIN, BUDDHIST STELE, Detail of the stele, *The Great Miracle of Sravasti*, showing worshipers (see plate 27).

29. THAILAND, NAKHON PATHOM, BUDDHIST STELE. This stele fragment in the Dvaravati style shows Buddha seated in the Western manner on a wonderful throne whose back is decorated with makaras (influence of the Srivijaya style, perhaps), which probably dates this work from about 800. Seated around him are members of the Samgha (monks) and brahmans or *rishis*. The delicately executed decoration below is chiefly floral. The folds of the robes and the details are incised. This stele appears to be of later date than the preceding one. *Nakhon Pathom Museum.*

30. THAILAND, STANDING BUDDHA. This very handsome torso in the Dvaravati style belonged to a statue of a standing Buddha, arms folded in front and his two hands in the vitarka mudra (preaching position). The treatment of the body and the folds of the robe covering the shoulders are very Indian, while still denoting a simplification in relationship to the post-Gupta style of the same period. Hard limestone. Height: 2 feet 8 inches. Source unknown. *Collection H.R.H. Princess Chumbhot, Bangkok.*

31. THAILAND, HAND OF A STANDING BUDDHA. (This photograph is turned to the horizontal.) Light-gray sandstone. Source uncertain. Length of the greater part: 5 inches. *National Museum, Bangkok.*

32. THAILAND, LOPBURI, STANDING BUDDHA. This was probably part of the decoration of an edifice. Sculpted from a block of limestone 5 feet high, rather hieratic, it is typical of the Dvaravati style, following here the post-Gupta style of the Ajanta caves rather closely. *Lopburi Museum.*

33. THAILAND, AYUTHIA, BUDDHA SEATED ON THE NAGA KING. A beautiful stele showing Buddha protected from rain and flood by the Naga king, Mucilinda. The very delicate treatment of the face seems to bear the stiffness characteristic of the early Dvaravati style (the nose has been badly restored); the robe covers only one shoulder. There is the same concern for balanced composition which here is emphasized by the curious small stupas supported by two *yakshas* (demons or nature deities) on either side of Buddha. The head of a grimacing kala is sculpted on the base of this stele, which probably decorated the gallery of a sanctuary or a niche in a stupa. Sandstone. Height: 4 feet 2 inches. Sixth–eleventh century. *National Museum, Bangkok.*

34. THAILAND, PRACCHINBURI, SEATED BUDDHA. This stele represents Buddha seated beneath the Bodhi tree. On either side, in low relief, are stupas with multiple roof-shaped parasols which somewhat resemble the *merus* of Bali. These parasols seem to spring from pots placed on square bases. Regular, composed features and serenity are the chief characteristics of this Buddha, whose body is naked to the waist. The legs are treated with great concern for realism despite flouting the laws of perspective and are simply executed. Sandstone. Height: 3 feet 4 inches. *National Museum, Bangkok.*

35. THAILAND, PRACCHINBURI, HEAD OF SEATED BUDDHA, *detail.* Profile view showing the details of the curled hair (see plate 34).

36. THAILAND, LOPBURI, HEAD OF BUDDHA. During the entire Dvaravati period (sixth–eleventh century) the types of Buddhas differed slightly according to local schools. Consequently, it is difficult to assign an exact place for each one in relationship to the others in chronological order. This Buddha of Lopburi, the shoulders covered, presents typically Mon features—thick nose, large lips emphasized by an outline in place of the mustache, eyebrows touching each other (a characteristic sometimes found also in Amaravati sculpture). Here, the curls of hair are more complicated and the modeling in the face shows great sensitivity. This head is part of a statue 5 feet high. Limestone. *Lopburi Museum.*

37. THAILAND, LOPBURI, VAT MAHADHATU, HEAD OF BUDDHA. This handsome face has the Mon characteristics of the Dvaravati Buddhas taken to extremes. The eyebrows form a continuous line, the eyes are emphasized by incised lines delineating the pupils, and a line also separates the forehead from the curled hair. This head seems to have belonged to one of the last periods of Dvaravati-style statuary, for a Khmer influence can be observed. Hard limestone, lacquered and gilded. Height: 2 feet ½ inch. *National Museum, Bangkok.*

38. THAILAND, LAMPUN, VAT KUKUT. Encompassed in Khmer art (known as the Lopburi style), Dvaravati art, which had disappeared in southern Thailand, nevertheless survived within the kingdom of Haripunjaya, in the northern part of the country. Vat Kukut, founded in the first half of the twelfth century by the Mon king Adichara (according to legend it was erected in 755 by the son of Queen Chamatdevi), then restored in 1218, shows architectural characteristics which, far from being new, are the logical result of many buildings which no longer survive but whose existence has been revealed by excavations at Phra Pathom. Built of brick and laterite, and 84 feet high, it consists of five cubic stories arranged somewhat like a pyramid and surmounted by square chattras, the whole resting on a square stone base. Each story is decorated with three niches holding standing Buddhas, which number 48 in all. The Sat-Mahal-Prasada of Polonnaruva at Ceylon, similar in conception, was perhaps built by monks from the Mon country. This style of edifice was followed at Lampun and in northern Thailand. The sovereigns who ruled the country erected structures copied from this model (Vat Maha That at Lampun, Chedi Si Liem at Xieng Mai). Its presence in the north and at so late a date is rather surprising.

39. THAILAND, LAMPUN, VAT PRAHTAT HARIPONCHAI, SECONDARY EDIFICE. This monument resembles Vat Kukut: square, with five stories, containing three Buddhas in side niches on each story, square parasols one above another, and resting on a square base. However, it is more slender and more delicately decorated. It could be attributed to King Sabbadisiddhi (early thirteenth century), who repaired Vat Kukut.

16

17

18

20

21

22

24

24

29

30

31

32

33   34

35

36

37

38   39

3. THE BEGINNINGS OF PAGAN (1044)

In 1057, the Pegu Kingdom having been encompassed in that of Thaton since the eighth century, a military expedition finally decided the fate of the Burmese Mons. But again, this industrious people did not disappear without leaving behind their techniques and style.

Many tribes related to the Pyus had long been established in the very fertile region on the banks of the Irrawaddy not far from its junction with the Chindwin. Chronicles relate that eighteen villages existed there, subsisting through the cultivation of rice, at the time when the Prome Kingdom, a prey to internal conflicts, sank into anarchy and fell into the hands of the Thaton Mons. Legends mention a list of mythical kings, from the supposed founder, Thammudarit, who probably lived from 107 to 152, to the real founder of Pagan, Anawratha (Aniruddha, 1044). During the seventh century, a priest named Popa Sawrahan tried to seize power, and in 638 created the "Small Era" to replace the Saka and Buddhist eras (the latter two having been in existence since A.D. 78 and c. 544 B.C., respectively) which were then the only ones in use. It continued in Burma as late as 1889. However, we know with some certainty that Pyinbya (848–78), the chief of the Pagan villages, united and fortified them with a brick enceinte wall in 849. Certain sections of this enceinte, especially a gate known as Sarabha, still exist. Several decades later, another king, Nyaung U Sawrahan (known also as Taungthugyi), the thirty-eighth king of Pagan according to the Hmannan Yazawin chronology (*The Chronicle of the Glass Palace*), anxious to create a lasting work in his fief, sent monks to Prome and Thaton to obtain plans of monuments and also workers. Indian influences had already penetrated Pagan, especially in the form of Mahayana Buddhism. Other sects, traveling by land from the north and the Tibetan frontier, "corrected" the Mahayanism which had entered the country by sea and across Arakan. These early "Burmese," who had descended from the Tibetan borders and settled at Pagan, were perhaps the originators of that Ari Tantric sect who had a form of worship marginal to official Mahayanism. These Ari monks worshiped the Naga gods (underworld spirits) and Buddha in his Lamaist form (veneration of the Buddha's *shaktis*), and led a less monastic life than is imagined, not hesitating in case of war to take up arms. To write down the canon of their faith they employed Sanskrit. Moreover, their faith soon influenced the local beliefs in the *nats*, or nature spirits (whose sacred home was the summit of Mount Popa), still venerated in Burma. Several Burmese kings, like Nyaung U, after whom a village near the capital is named, adhered to this doctrine.

These Burmese who had descended from the high Chinese plateaus had probably brought with them not only their magically inclined religious practices but also certain architectural forms. As a result, several outward-bulging stupas (pagodas) described in the annals as very ancient—such as the Bupaya attributed to the third king of Pagan, Pyusawdi (167–242), and the Ngakywenadaung Pagoda, which was probably built by King Nyaung U in the tenth century—have some association with the special form of Tibetan stupas (*chortens*). This would date their construction (the Bupaya especially) later than the eighth century. No inscription can assign an exact date to these stupas; those mentioned by Burmese chronicles appear very doubtful. Moreover, many of these stupas which bulge outward at the middle were often enlarged at different times. They are usually found incased one inside the other, sometimes covering a statue of Buddha. They are then known as *poromu*. Nevertheless they have retained their original form, which can often be seen when one of these chorten-stupas has half collapsed. These stupas seem to have been the only monuments that fell under Tibetan influence, and were probably built by the Ari sect, whose spiritual affiliation we have discussed. As their foundation was above all royal, these monuments were probably erected during the reign of the Ari kings, like Nyaung U, who was a usurper. From this it is easy to assume that this stranger to the normal dynasty was of Burmese-Tibetan origin and perhaps the first Burmese king in the country's history. But such a conclusion is impossible without strong proof, and until now there has been none.

The second influence discernible in Pagan architecture before the period of the historical king Anawratha is that of Mahayana Buddhism, which had entered central Burma from the Arakanese west coast. In fact, this region has many temples of distinct Indian design. We shall discuss them later. At Nyaung U, near Pagan, a single monument has this character, the Kyaukku-Umin, which, unlike all other edifices of central Burma, is built of sandstone. Set against a cliff, this massive cubic construction consists of a huge stone vault with many niches containing Buddhas. The sanctuary houses a large statue of the Sage in the Gupta style. The interior sculptures (depicting the life of Buddha) and the exterior ones (decorations of the door posts), as well as the frescoes, have the same characteristic. This monument is attributed to the "founder" of Pagan, King Pyinbya, while the upper terraces (added or restored) made of brick were probably the work of King Narapatisithu (1173–1210), the forty-eighth king on the traditional list. Rather different in type yet of the same influence, it is related to the Nat Hlaung Kyaung Temple, which is also at Pagan. Built entirely of brick with a vaulted entrance, it is the sole Hindu sanctuary at Pagan and is dedicated to the worship of Vishnu. Beautiful sandstone sculptures representing the avatars of this god decorate the outer niches, and four large figures of Vishnu, sculptured in the brick, adorn the sides of the massive central pillar. Frescoes, unfortunately in very bad condition, decorate the inner walls. This temple—again according to chronicles—was probably built by the Ari king Nyaung U, in 931.

Finally, there is the Pawdomu, a very special stupa of modest dimensions which was once incased in another brick edifice and uncovered by Scovels. Of unusual shape, built on three hexagonal terraces, the anda (part of the stupa known in Burma as the *thabaikhmauk*) is surmounted by a kind of sikhara, itself surmounted by a flower bud (*kyayaythi*) supported by a lotus (*kyar*). These two last elements, although somewhat modified, are found in many Burmese stupas (payas or pagodas). But it is difficult to determine to which influences this type of monument owes its curious shape. It may be an example of Ari architecture. In any case, it dates from before the eleventh century. This may very well be one of the aspects of the rather paradoxical genius of King Nyaung U.

In Arakan, on the west coast, there existed a unique style of architecture, directly influenced by India, which had a certain importance in the development of Burmese styles. Unfortunately almost nothing remains of these temples of Brahmanic design and persuasion. Since Buddhism did not appear in Arakan until the tenth century, eleventh-century art underwent a Pagan influence, then a Moslem one much later. In 1433 a capital was founded at Mrohaung, on the banks of the Lemro River, by King Narameikhla (1404–34), who made Arakan an independent country. We will discuss this in relationship to the Burmese kingdoms.

However, in 1055, Anawratha, the son of King Kunsaw Kyaungpyu, the thirty-ninth king on the lists, ruler of Pagan after having vanquished in single combat the last of the legal pretenders, became the forty-second sovereign. A young monk, Shin Arahan, who had come from Thaton to preach the Hinayana Doctrine (Lesser Vehicle), succeeded in converting the sovereign, who named him counselor. But the monarch needed the sacred writings, and these, written in Pali, could only be obtained at Thaton. A courteous request made to the ruler of Thaton was rejected. So Anawratha decided to procure the texts by force. Thaton was seized in 1057, pillaged thoroughly, and completely razed. On the return journey, Anawratha, his appetite whetted, pounced upon Prome, razed the city, and seized its relics. He returned to Pagan in triumph, followed by 39 elephants laden with sacred writings and relics and a huge procession of Mon captives—writers, artists, artisans—whom he installed at Pagan. The Mon king, Manuha, although well treated, was confined to his residence at Myinkaba, not far from the capital, where he was allowed to build (with his own funds, of course) a temple for his personal use. This military exploit and massive importation of specialists enabled Anawratha to inaugurate his newly established power with a construction program that was never surpassed. But more important, the monuments built by the king will ultimately help us to understand Mon architecture, since many of the

56

master workmen and artists were then originally from Thaton and Prome. Three phases of Pagan architecture soon come to light: the Mon period, with its reminiscences of Pyu architecture; a transitory period; and finally a style of architecture known as "classic Burmese," which ended with the brutal arrival of Kublai Khan's vanguard in 1287 and the flight of the last great king of Pagan, Naratihapati.

40. BURMA, PAGAN, BUPAYA PAGODA. Although tradition states it was built by the third king of Pagan in the third century, this pagoda, renovated and repaired by many sovereigns, certainly dates from the ninth or tenth century. Erected on a summit bordering the Irrawaddy where the river bends toward the south, it was used as a landmark by navigators. The ground descends steeply toward the river and has been arranged in concentric terraces bordered by crenelated parapets. The very shape of the pagoda, built on a low octagonal terrace bordered by pointed crenels, resembles that of Tibetan chortens, narrow at the base and swelling toward the top. An *amalaka* flattened like a cushion supports a very high point of concave lines on its summit, topped by a modern wrought-iron hti. The structure is solid. Leaves or petals decorate the summit of the bulb and the amalaka. In a modern wooden pagoda (Mondaing Nat) built alongside the Bupaya, a tempest nat (a nature spirit) is venerated, which clearly indicates the designed role of this pagoda, a guide to navigators.

41. BURMA, PAGAN, SARABHA GATE. This gate, standing east of the enceinte of the city of Pagan (the sole vestige of the city walls), on the road from Pagan to Nyaung U, has four brick pillars, and its summit has disappeared. It, as well as the city walls, were probably the work of the thirty-fourth king of Pagan, Pyinbya (848–78). Two niches made of brick and stucco contain the guardian nats of the city. These nats, who were brother and sister, were said to have lived on Mount Popa and the oracles they gave were famous. The female nat, on the right of the photograph (held in greater esteem than her brother), is perched on a raised pedestal at the head of a small stairway used by the faithful to lay their offerings at the feet of the statue. The type of architecture exemplified by this gate is probably the most ancient instance of the early Pagan style, at a time when Buddhism, introduced from the northwestern lands, was strongly marked by Tantric, Bengali, and Sino-Tibetan practices. The nats on this gate are still venerated by the local populace.

42. BURMA, PAGAN, NGAKYWENADAUNG PAGODA. According to tradition this stupa was erected in the tenth century by King Nyaung U, who seems to have reigned at Nyaung U after the Pagan leader Theinko (915–31), the thirty-seventh king listed in

The Chronicle of the Glass Palace. This date seems to be confirmed. It is similar in shape to the Bupaya Pagoda insofar as the bulb of the stupa is concerned. Unfortunately we cannot make any definite statement about the appearance of the base or that of the summit. One special characteristic of this pagoda is that it is partially covered with beautiful green glazed tiles.

43. BURMA, PAGAN, NYAUNG U, KYAUKKU-UMIN TEMPLE. This impressive structure is set against the side of a ravine situated somewhat east of the village of Nyaung U. It consists of a single vaulted room containing four massive pillars and a large statue of Buddha, and is surrounded by a half-vaulted corridor. The projecting entrance with its semicircular arch is decorated, like the base moldings, with bas-relief sculptures representing mythological figures and floral motifs. The inner walls hold many niches where statues and altars of the Thousand Buddhas were placed. The vaulting, covered with frescoes which are unfortunately in bad condition, is also sculpted with niches containing Buddhas and stupas. The upper terraces built of brick were added by the king of Pagan, Narapatisithu (1173–1210). The entire construction, made of brick and cut stone, was carefully executed. Light for the sanctuary is provided by the entrance door, whereas the corridor has grid-like windows. As this monument is unparalleled, the only one of its kind at Pagan, it is difficult to assign it an exact date, but it can be attributed to the tenth century.

44. BURMA, PAGAN, NYAUNG U, KYAUKKU-UMIN TEMPLE, VAULTING. This photograph shows the inner temple vaulting and the curious arrangement of the bricks creating the ogival arches. We can see the small niches in bas-relief and the remains of frescoes. At the far end and on the left are the half-vaults of the gallery.

45. BURMA, PAGAN, NAT HLAUNG KYAUNG TEMPLE. The only Brahmanic temple of Pagan, it may have been built in 931 by King Nyaung U. Relatively small, almost square in plan, with four superimposed roofs acting as false stories, this temple was surmounted by a sikhara adorned on its four sides by statues of divinities placed in ornamented niches. In the center of the sanctuary, an enormous brick pillar supports the sikhara, delimiting around its base a rather large vaulted gallery. Against the pillar are four large brick statues of a standing divinity (Vishnu?). The temple was dedicated to Vishnu, and his avatars were represented by sandstone sculptures placed in niches arranged on the outer four walls of the temple. The main door, which is reached by means of a small flight of steps, has a sandstone framing whose broken lintel has recently been replaced. On either side of the steps the statue of a guardian (dvarapala) once stood sculptured in the brick. The interior of the sanctuary, decorated with very nearly obliterated frescoes representing Vishnu and his procession of worshipers and devas, is very dark, only dormers and small, narrow windows providing light.

46. BURMA, PAGAN, NAT HLAUNG KYAUNG TEMPLE, VISHNU. This statue set against a central pillar perhaps represents Vishnu. Greatly damaged, the temple's Hindu-style statues, possibly inspired by Bengali art, make it impossible to determine whether this is Vishnu or Shiva. The statues are sculpted in brick and coated with stucco. On the left we can see the remains of the wall painting.

47. BURMA, PAGAN, PAWDAWMU STUPA. This structure, which was recently brought to light, was enclosed by a more recent stupa. Well preserved, it has an almost cylindrical anda placed on a very high, stepped base which resembles a temple structure. The anda is topped by a cone formed of a pile of rings of decreasing diameter, all different,

terminating in a lotus bud. The shape of this anda resembles that of a stupa erected in the eleventh century by Anawratha near Myinkaba. However, this stupa may be earlier in date, marking the beginning of a transition from the traditional stupa to the temple surmounted by a stupa. The base may be treated as a temple, although here it consists of a solid structure, with vertical walls and superimposed terraces. The treatment of the terraces and the cone rings of this stupa lead us to attribute it to the close of the tenth century, but as yet nothing enables us to assign an exact date.

48. BURMA, PAGAN, THIYIPYITSAYA, WEST PAGODA OF PETLEIK. The two pagodas of Petleik (the older one is probably that shown here) were conceived according to a Sinhalese type and stand not far from the Lawkananda Pagoda. They could very well be contemporary with it, although some authors attribute a more ancient origin (tenth century?). These pagodas have no special characteristics except their very large bases encircled by a covered gallery entirely decorated with fine terra-cotta plaques illustrating the *Jatakas* (episodes from the life of Buddha).

49. BURMA, PAGAN, EAST PAGODA OF PETLEIK, TERRA-COTTA BAS-RELIEF.

50. BURMA, PAGAN, EAST PAGODA OF PETLEIK, TERRA-COTTA BAS-RELIEF REPRESENTING A RISHI OR AN ASCETIC.

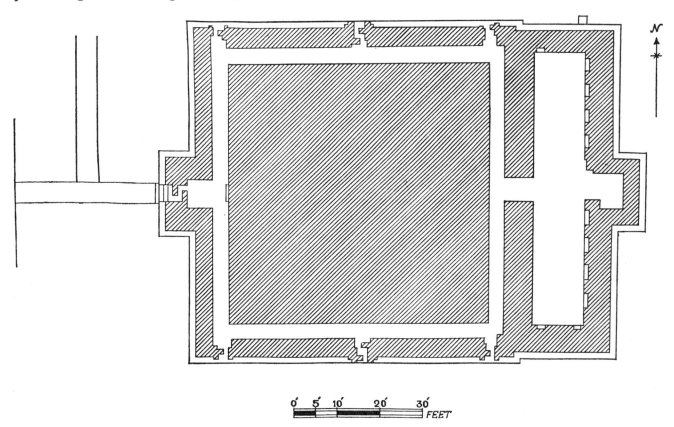

FIG. 6. GROUND PLAN OF THE EAST PAGODA OF PETLEIK AT PAGAN

49

48

IV. THE BURMESE KINGDOMS

1. THE ART OF THE PAGAN KINGDOM (1047–1287)

WITH THE ACCESSION to the Pagan throne by the Burmese king Anawratha (1044) and his conquest of the Mon country of lower Burma in 1047, there began a glorious period of construction which lasted for more than two and a half centuries and covered an area of almost 240 square miles surrounding Pagan. Included among the most important villages were those of Nyaung U to the north and Myinkaba and Pwasaw to the south and southeast. For a long time the Burmese capitals of Tampawadi (today the hamlet of Pwasaw), Thiripyitsaya, and Pawkkan (now unimportant villages around Pagan) had been abandoned. After King Pyinbya had transferred his capital of Tampawadi to Pagan (then known as Arimaddana), the embellishment of the city and its surroundings was begun. After surrounding the city with walls, architects who had come from Hmawza (Prome), Pegu, and Arakan began to erect monuments. But it was not until the Mon architects imported from Thaton (and probably from Prome also) were established at Pagan that the project assumed definite form. The region was then very rich in forests and rice fields well moistened by rainfall (the climate has since changed) and by the Irrawaddy and its tributaries. The clayey soil lent itself to the making of good-quality bricks. The Pagan Empire was huge and extended from the north of Mandalay to Thaton in the south, including the middle valley of the Irrawaddy and its rich rice lands of Kyaukse. To the east, the Thai and Shans, unsettled warring tribes, paid them an annual tribute. To the west were the Arakanese, separated from the Pagan Empire by a chain of mountains inhabited by hostile tribes. The king was therefore sufficiently wealthy to begin an unprecedented construction project which his successors were willing to continue. Thus we can still find the sites of more than 5000 monuments, while about a thousand, more or less ruined, are still standing. As the region became dry and arid after a climatic change, most of the monuments remained in better condition than if the monsoon rains had fallen on them regularly. As almost always during that period, the only buildings of hard material which resisted man and the elements—the last Pagan king demolished many constructions in order to erect ramparts against Kublai Khan's troops—were those of religious establishments. However, traces of palace foundations and other edifices have been found. But the structures built of perishable material have completely disappeared. The monuments which have remained belong essentially to five types:

1. Solid stupas or zedis
2. Sanctuaries whose internal structure consists of rooms and corridors
3. Monasteries
4. Structures copied from light edifices
5. Caves

But these types obviously include many variations, due more to the different artists and artisans who erected them than to a ruler's preference.

By examining these monuments, almost all of which were built of brick, we can attempt to classify them as follows, without respect to chronology:

1. Stupas or zedis
   a. Stupas in the form of a reliquary casket or of Tibetan inspiration: Bupaya, Ngaykywena-daung
   b. Sinhalese-type stupas: Sapada, Pebyingyaing, Petleik
   c. Bell-shaped stupas (Burmese type) with or without foundations terraced as a pyramid: Shwezigon, Shwesandaw, Mingalazedi (1274), Myinkaba, Seinnyet Myima, Lawkananda (1054), Dhammayazika
2. Sanctuaries
   a. With central pillar and enclosing corridor: Ananda, Shwegugyi (1131), Dhammayangyi (1167–70), Thambulla (1256), Nat Hlaung Kyaung (931)
   b. With central cella and surrounding corridor: Nagayon, Abeyadana, Kubyauk-Gyi, Pathothamya
   c. With sanctuary erected on a solid block: That Byinnyu (1144), Sulamani, Htilominlo, Gawdawpalin

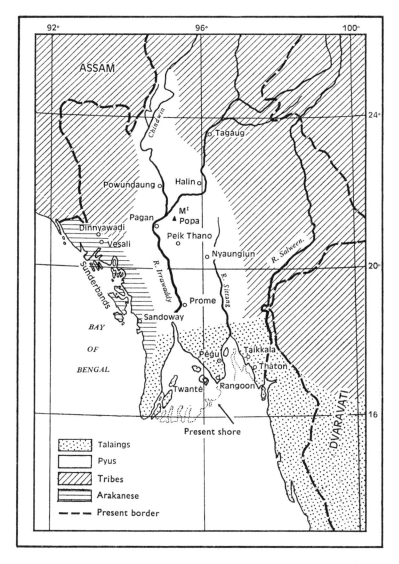

FIG. 7. THE PAGAN KINGDOM IN THE THIRTEENTH CENTURY

d. With single cella having one or several entrances (*gu* type): Lokhatlikpan, Hsinpyagu, Mahabodhi, Winidho, Kondawgyi, Nandamannya
3. Light edifices (unlike stupas)
    a. Ordination halls or long halls: Upali Thein, Shinbinthalyaung
    b. Libraries: Pithakat Taik, Mimalaung Kyaung
4. Monasteries
    a. Central courtyard surrounded by cella: Somingyi
    b. Without central courtyard: Shinbome, Theynpyie, etc.
5. Caves: (Umin) Thammiwet, Hmyathat, Kyaunzittha-Umin

However, in addition to this necessarily arbitrary and incomplete classification, there are unusual types; among the zedis, some are built on square, pentagonal, hexagonal, octagonal, or round terraces with three or five steps. Some, like the Dhammayazika, have a small gu-type sanctuary on each side (in this precise case); others, like the Minpyagu and the Petleik, have terraces in which corridors have been arranged.

As for the sanctuaries, each one is either surmounted by a tower in the form of a stupa— Kondawgyi (thirteenth century), Patothamya (tenth–eleventh century), Abeyadana (1084– 1112), Nandamannya (1248); or by a sikhara similar to those of the temples of northern India— Thetkyamuni (twelfth century), Htilominlo (1218), Ananda (1091), That Byinnyu (1144), Shwegugyi (1131), Gawdawpalin (1173–1210), Nanpaya (tenth century), Nagayon (1084), Seinnyet Nyima (eleventh century), Sulamani (1183), Thambulla (1255), Lemyethna (1222), Payathonzu (close of the thirteenth century); or by a tower of the Bodh-Gaya type—Mahabodi (1210–34), Kubyauk-Gyi (1113); or, finally, by a roofing that I shall qualify as Mon and which was probably used in a general manner in all light buildings of that period, here translated into more lasting material: sloping and curved terraced roofs, bordered on the diminishing corners by edifices or railing motifs in the form of a bird: Mimalaung Kyaung (1174), Pithakat Taik (1058), Shinbinthalyaung (eleventh century). Some temples combine both this roof form and a terminal tower: Kubyauk-Gyi (1113), Manuha (1059), Nagayon (1084), Abeyadana (1084–1112).

Chronologically we can classify the architecture of Pagan temples into four definite periods:

1. Before 1047: buildings of different types with Indian, Tibetan, Arakanese, Pyu, and Mon influences
2. From 1047 to 1160 (two definite types):
    a. Mon architecture
    b. Burmese architecture of Mon influence
    These two styles are characterized by simple plans with dark cella, corridors dimly lighted by fretted windows, and mural paintings with inscriptions in Mon characters
3. From 1131 to 1287: the style becomes frankly Burmese: the plans are more complicated, the sanctuaries higher, the galleries lighted by high windows, and the frescoes bear only Burmese inscriptions

This is the plan we are going to follow in order to classify the iconography.

ARCHITECTURE KNOWN AS MON STYLE

The general plan of this style was derived from the Pyu temples of Hmawza (Lemyethna and Bebegyi), but was qualified as Mon, however, to this day, because of the decoration of certain architectural details (clec motif of door arches and windows, Mon rather than Pali inscriptions on the frescoes, fretted windows, etc.).

The most typical temples of this style are Patothamya, Nagayon, Nanpaya, Manuha, Abeyadana, Alopyi, Kubyauk-Gyi, Myebontha Phayala, Kubyauknge, Lokhatlikpan.

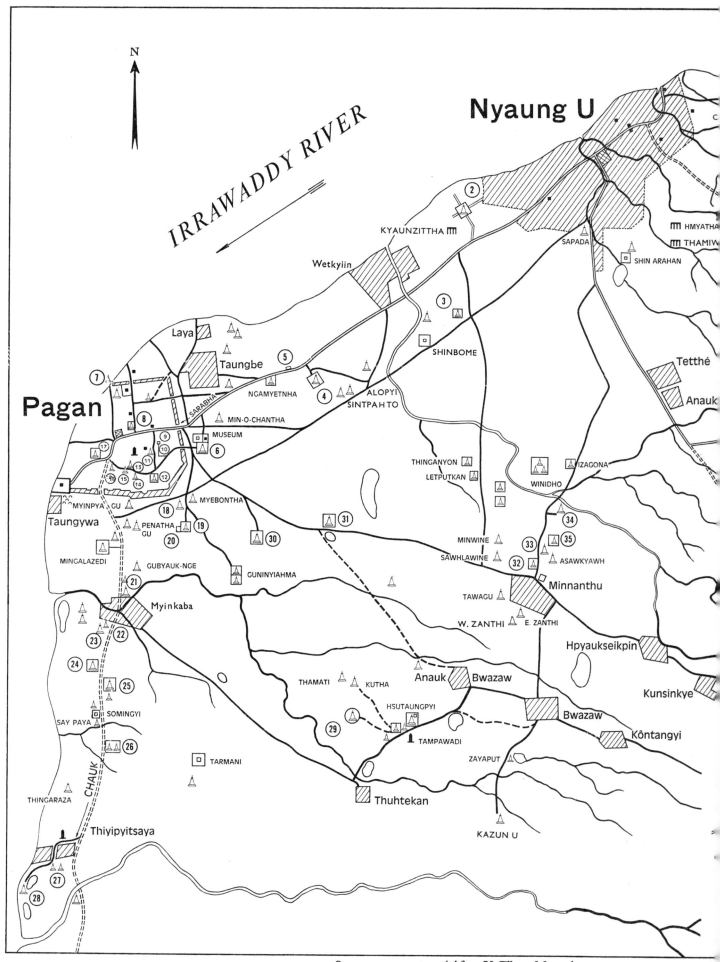

N

IRRAWADDY RIVER

Nyaung U

② KYAUNZITTHA 血

Wetkyiin

SAPADA

血 HMYATHA
血 THAMIW

SHIN ARAHAN

③

Laya

Taungbe

⑤

SHINBOME

Tetthé

Anauk

⑦

Pagan

NGAMYETNHA

④ ALOPYI
SINTPAHTO

MIN-O-CHANTHA

⑧

⑨ MUSEUM

THINGANYON
LETPUTKAN

IZAGONA

WINIDHO

⑩

⑥

⑰

⑪ ⑬ ⑫

⑯ ⑮ ⑭

MYINPYA GU

MYEBONTHA

⑱

⑱

③④

Taungywa

PENATHA
GU

⑲

③① ③①

MINWINE

③③ ③⑤

MINGALAZEDI

⑳

②⓪

SAWHLAWINE

ASAWKYAWH

③②

GUBYAUK-NGE

GUNINYIAHMA

②①

TAWAGU

Minnanthu

Myinkaba

W. ZANTHI

E. ZANTHI

②③ ②②

Hpyaukseikpin

②④

②⑤

THAMATI

KUTHA

Anauk

Bwazaw

Kunsinkye

SAY PAYA

SOMINGYI

②⑥

HSUTAUNGPYI

②⑨

TAMPAWADI

Bwazaw

Kôntangyi

ZAYAPUT

TARMANI

THINGARAZA

Thuhtekan

THINGARAZA

CHAUK

Thiyipyitsaya

KAZUN U

②⑦

②⑧

FIG. 8. MAP OF PAGAN (*After U Thau Maung*)

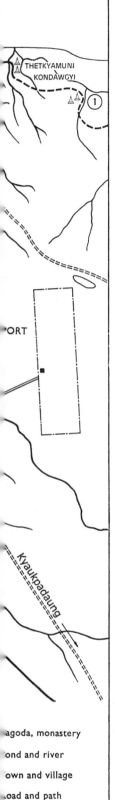

THETKYAMUNI
KONDÂWGYI

①

'ORT

Kyaukpadaung

agoda, monastery

ond and river

own and village

.oad and path

Valls of the
ncient city

ncient palace, site,
avern

KEY

1. Kyaukku-Umin Temple
2. Shwezigon Stupa
3. Kubyauk-gyi (Wetkyiin) Temple
4. Htilominlo Temple
5. Ordination Hall of Upali Thein
6. Ananda Temple
7. Bupaya Pagoda
8. Mahabodhi Temple
9. Pithakat Taik Library
10. Thandawgya Buddha
11. Shwegugyi Temple
12. That Byinnu Temple
13. Ngaykwenadaung Pagoda
14. Nat-Hlaung-Kyaung Temple
15. Patothamya Temple
16. Mimalaung Kyaung Temple
17. Gawdawpalin Temple
18. Lokhatlipan Temple
19. Shwesandaw Pagoda
20. Shinbinthalyaung Temple
21. Kubyauk-Gyi (Myinkaba) Temple
22. Manuha Temple
23. Nanpaya Temple
24. Abeyadana Temple
25. Nagayon Temple
26. Seinnyet Nyima Temple and Stupa
27. East and West Petleik Pagodas
28. Lawkananda Pagoda
29. Dhammayazika Stupa-Temple
30. Dhammayangyi Temple
31. Sulamani Temple
32. Lemyethna Temple
33. Payathonzu Temple
34. Nandamannya Temple
35. Thambulla Temple

ARCHITECTURE OF MON INFLUENCE

This architecture retained certain characteristics known as Mon (dark sanctuaries, fretted windows) but borrowed its plans from India. The most characteristic temple of this type is Ananda (1091). Dhammayangyi, another unfinished temple, built about 1170, belongs to this type.

BURMESE ARCHITECTURE

As early as 1131, this new type (construction of Shwegugyi) reveals a definite reaction against the Mon style. The stupa seems to have acquired its final Burmese form: a splayed bell surmounted by a long cone which becomes slender, like an arrow. The bell shape probably stems from a confusion in a continuous surface line of the base, of the main section (anda), and of the reliquary casket of the Indian or Sinhalese stupa: the slender spire with piled parasols is nothing more than an ornament. To recall the parasols, signs of royalty and divinity, the Burmese felt the need to add a triple wrought-iron parasol (hti) to the pinnacle. Finally, the bell itself was adorned with a band decorated with garlands and, often, the heads of monsters, the garlands perhaps inspired by those which decorate the andas of Amaravati stupas.

The temples were then built on a high, pyramidal platform with sanctuaries largely exposed to light.

That Byinnyu, Htilominlo, Gawdawpalin, Sulamani, and Lemyethna (1222) are typical examples of this style. However, alongside these massive structures were small temples which, instead of being built on a square plan, consisted of a simple sanctuary fronted by a vestibule with the main entrance at the far end. The most outstanding examples of this are Shwegugyi (1131), Thambulla (1256), Thetkyamuni (end of the twelfth century), Kondawgyi (thirteenth century), Kubyauk-Gyi—Wetkyiin—(1113), Nandamannya (1248), Payathonzu (end of the thirteenth century).

We shall therefore show, after the different types of stupas, first these temples and their decoration, then the "light" styles and the Mahabodhi type, and finally the caves which, scarcely decorated, are far from having the value of those we have already seen in India. It appears clear that, in spite of the word Mon given to many of these monuments of the early Pagan period, the principal types seem in general to have been more clearly derived from architectural styles used among the Pyus. It is obvious that Anawratha's conquest of the Mon countries of lower Burma greatly favored the flowering of this style, thanks to the contribution of artisans who were trained in the construction technique used by the Pyus of Hmawza before the ninth century. The Mon architecture of Thaton is unknown to us. The rare examples of stupas in the region (Zokhethok) offer no information concerning the type of sanctuary used. Did the Pyus borrow their art and plans from the Thaton Mons, or did they develop them themselves, basing the style on an architecture which has since disappeared and which seems to have flourished in Bengal and on the Orissa Coast in India at that period?

In Arakan, on the banks of the Lemro River, are the ruins of certain stone temples. If a study of these were made, they might furnish information on the development of this architecture. Since Mon writing had been used on the frescoes of many of the temples of the early Pagan period, people have concluded, somewhat too easily, it seems, that this architectural type is of Mon origin. As for the decoration of these sanctuaries—a decoration consisting of a thick coating applied to the brick walls, and then incised—nothing implies that it is more typically Mon than Pyu, with the exception of several simple geometrical forms which, moreover, do not belong exclusively to the Mon type.

The greatest originality of these Pagan temples lies mainly in the construction method of their vaults. In fact, in contrast to those of the Indian family, which has corbelled masonry, these are built of small blocks (usually brick or, in special cases, stone, like Nanpaya), designed in a radiating fashion to form a pointed ogival arch consisting of joined flattish arches. This peculiarity, which is reminiscent of ancient Persian arches, may have reached Burma through the Ganges Valley. A greater understanding of ancient Bengali architecture is necessary to offer some information about this form of arch which, it is rather interesting to note, had no known precedent in India. Nor does it seem to have been imitated among the other arts of the Indochinese peninsula. If the Dvaravati Mons were acquainted with this vaulting system, it is very probable that the Thai would later have been inspired by it. The method offered outstanding advantages, including dispensing with an arch. The Thaton Mons may have used this method, but evidence has yet to be furnished. It is only among the Pyus that we find this formula inaugurated. This may lead to a possible explanation of different Indian influences; as far as the Mons are concerned, the principal ones came from the southern coast of India (Telingana), by sea especially; and, as far as the Pyus are concerned, more exclusively by land, from Orissa and Bengal via Arakan.

Although the Pagan civilization was greatly indebted to the Thaton monks who introduced, in addition to Theravada Buddhism, a certain way of thought and probably writing, nevertheless the art of this kingdom remains indisputably Burmese—the Pyus being obviously of the same origin as the Burmese-Tibetan tribes who had long settled at Pagan.

We have already mentioned that many of the Pagan monuments were of brick. The reason was mainly the lack of building stone in the immediate neighborhood of the site, where the ground lent itself well to making this lightweight material which could easily be produced in great quantity. The bricks were fired in the open air, with brushwood used as fuel, and often made more even by rubbing them against one another. A legend concerning the Dhammayangi relates how during the construction of this temple by King Narathu (1167–70), the workmen were threatened with death if a needle could be inserted between any two bricks in the wall. This is sufficient to explain how carefully these bricks were formed and laid. Stone (a kind of rather soft sandstone) was use sparingly either to ensure greater rigidity for parts of the wall above the windows or to strengthen the corners of certain constructions. These cornerstones are often sculpted. At Sulamani, certain arches and wall sections consist of regularly alternating brick and rubble. In many of the Mon temples, the *jalis*, or fretted windows, consist of a single, pierced block of stone.

But in almost every case, stone is treated like brick, cut into small sections and laid like brick.

Decoration consists of stucco and wall paintings. Sculptures, with the exception of those representing Buddha, are rare. Wall decoration is usually executed in a kind of crude stucco applied to brick and sculpted. The ornament used at Pagan presents many similarities to that of the most ancient Orissa styles (the Mukteshvara Temple at Bhuvaneshvara), mainly the friezes formed of beading which usually decorate the upper spaces of the walls delimited by the pilasters. Geometrical motifs dominate, and often include people (Buddha, the Goddess of Fortune), animals, geese, monkeys, gazelles, or even mythical beings (*kinnaris*, makaras), in an iconography completely borrowed from India. Floral motifs are numerous, always stylized, used either as foliage with figures or animals, or as isolated decorative motifs, or even stylized to the extreme as more or less slender, flaming tongues to crown the tops of windows or doors. The most common motif used to decorate arches is the clec, a Mon word. Several authors have given this motif a specifically Mon origin, but I consider this somewhat premature, since no example of it has been discovered in Mon architecture of Thaton or of Dvaravati. It is even difficult to give it a Pyu origin, although I am inclined to do so, the Pyus having elaborated a gu-type architecture which was greatly developed at Pagan. Since the stucco reliefs of the Pyu temples at Hmawza are now lost, we can only state that edifices like Lemyethna and Bebegyi do not have arch motifs similar to, or at least foreshadowing, the clec. However, it seems that the clec owes its origin to India, for the raised corners are related (in a rather distant fashion) to the corner motifs of diverging makaras found on certain Indian monuments, and, in Khmer art, as far as Angkor. This would be confirmed by the presence, on the clec corners of certain monuments (Nanpaya,

Htsitaung, Theynpie Monastery), of reliefs representing makaras disgorging mythical animals and human beings. But again we must be careful. Did the decoration inspire the form? Or is it a decoration added to a pre-existing form? I should be inclined to accept the second solution, which seems more sensible. If the diverging makaras determined the form of the clec corners, what was the origin of the upward-thrusting leaves toward the top which form the true decoration of the arch? It appears more logical to see in this motif a stylization of flames, a motif common to most entrances—flames destined to purify those entering the sanctuary and recalling the fact that the spiritual flame lives forever in the holy place. As Nirvana can only be attained by the freedom of the soul from all earthly attachment, it would then seem normal to see the flames of the clec consume persons and animals, passions and desires. This would explain the presence of makaras and other decorative forms in the flames of the clec. Moreover, this motif, common to Pagan, is found only above the openings of doors and windows, which leads us to assume that this was actually a symbol of purification.

Another explanation seems plausible for its origin. The clec appears above the doors and openings of all the gu-type sanctuaries, that is, caves. It may be that this triangular-shaped motif derives its origin from the stylized form of the mountain in which a cave is usually found. Certain details of wall painting in Pagan temples (Abeyadana, for example) showing scenes which take place in caves topped by a stylized mountain, could very well support this suggestion. Yet I prefer the theory of purifying flames which seems closer to the Buddhist spirit, the other being merely a fortuitous relationship of representations. Following this type of reasoning, this clec motif may be compared to the one used by the Pyus in the form of a crown to adorn devas' heads and symbolizing a halo of fire, similar to the auras surrounding the heads of Islamic saints in certain Turkish miniatures of a later date.

This ornament of flaming tongues, associated with corner horns (derived perhaps from decorations formed by diverging makaras), contributes to shedding more light on the origin of the clec which, far from being Mon, may very well be of Pyu inspiration—that is, Burmese. This motif follows a very distinct development and, at the close of the Pagan period, became very slender and rigid, having little ornament. Only the emphasized corners still suggest the makara form. Sometimes the pediment, delimited by the clec and the window, is also decorated with an ornamentation which is generally a vase of abundance (Nanpaya), dear to Indian decoration but here treated with less exuberance.

Among the secondary motifs made by application of stucco is that of the head of a *kala* or *rahu*, a grimacing head provided with arms, about to devour something, or else sticking out an unusually long tongue which conceals the entire lower jaw. These heads of kala are often disgorging strings of beading belonging to friezes (Htilominlo). Dwarfs (ganas) and lions placed on the corners usually complete the decoration of the outer walls. Lions are treated in the Indian style and generally with much fantasy, the artists merely interpreting after their own fashion the models furnished by India. The historiated medallion—so common to Indian art long before Bharhut, Sanchi, and Amaravati—is here rarely seen (at Thetkyamuni, for instance). On the other hand, triangle and diamond shapes are commonly used.

Sculpture has less variety and generally consists of repetitions of Buddha in one of the four positions accepted by the Pali Canon. These images are almost always similar and scarcely appear to have undergone any distinct development during the Pagan period. Their type appears to be derived from the one used during the Pala Dynasty in Bengal, especially in the Nalanda Monastery in Bihar. The most common pose is the one representing the Sage in *bhumisparsa*—that is, in the act of touching the earth in witness of his resolution to conquer the Forces of Evil. The legs are crossed in the lotus position, the soles of the feet turned upward, the left hand, palm upward, resting on the right thigh, and the right hand touching the ground near the right knee. The garment clings to the body. Slightly bent, eyes half-closed, the head seems to be smiling at the ground. The hair is treated in small, tight curls and terminates in an ushnisha in the form of a lotus bud. The throne is almost always formed of a double lotus, sometimes placed on a high, recessed base.

We find several seated Buddhas treated in a mediocre manner (Manuha, Shinbinthalyaung), as well as standing ones (Ananda), and also several sculptures in the round, the most representative being those having the features of King Kyaunzittha and the monk Shin Arahan, now in the Ananda Temple. Another famous group, which represents the birth of Gautama Buddha and kept in the same sanctuary, has an unmistakable Pala stamp.

Although their sculpture in the round has little originality, Pagan artists showed definite talent in the many terra-cotta bas-reliefs which decorate temples and zedis (Petleik, Ananda, Shwezigon, Mingalazedi, Dhammayazika, Sintpatho), in which ardent naturalism reveals scenes of the Jatakas treated with humor and an acute sense of observation. These terra cottas are often glazed. A large number of sanctuaries at Pagan are decorated with wall paintings. Here again, the treatment is greatly influenced by the Pala school of Bengal, sometimes by a style which may have originated in Tibet (Tantric frescoes of Ari style at Nandamannya). The motifs are rosettes for the ceilings and compartments for the walls (Kubyauk-Gyi—Wetkyiin—Abeyadana, Nandamannya, Payathonzu, Lokhatlikpan, Thambulla). Some sanctuaries are decorated with paintings of the Mongol period (Kyaunzittha-Umin). The dominant colors are black, white, yellow, and dark red. Many of these paintings are unfortunately in a very bad state and their conservation presents great problems. The images are emphasized by many inscriptions and captions. They are generally written in Mon characters, translating Mon and Burmese texts. Lokhatlikpan, a very important temple from this point of view, studied and described by professors G. H. Luce and Ba Shin, shows the influences of Mon writing on the transcription of the Burmese language. Moreover, the most ancient inscription (dated in Burmese) is that of the four-language stele known as Myazedi (archaic Pali, Pyu, Mon, and Burmese) erected to dedicate villages to a sanctuary in 1084–85 by Rajakumar, the disinherited son of King Kyaunzittha.

51. BURMA, PAGAN, SHWESANDAW PAGODA. On his return to Pagan in 1057, after his victorious expedition to Thaton and the southern part of the country, King Anawratha felt it was his duty to build a pagoda to contain several of Buddha's hairs, relics offered to the new sovereign by the city of Pegu. Mon architects, who built the pagoda, added two terraces to the initial three to show how greatly the king venerated these relics. The first terrace is adorned with Hindu gods (dear to the Mon population, which came from India). The five square terraces have flights of steps, one on each side, reaching to the base of the stupa in the form of a bell, the finial of which is a modern addition. When this photograph was taken, the monks unfortunately had just given the brick structure a coat of whitewash.

52. BURMA, PAGAN, THIYIPYITSAYA, LAWKANANDA PAGODA. Erected on the banks of the Irrawaddy, not far from where the river harbor once existed, this cylindrical structure, regularly given a coat of whitewash, was a useful landmark for navigators along the intricate sand banks. The pagoda was erected by King Anawratha to venerate a replica of one of Buddha's teeth made by Ceylonese monks

who preferred to keep the original. On a triple octagonal base, flanked by four flights of steps, stands the shaft which is topped by flat, molded cushions, reminiscent of ancient parasols. A very restrainedly ornamented band encircles the middle of the stupa bell. The gilt-iron hti on the very top is a modern addition. This pagoda is still greatly venerated by the Burmese.

53. BURMA, PAGAN, THIYIPYITSAYA, SEINNYET NYIMA PAGODA. Very different from the preceding one, this pagoda shows the research of Burmese architects who were easily influenced by the arts of India, China, and Ceylon. It was probably built in the second half of the eleventh century. Built on triple square terraces decorated with crenelations, the stupa springs from a richly molded sixteen-sided base. Of medium height, the bell is encircled by a band containing four niches holding Buddhas, adorned with clecs, and surmounted by bracket sikharas. The tooth-ornament motif along the upper rim of the band creates a rhythm by a felicitous echoing of the lower decoration. Strings of beading hanging from the lower rim of the band are reminiscent of those which decorated the Amaravati stupas. On the summit, the square Ceylon-type reliquary casket is greatly recessed, a pleasant transition from the piled parasols which we have already seen at Ceylon. The square terraces, adorned with stupa-shaped stones at each corner, were decorated with lions and dragons treated in a very Chinese manner. The brick construction is carefully executed and the stuccowork has been well preserved. This pagoda is associated with a small square temple with four vestibules, traditionally attributed to Queen Seinnyet.

54. BURMA, PAGAN, NYAUNG U, SHWEZIGON PAGODA. This is one of the greatest of the Pagan complex. Begun in the reign of Anawratha in 1059 and finished by his son Kyaunzittha (1084–1112), based on a style inaugurated by the Lawkananda, this huge pagoda served as a model for many future stupas and later gave birth to Burmese-type zedis. Its form is more compact than that of Lawkananda and it stands on three high, square, step terraces, adorned with glazed terra-cotta panels relating in bas-relief episodes from Buddha's former lives. According to tradition it was built to honor a part of Buddha's forehead bone and a tooth, which partly explains why this pagoda is venerated. But it may also have been built to attract to Theravada Buddhism a people who still worshiped 37 nats whose home was the summit of Mount Popa, some 30 miles to the southeast. A unique instance in Buddhist architecture, the pagoda enceinte contains the effigies of these nats arranged in such a manner that they seem to render homage to Buddha in the form of a stupa, thus replacing Mount Popa. In fact, Anawratha said, "Men will not come for the new faith. Let them come and worship their old gods and they will gradually be won over to Buddha's Law." To finish this grandiose work, Kyaunzittha used stone blocks from the Tuywin hills, brought by shackled workmen. On each side of the pagoda is a small temple containing a standing statue of Buddha in a style similar to Gupta art.

55. BURMA, PAGAN, NYAUNG U, SHWEZIGON PAGODA, A NAT. Periodically covered over with stucco and gold leaf, and its lips painted vermilion, this pre-Buddhist spirit has retained nothing of the original except its form. However, we can easily imagine what these popular representations were like in the time of Anawratha. On festival days, these statues, still venerated by the people, are clothed and adorned with flowers.

56. BURMA, PAGAN, NYAUNG U, SAPADA PAGODA. During the reign of Narapatisthu, about the close of the eleventh century, several monks from Bassein went to study the holy writings at Ceylon. One of them, named Sapada, who was Talaing in origin, after spending ten years on the island, returned to Pagan with ordained monks and, about 1190,

erected a stupa which has since kept his name. In memory of his stay in Ceylon, he turned to the stupa style which he had often seen on the distant island. In addition, he brought the Burmese a new religious order to add to the theological conception already established at Pagan by Shin Arahan, considered invalid by the newly ordained monks. This caused a schism favoring relations between Ceylon and Burma. This simple stupa built of brick stands on a square base which is reached by gateways. The original stucco decoration has entirely disappeared.

57. BURMA, PAGAN, BEPINGYAUNG PAGODA. A small brick structure of the Sinhalese type which, according to tradition, dates from the tenth century. However, it was probably built several decades before the pagoda built by the monk Sapada, that is, toward the close of the eleventh century or the beginning of the twelfth—perhaps even on the return of the mission sent by Anawratha to Ceylon about 1071 to seek Buddha's tooth relic kept by the monks of that island. This pagoda may therefore be contemporary with Lawkananda and it may have been built by Sinhalese monks at their expense, which would account for its simplicity and its lack of decoration.

58. BURMA, PAGAN, PWASAW, DHAMMAYAZIKA PAGODA, FIRST BASE WALL. Here we can see the many recesses of the base forming a kind of frame for the

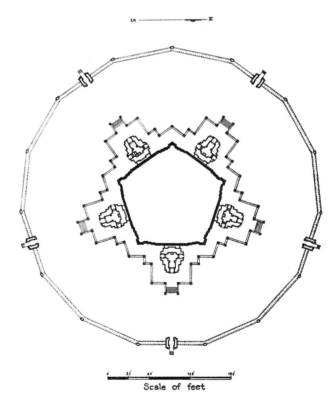

FIG. 9. GROUND PLAN OF THE DHAMMAYAZIKA PAGODA AT PAGAN

historiated panels. The flights of steps on each side of these bases begin on the far side of the small temples (we see one of them on the left). The original platform is paved with slabs of sandstone, while the entire building is of brick. Ink inscriptions can still be read on the inner walls of the porches of the small temples.

59. BURMA, PAGAN, PWASAW, DHAMMAYAZIKA PAGODA. This huge pagoda with a pentagonal base, and five small square temples, containing an image of Buddha set against it, was erected about 1196 by Narapatisithu in order to symbolize Buddha as King of Justice and Duty (*Dhammaraja*). Built after Shwezigon, standing on three low terraces decorated with terra-cotta panels illustrating the Jatakas, it has an unusual plan with evidences of Mon influence. The five small temples surmounted by sikharas are enclosed in a star-shaped terrace, where a flight of steps leads to each of the five sides of the stupa bases. The whole is surrounded by a huge outer wall in the form of a regular polygon of fifteen sides with five gates (see fig. 9).

60. BURMA, PAGAN, PWASAW, DHAMMAYAZIKA PAGODA, STUCCO DECORATION ON THE STUPA. This type of stucco is now common in Pagan. The lower garland of the band encircling the stupa's bell consists of beading disgorged by monsters. Above is a narrow beaded frieze.

61. BURMA, PAGAN, PANGU PAGODA, GLAZED TERRACOTTA DECORATION. Although the subject matter is somewhat banal, it perfectly illustrates the charming fantasy with which Pagan artists decorated their pagodas. Here we see two kinnaris (winged figures usually with human heads and bird's feet, but here having the heads of elephants, a theme probably borrowed from local folklore). The pagoda has been destroyed and only a few such curious fragments remain. Height: about 5¾ inches. *Pagan Museum.*

62. BURMA, PAGAN, MINGALAZEDI PAGODA, TERRACOTTA PANEL. This panel illustrates an episode from one of Buddha's former lives. On the right we see a hunter, probably a bodhisattva, holding a bow with one hand and a dog on a leash with the other, on his way to visit a crowned personage sheltered by a light roof. The balance of the composition, the graceful quality of the figures, and the litheness of the animal create a charming ensemble. Beneath the scene is an inscription. The pagoda itself is similar in type to the preceding one, but built on three square terraces and not flanked by small temples; it was finished in 1284. Construction of this pagoda took six years. A prophecy said, "When the pagoda is finished, the kingdom will fall." Despite this, however, the king hastily completed it. The perfection which marked its rise may now only be seen in the historiated capitals: three years after the pagoda was finished, Kublai Khan's Mongol troops pillaged the countryside, conquered the Pagan Kingdom, and forced King Narathihapati to flee.

63. BURMA, PAGAN, MYINKABA, NANPAYA TEMPLE. On his arrival at Pagan, the captive King Manuha (brought with his suite from Thaton by his conqueror Anawratha in 1057, and well treated by the latter) felt it was his solemn duty to build a royal dwelling which would also be a temple. Square in plan with a long vestibule open to the east, this temple is built of brick and sheathed with cut stone. Four huge stone pillars support the central vault, with light ensured by openings at the base of the sikhara above the edifice. The interior is dimly lit by means of Mon-type windows with perforated stone screens. These windows are surmounted by the clec motif, which was greatly developed at Pagan and throughout Burma. A vase of abundance, a typically Indian motif, decorates the pediments.

64. BURMA, PAGAN, ANAUK PWASAW, KUTHA TEMPLE, FRETTED WINDOW. This is from a small temple of the Mon type, probably slightly earlier in date than the Manuha Temple. Built of brick-shaped stone, its decoration is in excellent condition. The clec motif decorates the end of diverging makaras and a Buddhist divinity (Goddess of Fortune?) decorates its apex. The pediment contains a vase of abundance. The fretted window no longer consists of a single perforated stone but of a combination of cut stones incised with floral motifs. The columns are decorated with beautifully executed foliated triangles, while the friezes consist of ornamental foliage in the center of which are frolicking animals, a motif borrowed and developed by Burmese art.

65. BURMA, PAGAN, MYINKABA, INTERIOR OF THE NANPAYA TEMPLE. Here we see the four huge pillars which support the narrow vaulting. The throne of King Manuha probably stood on the center platform. It was here that he presumably held court during his early years of captivity. The pillars, decorated with figures of Brahma (?), attest the strong Hindu influence which formed Thaton Buddhism. The walls were originally decorated with paintings, now in very bad condition. The inner windows are also vaulted.

66. BURMA, PAGAN, MYINKABA, NANPAYA TEMPLE, DETAIL OF AN INTERIOR PILLAR. This detail shows Brahma (?) holding flowers. The effigy, however, may not be that of a Brahmanic god but rather of a Buddhist divinity taken from the Hindu pantheon.

FIG. 10. LONGITUDINAL CROSS SECTION OF THE PATOTHAMYA TEMPLE AT PAGAN (1 inch = 25 feet)

Although the hair clearly reveals a post-Gupta influence, the smile and general treatment doubtless belong to a very different style, probably Mon. The Buddhist halo around the three heads and the all over style may indicate that this style originated at the Nalanda Monastery in northern India. Strangely enough, the four sides of each pillar have the same motif. This divinity may well be King Manuha's personal *Ishvara* (tutelary deity).

67. BURMA, PAGAN, MYINKABA, MANUHA TEMPLE, HEAD OF A RECLINING BUDDHA. In 1057 the captive Manuha, sensing the approach of death, sold the royal ring and with the profit (six carts of silver) built a Mon-type temple to contain four huge statues of Buddha, their supine position perhaps symbolizing his own destitution. This reclining Buddha is over 60 feet long. The vigorous features and the slightly hooked nose are supposed to represent the king himself. Near the face is the vaulting of brick and painted stucco. Shortly after the construction of this prison-temple, the king and his suite lost all their rights and were given as slaves to the Shwezigon Pagoda.

68. BURMA, PAGAN, MYINKABA, NAGAYON TEMPLE. Legend relates that when Prince Kyaunzittha, forced to flee from his brother, Sawlu, stopped to rest at Myinkaba, a serpent Naga emerged from the ground and sheltered the sleeping prince with his hood. In memory of this, Kyaunzittha, on

becoming king in 1084, ordered this temple to be built by Mon (Talaing) architects whom he had probably brought back with him from exile. Square in plan with a long vestibule opening on the north, this temple has many new features. More directly inspired by the wooden buildings of the period, it has a roof composed of three sloping terraces, at the corners of which rise pagodas. On the last terrace, a sikhara topped by a reduced stupa gives the whole edifice (which retains all the characteristics of Mon architecture) the impression of a slender pyramid with concave groins. This prototype later served as the model for Kyaunzittha's masterpiece, the Ananda Temple. This type of architecture was also used for many adjacent buildings, libraries, and ordination halls. Although it was built of wood, this is what the royal palace may have looked like. The inner walls are decorated with paintings and the plinth of the central doorway is of carved wood, reminiscent of the wooden buildings which have since disappeared. In the center of the sanctuary are two seated Buddhas.

69. BURMA, PAGAN, MYINKABA, ABEYADANA TEMPLE. This temple was built by the wife of King Kyaunzittha. Oriented to the north, it follows the architectural traditions of this reign. The porch has three entrances leading to the sanctuary which has a central pillar and an enclosed corridor whose light is provided by Mon-type perforated stone screens. Deeply hewn in the north side of the

78

central pillar supporting the entire roof (which is in the form of a stupa) is a niche with an image of Buddha seated in the earth-touching pose (bhumi-sparsa). The image is of brick and stucco. In this building, the fretted windows begin to let in more light, and the vase of abundance in the pediment has disappeared, replaced by another perforated screen. Alongside the temple is a pagoda of the same period, once part of the sanctuary.

70. BURMA, PAGAN, WETKYIN, ALOPYI TEMPLE. This sanctuary is similar to the preceding one, especially in plan, but the openings in the cella are replaced by fretted windows of brick rather than perforated stone. This seems to suggest that Mon artisans had already disappeared and had been replaced by Burmese. The clec motif is modified, its slender tongues pointing skyward. A dormer-type opening in the base of the roof allows more light to enter the inner sanctuary.

71. BURMA, PAGAN, MYINPYA-GU PAGODA-TEMPLE. This special Mon sanctuary consists of a stupa erected on a high hexagonal base of three terraces. The interior of the base contains two levels of surrounding galleries, lit by narrow fretted windows and decorated with many niches. The niches contain Buddhas in the earth-touching position, seated on thrones of different styles. The upper gallery cannot be reached; the architect seems to have overlooked a means of access. The lower gallery has a vault decorated with wall paintings. This is one of the most curious edifices of the Pagan group and was probably built during the early reign of King Kyaunzittha, although some authors place it at the end of Sawlu's reign (1077–84).

72. BURMA, PAGAN, MYINPYA-GU PAGODA-TEMPLE, BUDDHAS IN THE LOWER GALLERY.

73. BURMA, PAGAN, PATOTHAMYA TEMPLE. Traditionally attributed to the tenth century, it is perhaps later in date and may have been built during the early reign of King Kyaunzittha (end of the eleventh century). It is of the Mon type, and the inner walls are decorated with paintings illustrating scenes from the life of Buddha, with captions in archaic Mon characters. The stupa above the sanctuary has very pointed ogival vaulting. The far wall, against which are set three seated Buddhas, is enclosed by a half-ogival vaulted gallery with facing fretted windows. The statues are directly lit by means of an opening leading to the terrace. The latter contains small cubic sanctuaries containing sculptures of Buddha. On the east, the sanctuary is fronted by a very long hall. Within the thick vestibule wall, a steep staircase leads to the terrace (which has been mostly uncovered), directly below.

74. BURMA, PAGAN, MYINKABA, KUBYAUK-GYI TEMPLE, WALL PAINTING OF A MONK. Similar in outline to the preceding temples, this square sanctuary, built in 1113 by Rajakumar, the son of King Kyaunzittha, has a central altar surrounded by a vaulted corridor adorned with niches containing sculptured stone Buddhas, and lit by windows with perforated stone screens. In addition to the fact that the famous four-language inscription of the Myazedi Stele mentions its erection, this temple is outstanding for the remarkable wall paintings which decorate the sanctuary and the corridor. Contemporary with the temple, they are probably the most ancient to have survived. Here we see a monk worshiping the central Buddha. The drawing is restrained. The colors are red, yellow ochre, black, and white. Unfortunately, clumsy restoration ruined the paintings, which are now covered with spots. Thanks to many inscriptions in old Mon characters, we have been able to identify the scenes.

75. BURMA, PAGAN, LOKHATLIKPAN TEMPLE. This small sanctuary, which stands near the Shwesandaw Pagoda, has become very important in the history of Pagan since the scholarly study made by U Ba Shin. According to him, it seems to represent a transition from the Mon culture imported from Thaton to a Burmese attempt at cultural independence. Dr. G.-H. Luce, who made a special study

FIG. 11. CROSS SECTION OF THE LOKHATLIKPAN TEMPLE AT PAGAN

of this temple, discovered wall paintings with captions in old Mon characters as well as numerous specimens of archaic Burmese writing. Both authors agree that this temple dates from Alaungsithu's early reign, that is, shortly after 1113. The very

79

name of the sanctuary means, "He who adorns the summit of the world." Its dimensions are modest: about 51 feet in length, the same in height, and 36 feet in width. The interior of the principal part of the monument contains a colossal seated Buddha on a high base. Made of brick and stucco, the statue stands in the center of the room, which is relatively better lit than the old Mon temples by an ogival-vaulted hall and three fretted brick windows (see fig. 11). Here, as in old Mon temples, the vaulting begins at the floor, which is paved with large bricks. But the chief interest of this temple lies in the paintings which decorate the hall and sanctuary, portraying scenes from the life of Buddha (south wall), effigies of 28 Buddhas (north wall), various miraculous events (east wall), and typically Mon Jatakas (west wall).

76. BURMA, PAGAN, BUDDHA AS PREACHER. This gray sandstone sculpture represents Buddha as preacher. The face is typical of the Kyaunzittha period. The delicate, slightly hooked nose and finely drawn smile indicate an Indian type rather than a Burmese. This sculpture was probably by Talaing Mon artists. The treatment of the robe clinging to the body indicates a Gupta influence, which relates this work (in its pose, robe, and position of the hands) to the celebrated Buddha of Sarnath. But here the body halo is ogival and unadorned, and the general treatment less skillful. Total height: 3 feet 7¾ inches. *Pagan Museum.*

77. BURMA, PAGAN, BUDDHA AS PREACHER (*detail*).

78. BURMA, PAGAN, GAUTAMA BUDDHA CUTTING HIS HAIR. On leaving his father's palace in quest of truth, Buddha sacrificed his long hair which he cut off with his sword. The somewhat stiff attitude is lightened by the movement of the fingers, only here the almost stereotyped face is less expressive and the treatment of the garment less vague than that shown in plate 76. The stele was originally painted. This sculpture probably dates from the early twelfth century. Sandstone. Height: 3 feet 4 inches. *Pagan Museum.*

79. BURMA, PAGAN, ANANDA TEMPLE. According to tradition, Kyaunzittha built this temple in 1091 after hearing Indian monks describe their own which stood on the Udayagiri Hills in Orissa. Square in plan with a projecting porch on each side, it consists of a central massive pillar enclosed by two concentric corridors and connected by narrow passages in the form of windows. Each porch consists of four massive pillars separated by passages at right angles and surrounded by a gallery lighted by small independent windows (see fig. 12). The four sides of the cental pillar have deep niches containing standing Buddhas, each lit

by openings facing the first terrace of the roof and forming a projection with it. The corners of the

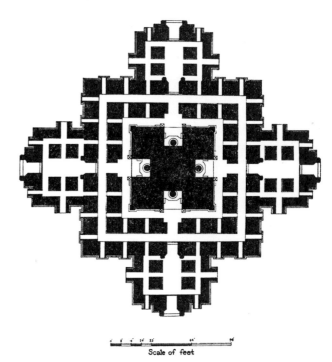

FIG. 12. GROUND PLAN OF THE ANANDA TEMPLE
AT PAGAN

second terrace support reduced temples. The whole edifice is topped by a splendid sikhara with convex sides, terminating in a very slender stupa supporting a gilt-metal hti. This temple (Ananta Pannya) glorifies Buddha's all-powerful wisdom. Its dimensions are impressive: about 196 feet per side, not including the projecting porches. The total height of the monument is 180 feet. The roof consists of increasingly sloping terraces (six in all) which become narrow toward the top. Each porch has a main entrance, with two side ones. From each vestibule we can look down the corridor and see one of the four gigantic Buddhas, each measuring nearly 33 feet high. Many small niches in the corridor walls of the west sanctuary contain statues, the most famous being those of King Kyaunzittha, represented kneeling, and his religious counselor Shin Arahan. Many of these statues represent episodes in the life of Buddha and were probably executed by Indian artists. At the base of the outer walls are two rows of terra-cotta slabs (about 1500 in all) incised with Mon and Pali characters, illustrating the Jatakas. According to legend, the local architect, probably in obedience to an old native custom, was sacrificed by the king when the monument was dedicated in 1091. The Ananda, the logical result of the architectural style inaugurated by Kyaunzittha with the Nagayon, with its correct proportions and fine, restrained lines in spite of its dimensions, was the first great Pagan monument. This temple is still used and greatly venerated by Burmese Buddhists.

**80. BURMA, PAGAN, ANANDA TEMPLE, LARGE STAND-
ING BUDDHA.** The canopy above the head of this
huge, 33-foot, gilt-bronze sculpture is modern, as
are the decorations on the body halo. It is the
work of Burmese artists who clumsily copied the
work of Mon artists.

81. BURMA, PAGAN, GILT-WOOD BUDDHA. This
charming small statue (23¾ inches) probably
represents Buddha descending from Trayastrimsa
(Heaven of the Thirty-Three Gods), suggested by
the ladder at the far end. He is assisted by two
divinities: one is female and has three heads
(Tara?), the other carries an alms bowl. Kneeling
at his feet is a worshiper. This sculpture is difficult
to date (it is perhaps contemporary with the
Ananda Temple), and retains the Mon characteristics we have seen in the seated Buddhas (see plate
76). The garment is in the Gupta style, and the
graceful shoulders indicate a strong Indian influence. *Pagan Museum.*

**82. BURMA, PAGAN, VIEW OF THE SITE FROM THE
TERRACE OF THE THAT BYINNYU TEMPLE, LOOKING
TOWARD THE NORTHEAST.** In the center is the
Ananda Temple. Somewhat to the left, in the
distance and dominating the horizon line, is the
Htilominlo Temple. On the horizon, to the left, is
the Shwezigon Stupa.

83. BURMA, PAGAN, DHAMMAYANGYI TEMPLE. After
succeeding his father Alaungsithu, whom he killed
with his own hands, the cruel, despotic King
Narathu (1167–70) felt that it was his duty to build
a huge sanctuary in order to be pardoned for his
crimes. His model was the Ananda Temple, but he
failed to achieve a similar refined elegance.
Assassinated by men from Chittagong who wanted

to avenge their leader's wife who had been killed by
the king, Narathu disappeared from the political
scene before the temple was finished; it remains,
however, the greatest sanctuary of this type in
Burma. Narathu built it with the utmost care so
that his work might defy time. This monument is
one of the most carefully constructed at Pagan and
more massive than Ananda. With its single niche
facing east to contain the image of Buddha (see
fig. 13), surrounded by a single corridor, the central
block measures almost 164 feet on each side. The
sikhara, which was to surmount the structure, has
disappeared. Behind the temple (here seen from
the top of the terrace of the Sulamani) is the
Irrawaddy and the hills of the west bank of the
river.

**84. BURMA, PAGAN, DHAMMAYANGYI TEMPLE, SIDE
GATE.** One of the rare gates still with its original
stucco decoration. It has been partly obstructed by
a low brick wall, erected by the archaeologists to
prevent animals from penetrating the sanctuary.
Here, the motif which decorates the double
projection of the entrance has become rigid and
very slender. We can still distinguish the effigy of
the Goddess of Fortune in the center of the upper
clec decoration, and the makaras on the corners of
the lower clec. The finely curved ogival vaulting
is rather high. The whole is well balanced and has
pleasing proportions. The angled stones of the base
of the porch jambs reproduce the clec corners and
are a decorative motif probably related to the ones
often used by Cham artists.

**85. BURMA, PAGAN, DHAMMAYANGYI TEMPLE, ORIG-
INAL BUDDHA IN THE ENTRANCE.** Of massive proportions, this statue is related to the popular representations of nats rather than to the effigy of the Sage.

EAST   WEST

FIG. 13. CROSS SECTION OF THE DHAMMAYANGYI TEMPLE AT PAGAN (1 inch = 65 feet)

Here, Burmese artists, somewhat free of Indian and Mon influences, have attempted a return to traditions anterior to the introduction of Thaton Buddhism. Although the pose remains conventional, the treatment of the garment (probably restored during a more recent period) and the face have become Burmese. Only the hooked nose remains, reminiscent of the Indian origin of these models. The hair is now clumsily stylized. The general effect, although heavy, nevertheless has a certain character.

86. BURMA, PAGAN, SHWEGUGYI TEMPLE. With this edifice, erected in 1131 near Alaungsithu's royal palace, we find the true Burmese type of temple freed of Mon influence. The temple surroundings are now largely cleared away. Square in plan, it has a central block of reduced dimensions surrounded by a large corridor lit by four doors and six windows and fronted on the north by a vestibule, which is also square (see fig. 14). A flight of steps leading to the terrace was hewn into the thickness of the wall. The temple is entirely built on a high, rectangular platform enclosed by walls. Access is gained by means of a narrow flight of steps on the northwest corner. This elegant building, with three practical terraces surmounted by a sikhara of attractive proportions, was built in seven months. It was consecrated by the royal prayer, which is still inscribed in Pali on the walls: "... But I would like to raise a bridge across the Samsara River [referring to the transmigration of souls] so that all can take it to reach the blessed city [meaning Nirvana]."

An extraordinary coincidence occurred when the king was brought here during his illness: he was smothered to death in his own temple by his son Narathu, who coveted the throne.

87. BURMA, PAGAN, SHWEGUGYI TEMPLE, OUTER FRIEZE OF THE PLATFORM BASE. The decoration is of brick and stucco and represents worshipers (hands joined at breast).

88. BURMA, PAGAN, THAT BYINNYU TEMPLE. This temple symbolizing Buddha's omniscience was built by Alaungsithu in 1144. It is almost 229 feet high, is entirely coated with stucco which was then whitewashed, and has special characteristics. It is built on a very high platform within which corridors extend around all four sides, and a flight of steps leads to the sanctuary (see fig. 15). The sanctuary proper no longer consists of a niche hewn from a central pillar supporting the superstructure, but of a vaulted room situated in the center of the building. It contains a very fine statue of a seated Buddha. The platform, over 65 feet high, contains on the east side a kind of antechamber set within the thickness of the walls. From this rise staircases leading to the sanctuary level. At the far end of this vestibule is a flight of steps leading to the upper enclosed gallery. Two entrances arranged on each side of the main vestibule stairs, and entrances in the center of each of the other sides (north, west, and south) of this platform, lead directly to the upper gallery.

On the elevated terrace, the sanctuary itself is fronted on the east by a vaulted antechamber.

Three shallow recessed terraces separate the summit of the platform from the base of the sanctuary. The latter is surmounted by three recessed stories culminating in an almost cubic sikhara whose tip is decorated with the traditional hti, giving the building a pyramidal appearance. Divided thus into five stories, the temple served as both a monastery and a sanctuary: the ground level and

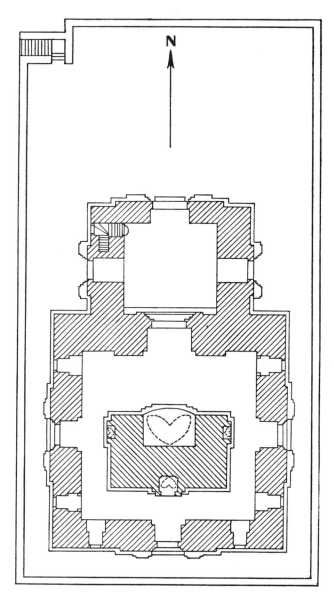

FIG. 14. GROUND PLAN OF THE SHWEGUGYI TEMPLE AT PAGAN (1 inch = 30 feet)

first floor (galleries) served as dwellings for the monks; two split-level rooms below the sanctuary proper contained the holy images and the library; and the last story was the sanctuary. Each corner of the terrace had a small cubic temple surmounted by a small stupa, which rather curiously recalled the form of Tibetan chortens. The entire structure

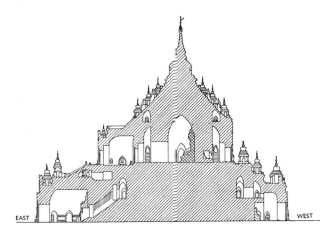

FIG. 15. EAST-WEST CROSS SECTION OF THE THAT BYINNU TEMPLE AT PAGAN (1 inch = 108 feet)

is a pleasant combination of *vihara* and *chaitya*, which probably remained unique in its conception.

89. BURMA, PAGAN, THAT BYINNYU TEMPLE, INNER STAIRCASE. Each ogival arch consists of several thicknesses of cemented bricks.

90. BURMA, PAGAN, MINNANTHU, SULAMANI TEMPLE. In 1183, King Narapatisithu built this huge temple somewhat distant from the village of Nyaung U, to the south. The general plan is similar to that of That-Byinnyu. However, it differs in that each of the two main stories of this temple are somewhat similar in plan. The very massive base consists of a huge central section (approximately 164 feet square) containing an inner encircling gallery decorated with statues. Access to this gallery is effected by the projecting porches, the eastern one having a niche containing a statue of Buddha. A flight of steps let into the thickness of the corner of the southeast wall leads to a vestibule of the upper structure, which is placed on the third terrace, and whose main entrance is on the north side. From the sides of this entrance porch a stairway descends to the second terrace. This upper section is also different from that of That Byinnyu, since it consists of a solid central core encircled by a gallery open on the four cardinal points. Three other terraces with small temples on their corners lead the eye to the sikhara which tops the structure. Walls and vaulting still contain fragments of paintings, unfortunately mostly destroyed by awkward additions made by artist monks during the last century.

91. PAGAN, GENERAL VIEW. Taken from the terrace of the That Byinnyu Temple, looking toward the west. In the left foreground, we see the Nat Hlaung Kyaung and immediately behind, the Patothamya. In the background is the small library building of the Mimalaung Kyaung. In the center stands the ruined pagoda of Ngaykwenadaung. Finally, on the right, rises the majestic temple of Gawdawpalin built by Narapatisithu and finished by Htilominlo in order to pay homage to the dead souls of his ancestors. More slender than That Byinnyu, it is obviously built on the same plan and has the same characteristics. Beyond we see the Irrawaddy and the hills of the west bank of the river. On the summit of the highest hill we see a modern monastery. A child standing to the left of the Nat Hlaung Kyaung indicates the scale.

92. BURMA, PAGAN, HTILOMINLO TEMPLE. The last of the series of great Pagan temples that began with the That Byinnyu, this temple differs little from the others. It was built by King Htilominlo (1210–34) in 1218 to commemorate the "miracle" (a parasol dipping, or bowing, by itself) which caused him to be elected over Narapatisithu's four other sons.

93. BURMA, PAGAN, HTILOMINLO TEMPLE, DECORATIONS. Detail of the decoration adorning the upper part of a corner pilaster. This motif was often used in Pagan art.

94. BURMA, PAGAN, MINNANTHU, LEMYETHNA TEMPLE. In 1222 Anantathuryia, King Htilominlo's prime minister, built this small, attractive temple on a high platform in imitation of the Ananda. The decoration is simple. On the clee corners, the makaras which still appear on those of the Htilominlo Temple have disappeared. This temple is still in use.

95. BURMA, PAGAN, HEAD OF BUDDHA. This beautiful stucco head with somewhat heavy lines decorated the Lemyethna Temple. Mon characteristics are completely absent in the face. The eyelids are described in a wavy line which became one of the outstanding traits of Burmese faces. However, the quivering nostrils and the well-drawn, fleshy lips betray this artist's certain concern for realism which unfortunately spoils the very heavy lower jaw. Height: 12 inches. *Pagan Museum.*

96. BURMA, PAGAN, WETKYIIN, KUBYAUK-GYI TEMPLE. This charming small temple was probably built during the reign of King Kyaunzittha (1084–1112) and repaired in 1463, as indicated by an inscription. It is the first of a series of simple sanctuary temples. Two features are noteworthy: (1) the sikhara, somewhat an imitation of that of the Mahabodhi of Bodh-Gaya (Bihar) in India, differs by its rigid aspect from those commonly used at Pagan which have convex lines; and (2) the paintings which decorate the walls are treated as small surfaces and form charming panels with captions in Pali and archaic Burmese. The Chauk Phalaya, a small temple erected near Nyaung U by Narapatisithu, has a similar sikhara. It lacks decoration, however, which may have been lost through adverse weather conditions.

97. BURMA, PAGAN, NYAUNG U, THETKYAMUNI TEMPLE. Somewhat later in date than the preceding, this temple contains attractive paintings depicting the life of the great Indian emperor Ashoka, and also beautiful stucco decoration.

98. BURMA, PAGAN, NYAUNG U, THETKYAMUNI TEMPLE, DECORATIONS. This shows the upper frieze on a wall and the stucco decoration of a corner pilaster. In the frieze, the garlands are stylized and surround female worshipers. Kalas' tongues separate each unit from the next. The pilaster has a triangular motif with a stylized floral décor.

99. BURMA, PAGAN, NYAUNG U, KONDAWGYI TEMPLE, ENTRANCE. This doorway, marvelously decorated with stucco on brick, illustrates how extremely skillful the Burmese artists were. The pilasters are decorated with ornamental foliage in which birds, animals, and figures are combined. The clec above the perfect ogival arch is profusely adorned. The corner makaras are surmounted by kinnaras, with ornamental foliage containing animated subjects in the vertical tongues of the clec, and, finally, a lion and Goddess of Fortune in the center.

100. BURMA, PAGAN, NYAUNG U, KONDAWGYI TEMPLE. This sanctuary was built in the thirteenth century on the same plan as the two preceding ones. However, instead of a terminal sikhara, it has a stupa whose spire, representing parasols, is as important as the stupa bell itself, thus giving the edifice a conical appearance. The interior is decorated with fine paintings illustrating episodes from the Jatakas.

101. BURMA, PAGAN, MINNANTHU, NANDAMANNYA TEMPLE. Similar to the Kondawgyi, this small temple with its many small, recessed terraces seems to combine the aspect of a pagoda and the function of a temple. It has but a single entrance (shown here) on the east. However, it differs from the Kondawgyi by its recessed square plan. The rather dark inner sanctuary is decorated with interesting Tantric paintings. According to an inscription, it probably dates from 1248.

102. BURMA, PAGAN, MINNANTHU, NANDAMANNYA TEMPLE, WALL PAINTING. This attractive subject,

painted on the inner temple walls, was part of a series of Tantric (magical) paintings, probably executed by monks of the Ari sect. Strong Chinese-Tibetan influences can be seen not only in the incised treatment of the forms but also in the clouds on which this divinity is kneeling. These clouds are part of the Chinese theme known as "wind and clouds," combined with an extremely Tibetan type of zoomorphism. The yellow, dark red, yellow ochre, and white tones of the painting are outlined with black.

103. BURMA, PAGAN, MINNANTHU, NANDAMANNYA TEMPLE, FRETTED WINDOW. This was made by perforating a slab of sandstone included in the masonry. The thickness of the slab, together with its very small openings, allows little light to enter. The stucco decoration is here summarily executed by incising.

104. BURMA, PAGAN, MINNANTHU, THAMBULLA TEMPLE. Similar to the Thetkyamuni, this temple was erected in 1255 by Queen Thambulla, the widow of King Uzana (1250–54) who was killed during an elephant hunt. Several wall paintings decorate the corridor surrounding the central pillar.

105. BURMA, PAGAN, MINNANTHU, PAYATHONZU GROUP, WALL PAINTING. Mahayana wall painting portraying a bodhisattva. The crown is in the form of a clec, adorned with diverging makaras on each side. This crown may be the source of the clec motif above the doors of Pagan temples.

106. BURMA, PAGAN, MINNANTHU, PAYATHONZU GROUP. This particular temple, consisting of three identical sanctuaries connected by two narrow, vaulted corridors, was built at the close of the thirteenth century and probably abandoned before completion. The paintings that decorate the vaulting and walls of the sanctuaries belong to the Mahayana school and to the Ari sect. The west temple is not decorated. Each sanctuary is erected on an independent plinth. The windows are blind so as to emphasize the secret character of Tantric practices. The stucco decoration has entirely disappeared.

107. BURMA, PAGAN, MAHABODHI TEMPLE. About 1120, Alaungsithu sent money and architects to Bodh-Gaya in Bihar, India, to repair the Mahabodhi Temple which had been built on the very site where Buddha attained Enlightenment. An inscription relates this event, with the title "Lord of Millions of Pyus" referring to the Burmese king. Several years earlier Kyaunzittha had also ordered repairs. After Burmese architects had returned from their mission with plans and drawings, King Htilominlo (1210–32) decided to build a copy of the

84

famous temple within the walls of his city. The quadrangular building, supporting a very high sikhara with rectilinear lines, is flanked on the corners by miniature edifices. The Indian temple at Bodh-Gaya was probably repaired in the Burmese fashion and many non-Indian additions were made to the original design. The Pagan copy is the only sanctuary of its kind in Burma.

108. BURMA, PAGAN, PITHAKAT TAIK LIBRARY. When King Anawratha returned victorious from Thaton, followed by 39 elephants laden with precious manuscripts, he erected this edifice to contain them (1058). This is the first building made of lightweight, perishable materials to be found intact. It perfectly illustrates what wooden architecture was then like, having brick walls and many recessed roofs. Repaired in 1783 by King Bodawpaya, this edifice has kept its original design, although we think the *dubika* on top and the motifs bordering the roofs were the work of restorers. Small square windows of slabs of pierced sandstone allow light to filter into the interior.

109. BURMA, PAGAN, MIMALAUNG KYAUNG TEMPLE. This small structure was erected on a very high base forming a terrace, flanked by a single flight of steps. It was built by King Narapatisithu in 1174, out of reach of fire and flood (which explains the name), and probably represents a type of wooden architecture of the period. A fine pagoda terminates this small architectural jewel. Its three terrace-roofs are adorned with horned motifs which some authors have compared to peacocks, but which more likely represent a stylization of guardian-dragons, whose origin is certainly Sino-Tibetan, the model having been lost in King Narapatisithu's time.

110. BURMA, PAGAN, MIMALAUNG KYAUNG TEMPLE, ROOF. The terminal spire measures about 10 feet in height. Here we clearly see the decorative motifs which adorn the corners of the tiered roofs, consisting, as throughout the building, of bricks coated with stucco.

111. BURMA, PAGAN, UPALI THEIN, ORDINATION HALL. This is a second type of "light" architecture translated into masonry. It is a long low structure with barrel vaulting, terminating at each end in a false door similar to temple entrance porches. Windows are at the ends, whereas entrance and exit are at the sides, with openings large enough for only one person at a time. On the summit, as though to indicate the sanctity of the place, a small pagoda has been erected. Light for the rather dark interior is afforded by perforated stone openings. This elegant edifice, built between 1220 and 1250 by the primate of Burma, Upali, for the ordination

ceremony of monks (and probably still in use until the last century), was decorated about the close of the eighteenth century with fine wall paintings which are still in very good condition.

112. BURMA, PAGAN, WETKYIIN, SHINBOME MONASTERY. Alongside the temples were monasteries, some of which, built of brick, are rather well preserved. This one, probably built in the time of King Kyaunzittha, is a massive quadrangular structure consisting of huge walls enclosing a high gallery arranged around a massive central tower. Floors of wood planks or masonry formed two stories where the monks lived. Entrance to these stories, lit by small square windows, was by means of flights of steps built in the interior of three of the walls, and entrance to the terrace was by means of a spiral staircase in the central block. The top of the outer walls is decorated with stucco friezes of garlands and praying figures. A simple ogival door, fronted by a flight of steps, leads to the lower gallery. Bricks of lighter color indicate conservation work.

113. BURMA, PAGAN, MINNANTHU, MINWINE MONASTERY. Rather similar to the Shinbome, this ruined monastery displays the thickness of its walls. It has a single story but probably included a sanctuary on the terrace. We can still see one of the four small temples on the corners of the terrace. This curious small building is surmounted by tiers of roofs which strangely recall the Nepalese architecture of Bhatgaon stupas or that of certain Chinese pagodas. The terrace corners and roofs of the small temples are adorned with stucco masks.

114. BURMA, PAGAN, THEYNPIE MONASTERY. This shows the vaulting of the inner gallery. Here seen is the upper part, showing the arrangement of the bricks, which are still coated with the remains of stucco.

115. BURMA, PAGAN, NYAUNG U, KYAUNZITTHA CAVE. A cave which is actually part of a monastery, both hewn in the hill and built on the surface. (Burmese caves cannot begin to compare with those in India.) This one, probably built by Kyaunsittha, was used to house monks rather than as a place of worship, the interior being merely a series of narrow corridors broken at right angles. These corridors are decorated with wall paintings, some of which are probably by Mongol artists who arrived in 1287 with Kublai Khan's troops.

116. BURMA, PAGAN, PAWDAWMU BUDDHA. Certain pagodas or sculptures considered too small were enlarged by building over the original layers of brick and plaster, reproducing in greater size the forms covered. Thus, certain pagodas or sculptures were contained one within the other, like Russian dolls. Pagoda pillagers and bad weather have often led to the discovery of these "boxed-in" structures. This sculpture of Buddha, in a small sanctuary lying directly south of the city of Pagan, near the Myinypa-Gu Temple, clearly shows the method employed. The core of the sculpture is usually better preserved than the outer part.

117. BURMA, PAGAN, NYAUNG U, THAMMIWET CAVE, WALL PAINTING. Although according to popular tradition this cave dates from the second century, it cannot date earlier than the beginning of the thirteenth. Used as a monastic residence, its long, zigzag corridor walls are covered with rather well-preserved wall paintings, the treatment of which is somewhat clumsy and stiff.

52

53

56

58

60

61

62

63

64

68

69

73

74

77

78

79
80

81

86

87

88

89

97

98

99

100

101

103

104

105

109

110

111

112

113

114

115

2. THE BURMESE RENAISSANCE (1287–1885)

The appearance of Kublai Khan's Mongol troops in northern and central Burma put a sudden end to architectural and artistic production. Ruined and politically unstable, the country no longer enjoyed a rich, peaceful period marked by building projects. It lacked a strong, organized central government. Almost at the same time, Thai tribes descended from the north and gradually replaced Burmese kingships. In 1364 upper Burma became the seat of the Shan (Thai) Kingdom with Ava as capital. Five years later, in the south, the Mon restored their kingdom with Pegu as its center. The Burmese established themselves in southeast Burma, however, near Toungoo, and two centuries later attempted to restore Burmese unity; they embellished their capital, transferred in 1546 to Pegu, and erected many monuments. The style then became evident and the pagoda with concave lines (zedi or *paya*) began to be used everywhere, based on the Pagan model of Shwezigon. Many old monuments were rebuilt or renovated (Schwenandaw, Swetalyaung, and Kyaik Kpun at Pegu), others were erected (Tupayon and Pon Nya Shin at Sagaing). In 1636 the city of Sagaing, the capital of upper Burma in 1315, again became the principal city of northern Burma. The huge Kaung Hmu Daw Stupa and the Ngadatkyi date from this period. Tabinshweti (1531–50), king of Toungoo, rebuilt the Schwenattaung Stupa at Prome. In the fifteenth century the Thai built the Schwegule Pagoda at Pegu, returning to a cherished theme in Mon architecture. This was followed by another period of political instability and constant warfare between the Burmese and the Thai of Ayuthia, the Thai of the north (Shans), and Arakan. Arakan had regained its independence when King Narameikhla, aided by Moslem troops, returned to power (1430) after fleeing before a Burmese invasion, and art was concentrated in the new capital, Mrohaung, founded in 1433. A mosque was erected. The sovereigns now had two names, one Burmese and the other Moslem. Minbin (1531–53), a very energetic king, reinforced the defenses of Mrohaung to preserve the city from Burmese raids, and erected numerous pagodas. Those of Shittaung, Dukkanthein, Andaw, and Shwedaung, strongly influenced by India, retained in their architecture as well as in their decoration certain characteristics which later related them to the art of India rather than to that of Burma. King Minbin's successors, especially Minhkamaung (Hussein Shah, 1612–22) and Sandathudhamma (1642–84), continued to erect pagodas in the capital.

Meanwhile the Arakanese had become terrible pirates and greatly hampered the Indians' commercial activites in the Gulf of Bengal. To end this, Aurangzeb collected a fleet of 188 armed ships and captured Chittagong, the Arakanese city, in 1665. The royal power was overthrown, and complete chaos followed.

In 1635, Ava again became the capital and Sagaing, Mingun, and Amarapura wrestled for supremacy until at last the English established order by deposing the tyrant King Thibaw in 1885. It was during the Alaungpaya Dynasty (Konbaungset) that most of the modern Burmese monuments were erected. Influenced by the art of the Thai, Burmese art became somewhat "Chinese-like" and revealed a decided preference for the baroque and excess decoration. Light wooden architecture was used especially for monasteries and palaces, while brick remained the favorite material for stupas. Certain projects tended to be gigantic (Kuthodaw, Jaung Hmu Daw, Mingun Paya); others returned to themes dear to Pagan dynasties (Maha Aung Mye Monastery, Kyauktawgyi). But this late period is outstanding for the wonderful wooden carvings which decorate the monasteries. Statues of Buddha became stereotyped, and series of them were executed in alabaster (found in large quantity on the outskirts of Mandalay). Lacquer art spread and resulted in wonderful statues covered with gold and precious stones. Finally, the roofs were adorned with slender motifs of carved wood or wrought metal, giving the buildings a lacelike design. But art succumbed to a precious and meticulous handicraft. Inspiration was lacking to recall Pagan's glorious past. Pagodas were covered with gold leaf and raw lacquer (known as *htsi*), walls were painted in lively colors, and bad taste spread everywhere. Everyone built his pagodon to suit his own taste, gilding or whitewashing it, which explains why the landscape seen from the distance has a gay aspect. But we must not look too closely. Even the marvelous Shwe Dagon, in the heart of the city of Rangoon, rebuilt twenty times, has now disappeared beneath the accumulation of gilt and strange chapels connected by electric wire. When night falls, the splendid spires on the pagodas, illuminated with neon tubes, create the most disgraceful effect.

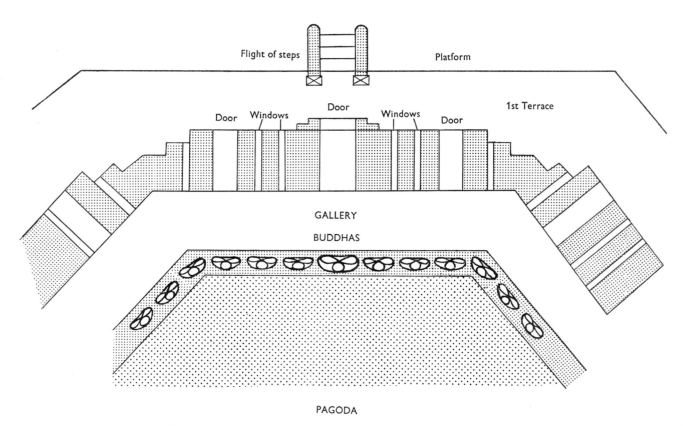

FIG. 16. PARTIAL GROUND PLAN OF THE SCHWEGULE PAGODA AT PEGU

118. BURMA, PEGU, KYAIK-PUN COLOSSUS. An impressive mass, this curious unfinished monument of brick and stucco was erected in 1476 in the reign of King Dhammaceti. Around a colossal square pillar were four statues over 98 feet high, representing a seated Buddha and his three ancestors. One of them has completely collapsed. The monument is now undergoing repairs.

119. BURMA, PEGU, SCHWEGULE PAGODA. According to tradition, this pagoda was built in the fifteenth century by the Thai, but its Mon characteristics are so obvious that it seems to be the work of native architects. It is quite probable that the base of this pagoda was originally Mon and that the Thai built (or ordered built) the pagoda which surmounts the base. Octagonal in plan, it contains a hewn gallery which takes its shape from the base's contours. It is lit by doors—three on each side—and by cross-shaped windows running along the entire wall (see plan). Sixty-four seated Buddhas are arranged on a pedestal running along the entire

gallery, which is narrow and vaulted. Above the main door of each side is an octagonal pagodon. One of the peculiarities of the pagoda itself is that the sides of its terraces on each story are alternately notched or smooth.

120. BURMA, SAGAING, TUPAYON STUPA. This stupa, begun in 1444 by King Narapati of Ava, was left unfinished. Its three circular terraces, 98 feet high in all, were to be surmounted by the usual Burmese stupa. Each level is adorned with niches having window frames, the only example of this type in Burma. The niches were probably meant to contain images of Buddha. The pagoda is entirely built of large-size bricks. Beneath a nearby shelter is a collection of fourteenth- and fifteenth-century steles.

121. BURMA, PEGU, SCHWENANDAW PAGODA. This gigantic pagoda was built at an uncertain date (probably about the fifteenth century) on the site of another pagoda which, according to tradition, was founded in 825. Only the terraces are original; the entire upper part was rebuilt several times. This was partly destroyed by earthquakes in 1910 and 1930, after which the pagoda was rebuilt and regilded.

122. BURMA, ARAKAN, MROHAUNG, DUKKANTHEIN PAGODA. This modest pagoda, built during the reign of King Minbin (1531–53), stands in the center of a high, square, three-story terrace flanked on each corner by a pagodon, and is typically Indian. The construction, a mixture of brick and stone, is rather crude. The sides of the terraces were adorned with sculptures. At the foot of the stupa was a small sanctuary. The entire structure is now in very bad condition.

123. BURMA, ARAKAN, MROHAUNG, SHITTAUNG TEMPLE, MAHISHASURA. This curious section from the Shittaung Temple (erected in Mrohaung, the Arakan capital during the reign of King Minbin), represents Mahishasura, the buffalo-demon, familiar to Indian iconography. In fact, Brahmano-Buddhist syncretism in Arakan influenced not only art but daily life as well. This rather clumsy work probably decorated one of the temple walls.

124. BURMA, SAGAING, NGADATKYI TEMPLE, BUDDHA. Erected in 1657 by the son and successor of King Thalun of Ava, this temple contains a huge seated Buddha which is periodically repainted and decorated with gilt-metal garlands. An impressive work, but one lacking style or grace.

125. BURMA, SAGAING, KAUNG HMU DAW STUPA. Sometimes also called Rajamanicula, this gigantic stupa was erected by King Thalun of Ava in 1636 to commemorate the capture of the capital. The model for this structure was the Anuradhapura Mahaceti at Ceylon. The stupa stands on three plainly decorated circular terraces. About 164 feet high, its base is surrounded by 812 lantern-pillars 4 feet 11 inches high (with oil lamps) and by 128 small sanctuaries containing images of nats. The stupa is surmounted by a gilt hti, in a modern form.

126. BURMA, MINGUN, SETTAWYA TEMPLE. This temple, modeled after those of Pagan, reveals no innovations except the fact that it was erected on the banks of the Irrawaddy on a square terrace decorated with five flights of steps with notched ornamentation.

127. BURMA, AMARAPURA, U BEIN BRIDGE. When the capital was transferred from Ava to Amarapura, the mayor of the city, using the remains of the royal palace, had a bridge built almost 4920 feet long across Lake Thaung Thaman. Entirely of teak, the pillars, 13 to 16 feet in height, have resisted more than two centuries of water soaking. This bridge leads to the Kyauktawgyi Temple, which was built in 1847 in the style of the Ananda in Pagan and decorated with many wall paintings.

128. BURMA, RANGOON, SHWE DAGON PAGODA. According to tradition, this huge pagoda dates from the time of Buddha. In fact, two of his disciples are said to have come from India, bringing with them some of Buddha's hair, and to have built a stupa 60 feet in height on the Okkala Hill, which is the site of the present city of Rangoon. The pagoda was successively repaired and enlarged in 1372 by Binnuya U, king of Pegu. Other sovereigns followed suit. In 1460 Shinsawbu, queen of Pegu, built the terrace and the walls, gilding the pagoda with the equivalent of her weight in gold. Finally, Sinbyushin, king of Ava, raised it to a height of more than 328 feet and gave it its present form. Later kings gave increasing amounts of gold to the pagoda. The dimensions of this monument are impressive: perimeter at the base, 1476 feet; total height, 344 feet; and height of the hti, 36 feet (weight of the hti, 2756 pounds).

At the very tip (*seinbu*) of the hti is a ball of pure gold 10 inches in diameter inlaid with diamonds and precious stones. The part supporting the hti is of gold and silver and is inlaid with 5440 diamonds and 1317 precious stones. The entire surface of the bulb is covered with gold leaf. The octagonal base of the pagoda is surrounded by 64 pagodons, all similar. Four of them, much larger, are placed on the cardinal points. The inner side of the platform is bordered by 74 chapels with images of nagas, nats, and devas. The rest of the platform is cluttered with various structures. Finally, four huge covered flights of steps lead from the ground to the platform.

129. BURMA, MINGUN, PONDAW PAYA. In 1790 King Bodawpaya conceived the plan of erecting the greatest pagoda in the world. On a base of five terraces measuring almost 492 feet square, he wanted to erect a pagoda 213 feet square and almost 524 feet high. Someone predicted that if the pagoda were finished the country would be ruined. Seven years later the king abandoned the project, although the terraces and the first story were already built. More than 100 million bricks 16 by 8 by 2¾ inches had been used. This is the greatest mass of brick in the world. The model of this huge monument, known as Pondaw Paya, stands on the banks of the Irrawaddy and is only 15 feet high.

130. BURMA, MINGUN, MANTALAGYI PAGODA. View of the terraces and first story of King Bowdawpaya's unfinished pagoda. In 1838 an earthquake caused considerable damage. The height of the first story is 164 feet, and is of solid brick.

131. BURMA, MINGUN, MANTALAGYI PAGODA, FAÇADE. This huge niche once held a statue of Buddha.

132. BURMA, MINGUN, SHINBYUME PAGODA. Also known as Mya Thein Daw, it is surrounded by seven concentric terraces symbolizing the seven rows of mountains around the mythical Mount Meru—the celestial home of Indra in his paradise Trayastrimsa. This monument was erected in 1816 by Bagyidaw, shortly before his accession to the throne, in memory of his first wife, Shinbyume. Four flights of steps lead to the foot of the central sanctuary, surmounted by a small pagoda. Greatly damaged by the earthquake of 1838, this attractive pagoda was repaired by King Mindon in 1874.

133. BURMA, AMARAPURA, PAHTODAWGYI PAGODA, GATEWAY. Built by King Bagyidaw in 1861, its highest section, standing on five stories, dominates the landscape. There is one original detail, namely, the gateways in the enceinte are surmounted by terraced roofs similar to those of "light" Pagan architecture. A modern structure of wood and sheet metal translates a very original and at the same time perfectly Burmese type of roofing. The walls are covered with good but very recent paintings.

134. BURMA, AMARAPURA, BUDDHA. This sculpture of brick and stucco decorates the entrance to a small temple founded in the twelfth century by a Pagan king and built in the style of the region. However, the present structure is of a later date and was built in the early nineteenth century by one of the kings of Ava or Amarapura. The style is the one which prevailed at that time.

135. BURMA, AMARAPURA, NAGAYON TEMPLE. This temple is a very special type, as the peak is represented here by a naga, or stylized mythical dragon. It is a charming small sanctuary, with its very elaborate decoration—still covered with a stucco coating applied by monks, erected on a high terrace guarded by griffins with human heads—and is one

of the most curious of the early nineteenth-century structures. In the foreground a modern structure in the traditional style can be seen.

136. BURMA, MANDALAY, KUTHODAW PAGODA. Also known as Maha Lawka Marazein, this large pagoda was erected in the reign of King Mindon in 1857 and modeled after that of Shwezigon at Pagan (Nyaung U). It is surrounded by 729 slabs of white marble, each placed in a small tabernacle, and on which are inscribed the texts of the *Tipitaka* (Buddhist Canon), as defined by the Fifth Buddhist Synod held by King Mindon.

137. BURMA, MANDALAY, SCHWENANDAW MONASTERY. Entirely built of wood, this wonderful building was spared when fire destroyed all the other edifices of Mandalay during World War II. It formerly consisted of one of the suites of Queen Setkyadevi, the wife of King Mindon (1853–78). When King Thibaw (1878–85) no longer wished to live in this building, he had it transported beyond the palace grounds and transformed it into a monastery. Thanks to this, we can admire the wonderful wood carvings which decorate its railings, walls, and doors, for the royal palace was utterly destroyed by aerial bombardment during World War II.

138. BURMA, MANDALAY, SCHWENANDAW MONASTERY, TEAK DOOR DECORATION. The figurines are about 12 inches high and were carved independent of the door to which they are attached.

139. BURMA, MANDALAY, THE FORT OR PALACE. Known in Burmese chronicles as "The Center of the Universe," this palace was entirely built of wood, surrounded by crenelated walls 29 feet high and 10 feet wide, and had a moat 246 feet wide and 13 feet deep. It was completely destroyed by aerial bombardment during World War II. All that remain are the walls and the wooden *pyatthats* which sheltered the guards above the gates. The palace stood in the center of the royal city which witnessed the surrender of King Thibaw, who was defeated by English troops in 1885.

119

120

122

123

129

130

133

134

137

138

139

V. THE ISLAND KINGDOMS

GENERAL REMARKS

SOUTH of the Asiatic continent are chains of islands which seem to protect it from the Indian and Pacific oceans. These islands, numbering more than 3000, are concentrated in the shallow waters arching below the huge mass of Borneo, separated from the continent by the Malay Peninsula. Known as Indonesia, this group consists of four principal islands. To the west is Sumatra, 648 miles long and more than 400 miles wide, very mountainous and wooded, with its northern part covered with swamps. It almost touches the Malay Peninsula.

To the south, separated from Sumatra by the Sunda Strait (unfortunately famous—or infamous—for the volcano Krakatoa which rises from its waters), the island of Java extends for almost 720 miles, a dorsal thorn emerging from the ocean. Bristling with volcanoes, rich with fertile soil and equatorial vegetation, it has been called "the richest island in the world."

Further toward the east, in the direction of New Guinea (which is still largely in the Stone Age and as yet to be completely explored), is a scattered string of islands with magical names: Bali, land of gods and dances; Flores, the island of the huge Komodo lizards; Timor, which is shared by Portuguese and Indonesians. The Flores Sea separates these islands from Celebes (Sulawesi), lying more to the north—the group known in the time of sailing ships as the "Spice Islands," and the source of Macassar ebony. At the center of these islands is the still relatively unknown island of head-hunters, Borneo (Kalimantan), with its swampy coasts.

Stretching across the Pacific, these islands were the scene in prehistoric times of many migrations. The most important was that of the Indonesians who, after coming from the continent, swarmed across the archipelago. In historic times, the wealth of these countries attracted merchants, missionaries, and Indian colonists. The Malacca Strait provided an easy passage for ships sailing to the China Sea, but the route was dangerous, as the waters were often infested with pirates. Meanwhile, other routes were created in the Malay Peninsula. They were relatively easy to cross, and several harbors were established on both coasts. However, the islands received constant influxes from India. We have already discussed the ways and means of Indian colonists. Cities were founded, harbors opened to trade, kingdoms established—first along the coasts, then inland. Traces of these Indian travelers have been found not only in Sumatra and Java but also in Borneo and Celebes, although these last two islands were rarely visited because of their distance and perhaps also because of their inhospitable shores. Our interest here is drawn only to those islands which, influenced by India, developed a special, lasting civilization and art. In geographical order, which is arbitrary from a historical viewpoint, we are going to study the civilizations that developed an art and architecture termed Indo-Javanese, or even Indonesian, in the Malay Peninsula, Sumatra, Java, and its immediately southern satellite, Bali.

1. SRIVIJAYA AND THE MALAY PENINSULA (A.D. 900)

The Malay Peninsula was the center of a civilization brought from India. Its position between India and the Far East was from the very first a natural barrier opposing penetration of Indian influence by land. But its coasts extending toward the south led, on the one hand, to the island of Sumatra and, on the other, opened a gateway to the Sunda Isles and the Far East. It was natural that a power able to guard the strait should have imposed itself as the necessary intermediary between east and west in Southeast Asia and derived the greatest benefit thereby. Already in the time of Ptolemy, the peninsula was known as the "Golden Chaeronea." In the sixth century, Chinese chronicles gave it the name Lang Ya Sseu Kia and described it as forming a vassal kingdom of Funan (a strongly established Hinduized empire in Indochina) and dating from the first century. It seems then that the colonization of the peninsula, known as Lankasuka by the Indians, dated from about the second century after Christ. These Indians were primarily Buddhists and probably Mahayanists, according to the many vestiges of stupas and sculptures found on different sites of the peninsula. About the sixth century, the cities were surrounded by brick walls and (again according to Chinese chronicles) the dwellings were erected on high terraces. But no great political state seems to have existed, at least in the beginning. These fortified cities, somewhat distant from one another and generally situated near the mouths of rivers, were really small kingdoms. Here again Chinese chronicles are our source of information: the cities of Kedah and Perak (Lankasuka) were known as Lang Ya Sseu Kia. The region of Palatung was the seat of the kingdom of Che-T'u, while the present city of Nakhon Sri Thammarat (Ligor in Thailand territory) was the capital of the state of Tambralinga. The port of Tokkala, on the Isthmus of Kra, has recently been identified with the site of Takuapa. One of the first states, named P'an P'an by the Chinese and situated on the edge of the Bay of Bandon on the southeast coast (near the city of Chaiya), probably transferred its culture to Funan about the second century. No vestige of any city remains for us to draw conclusions about its art and inhabitants. However, the few statuettes found show decided affinities with the Amaravati and Gupta styles, which would date them from the fourth and fifth centuries. Nevertheless, it is certain that these kingdoms conducted continuous trade, probably commercial, with India on the one hand, and the Dvaravati and Funan kingdoms and China on the other.

Toward the close of the seventh century, a kingdom already appears to have been formed on the island of Sumatra which gradually encompassed and united under its rule all the small kingdoms of the peninsula and extended itself even to the western part of the island of Java. This Srivijaya Empire, known to the Chinese as Chi-Li-Fo-Che, or simply Fo-Che, had its capital on the site of the present city of Palembang, formerly a seaport and now situated inland. The Chinese pilgrim, Yi-Tsing, who stayed three times at Fo-Che, in 671, about 687, and about 693, describes the city which, according to him, contained more than a thousand Buddhist monks and the seat of an important university, and was a convenient stop for pilgrims on their way from China to Nalanda in northern India. Moreover, in 670, the Srivijaya Empire was sufficiently important to send an ambassador to the court of China. Coinciding with the fall of the Funan Kingdom, which was destroyed by Chen La, the mostly maritime Srivijaya Empire began to develop, conquering the Malay Peninsula, the neighboring islands, and a part of Java. In 775 a foundation stele erected at Chaiya reveals the sudden advance of Fo-Che's army. Since Central Java was strongly held by the Javanese dynasty of the Sailendras, or "Kings of the Mountain," the Srivijaya Kingdom was unable to spread in that direction. But, according to Coedes, one of these "Kings of the Mountain" became ruler in the ninth century. Srivijaya power was thus affirmed and the kings extended their conquests, but in the eleventh century they soon came in contact with the powerful Cholas of southern India, who destroyed them at sea and invaded their territories. Here historical evidence is doubtful and authors fail to agree as to the succession of facts. According to Majumdar, it was first the Sailendras of Java who replaced the Srivijayas in the Malay Peninsula toward the close of the eighth century and who, from their capital, Ligor, established their supremacy over Java. According to Quaritch Wales, the Srivijaya Kingdom at Sumatra was replaced in the eighth century by one known as Javaka, headed by Mahayana sovereigns of the Sailendra Dynasty who had come from India and had established their capital in the state of Perak. In any case, vestiges of this period are more numerous in the Malay Peninsula than in Sumatra The reason for this is perhaps explained by the island's swampy coast and its equatorial climate which are scarcely conducive to the preservation of edifices or sculptures. The types found in the Malay Peninsula are mainly related to the Pala style of Buddhist representations, and were given the generic name of the Srivijaya style. We can thus date them from the eighth to the eleventh centuries. But many non-Buddhist colonies had also prospered on the peninsula, leaving several interesting representations of Brahmanic divinities, especially in limestone and schist, in a heavy style quite different from the Pallava Indian one. On the other hand, surviving Mahayana sculpture, related to the Pala style, is represented by wonderful examples of representations of Lokeshvara (Avalokiteshvara) in carefully executed bronze or stone.

Architectural remains offer little information. Here and there on the sites of ancient cities, especially at Chaiya, are fragments of brick stupa bases completely covered by vegetation. The sole example of a stupa able to furnish some indication of the construction styles of the period and region is the one at Chaiya, in the center of Vat Phra Borom Dhatu, which has often been rebuilt and restored.

In a cave at Yala, near Nakhon Sri Thammarat, there are fragments of wall paintings tracing the life of Buddha, perhaps dating from the thirteenth century. They are now almost invisible.

140. THAILAND, SURAT THANI, STATUE OF VISHNU. This hieratic sandstone piece had four arms. Found in the Malay Peninsula, it belongs to the Funan and Sri Deb styles rather than to that of Srivijaya. On the face are traces of gold leaf. We have included this statue to show the coexistence of Brahmanic and Buddhist faiths and kingdoms in the Malay Peninsula. Height: 5 feet 8 inches. *National Museum, Bangkok.*

141. THAILAND, CHAIYA, VAT PHRA BOROM DHATU. This stupa is the only one in the Srivijaya style to have survived. Although it has been rebuilt several times, it seems almost to conform to the original design. Cubic in form, of modest dimensions, set on a high platform, it is surmounted by recessed platforms. At the corner of every other platform or story—as well as above the ornaments (modifications of Indian *kudu*) centered on each side of the stupa—is a small stupa. The main section is adorned with three false projecting doors and a niche, also projecting, on the fourth side. The pediment décors of these niches and false doors are certainly recent additions. The stupa was probably erected in the reign of King Indra (of Sailendra?) in the eighth century and symbolized the Four Truths and the noble Eight-fold Path to Nirvana. This type of temple is perhaps related to Tjandi Pawon and to the temple of the Sailendra kings of Java. The finial is a recent addition.

142. THAILAND, CHAIYA, VAT PHRA BOROM DHATU, BUST OF AVALOKITESHVARA. This wonderful bronze bust (which may have been dedicated to King Indra by his son, Vishnu, in 775), is one of the most representative and finest sculptures of the period. Heavily decorated, its features are probably those of the king who commissioned it. The upper part of the headdress, which contained a small representation of Buddha, has disappeared. Without assigning as exact a date as the local chronicle, we can approximate that the piece dates from the eighth century. Height: 2 feet 1 inch. *National Museum, Bangkok.*

143. THAILAND, CHAIYA, VOTIVE TABLET. Stamped terra cotta showing Avalokiteshvara seated on a throne. To his right is a small Indian-style stupa beneath which is an inscription in Nagari characters. Eighth–ninth century. Height: 2½ inches. *Chaiya Museum.*

144. THAILAND, CHAIYA, STATUETTE OF BUDDHA WALKING. This small bronze found near Vat Phra Borom Dhatu is of a late date and although still related to the Srivijaya style, already shows Khmer influences. It can be attributed to the close of the eleventh century, perhaps even to the beginning of the twelfth. Height: 8 inches. *National Museum, Bangkok.*

140

143   144

2. THE JAVANESE AND BALINESE KINGDOMS
(Eighth–Fifteenth Century)

Although the Hinduized kingdoms of the Malay Peninsula and Sumatra are familiar to us only through rare traces and the rather uncertain accounts of Chinese travelers, this is not the case with the kingdoms of the island of Java known as Indo-Javanese. Many fine examples of architecture and sculpture attest to a flourishing civilization. Many monuments, built of volcanic stone, have lasted for centuries. Moreover, the inhabitants have preserved them. Even when converted to Islam, the Javanese were unwilling to destroy the images of their ancient gods. Thanks to a flowering of wonderful works, we are able to read the island's past and, with it, that of almost all of Indonesia. A rich, fertile island, Java became a cultural center as early as the Indian colonization period, attracting people from every part of the subcontinent. The first colonists undoubtedly came from the Amaravati region, introducing Mahayana Buddhism. They were followed by Pallava Hindus and Brahmans who came from the Gujarati coasts during the period of Gupta power. Later, the introduction of Islam followed a similar pattern. Ceylon itself shared this influence. Northeast India, whose center was the celebrated Buddhist monastery at Nalanda, had a lasting influence on Indo-Javanese styles and civilizations. Early Indian influence in Java is almost unknown. Yet many statues of Buddha exist. They were probably made in India and brought to the island by Buddhist missionaries. As a matter of fact, they are similar in every respect to those common in India before the fifth century. Between the fifth and seventh centuries, Hindu kingdoms had been founded in western Java, where sculptures in a distinctively Pallava style have been found. However, no important architectural vestiges exist from these states; the name of one of them—the Taruma Kingdom—has survived in an inscription in Pallava Grantha Sanskrit characters.

About 800, a Brahmanic city existed on the volcanic Dieng Plateau in Central Java, at an altitude of 6500 feet, near sulfur springs—a well-planned city with sewers to drain the water from the swampy plateau, temples all dedicated to Shiva, and *mandapas* (temples) and palaces whose foundations have been discovered. These temples, eight of which are still standing, are small and are built on the Indian plan with a single cella on a high base. All reveal strong affinities with the Pallava styles of southern India. They are built of volcanic stone. The kala motif (head of a demon placed above gates and false doors) and diverging makaras, typical of later Indo-Javanese styles, are distinctly developed. Many statues of a powerful style were found on the spot.

The city seems to have been suddenly abandoned about the beginning of the ninth century, probably because of a volcanic eruption.

Almost at the same time and under the influence of the Sailendra Dynasty, a Mahayana-inspired Buddhist civilization developed somewhat to the south, leaving wonderful monuments, including the Borooudur Stupa, which for its size and distinctive architecture has no equal anywhere in the world. The fact that Buddhism and Brahmanism flourished at the same time is not at all surprising in Asia, where often religious syncretism suited populations who were of a different religion than their leaders. When the Borobudur Stupa was erected, many people had probably remained Shivaists, some still faithful to the Hinayana Doctrine which once flourished on the island. Between about 750 and 850, two dynasties ruled Central Java—the one of Buddhist obedience, which was that of the Sailendras of Srivijaya, the other Brahmanic (Shivaist), from Sanjaya (or the first Mataram Dynasty). About 850, a Sailendra princess married a Sanjaya prince and only the Mataram Dynasty reigned in Central Java. The Sailendra Dynasty emigrated to Sumatra, where it reigned over the Srivijaya Empire and the Malay Peninsula. Combined efforts of two rival houses led to the creation of many monuments not only in Central Java (Tjandi Placsan) but in the eastern part of the island as well.

About 930, for some unknown reason, the Mataram kings decided to change their capital and settle in eastern Java, although small dynasties continued to reign in the central part. The sovereigns soon ruled over the entire island and the dynasties often changed capitals.

About the close of the tenth century, the daughter of a sovereign of eastern Java married the king of Bali. Brahmanic doctrines and animistic practices combined to produce a special form of Hinduism in Bali, which has lasted to this day without being replaced by Islam. Of this marriage a prince was born who became the hero-king Airlangga. Married to another princess of eastern Java in 1006, at the time when the Srivijayas destroyed the kingdoms of Central Java in a revengeful raid, Airlangga undertook to reconquer the territories he had inherited, and by 1037 he finally ruled the entire island. Internal disorder probably prevented future sovereigns from

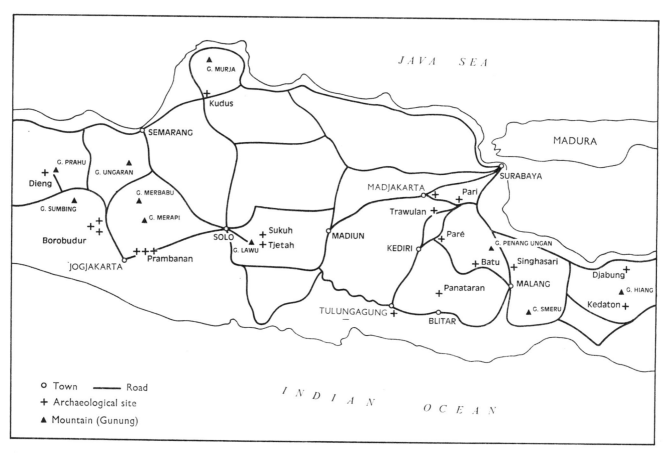

FIG. 17. ROADS AND ARCHAEOLOGICAL SITES IN CENTRAL JAVA

building lasting monuments, with the result that none from this period have survived. Construction tended perhaps toward lightweight buildings reinforced with wood, which have since disappeared. In the early thirteenth century a new dynasty, that of the Singhasari, seems to have had the impetus to build new monuments. A new wave of Indians from Bengal, coming from Nalanda, may have inspired the Singhasari sovereigns and introduced elements of the Pala style. A new style was developed, strongly contrasted to that of Central Java. The country was covered with both Buddhist and Shivaist religious buildings. The sovereigns neglected their tribute to China and as a result Kublai Khan sent a fleet in 1292. The country, then in the throes of internal dissensions, became peaceful with the advent of a new dynasty, that of Majapahit. Their capital was no longer Blitar but Madjakerta (the present village of Trawulan), somewhat more to the northeast. Brick seems to have been preferred here, although stone continued to be used in the southern part of the kingdom, especially at the Panataran Sanctuary, whose construction covered a period of 125 years, the last monument of this group having been erected in 1454.

During the reign of this dynasty, religions tended to unite, and Buddha and Shiva were proclaimed identical.

About 1350 a king of Malayu, Adityavarman, founded the independent kingdom of Minangkabau in Sumatra. As early as the thirteenth century the first preachers of Islam came from Gujarat, on the western coast of India, to Java, and the traffic increased after the foundation of the Moslem Kingdom of Malacca in 1402. Hindu dynasties were soon replaced by the Islamic ones of Wali, then of Mataram. Only the island of Bali escaped Islamic invasion. In 1600 the Dutch colonized Java and ended its independence.

This brief history will help in understanding the development of styles as indicated in this tabulation:

I. *Second–fifth century*. Bronzes imported from India or copied from them locally, scattered throughout Java and also Sumatra, Borneo, and Celebes.

II. *Fifth–seventh century*. Kingdoms of western Java: distinctively Pallava Indian style.

III. *Seventh–tenth century*. Kingdoms of Central Java: styles strongly influenced by those of southern and northeastern India. Typically Indian motifs reused and adapted, such as the head of kala and makaras (motifs borrowed again in the ninth century by the Khmers). This period includes three series of temples:

   1. Temples of the Dieng Plateau (seventh–eighth century). Shivaist and greatly influenced by southern India (except an unusual type, the Tjandi Bhima, whose roof in the form of a north Indian sikhara is adorned with kudus on the sides of many recessed stories. Generally open to the west (except the Tjandi Bhima, open to the east), these temples were enclosed by barriers of which only the stone bases remain.

   2. Buddhist temples of the central part (eighth–ninth century). Borobudur, Tjandi Pawon, Tjandi Mendut, Tjandi Kalasan, Tjandi Sari, Tjandi Sewu, Tjandi Plaosan, Tjandi Ngawen, and Tjandi Lumbung. All of various types, and all richly decorated.

   3. Brahmanic Prambanan complex (early tenth century). Built for the first Mataram Dynasty, consisting of the most important group built in Java. Symmetrical, surrounded by additional small temples, the influence of Indian styles is still very noticeable in both architecture and sculpture.

IV. *Oriental temples of central influence, eighth–eleventh century*. Tjandi Selamangleng, Tjandi Sanggariti, Tjandi Badut, Djalatunda; dedicated to Shiva and greatly influenced by Indian types.

V. *Oriental kingdom styles*. Native influence is strong (*Wayang* style, wayang means "shadow-play puppets"), stone construction and, during Majapahit Dynasty, brick. Appearance of "broken doors."

   1. Singhasari Dynasty. Tjandi Kidal, Tjandi Djago, Tjandi Singhasari foundation, Tjandi Djawi, Panataran complex.

   2. Majapahit Dynasty. Baths of the Panataran complex, Tjandi Djedong, Tjandi Kedaton, Tjandi Tigawangi, Tjandi Tikus.

VI. *Islamic kingdoms*. Persistence of former styles: Kudu minaret, Tralaja tombs, Sendang-Duwur cemetery, Mantingan mosque reliefs, tomb of Ratu Ibu at Air Mata, Madura, with renewed decoration, especially vegetal.

VII. *Balinese styles*. Converted to Buddhism in the eleventh century and colonized in 1343 by kings of the Majapahit Dynasty, the island of Bali has remained Brahmanic to this day. A special style developed which was a happy combination of native styles of the Pedjeng Kingdom and of Tirta Empul (928–50) and of those of eastern Java, with a luxuriant decoration which caused it to be termed "baroque." A special type of sanctuary built of lightweight material, already existing in eastern Java, was further developed—the meru, with multiple, superimposed roofs, sometimes as many as eleven. The principal monuments on the island are, in chronological order: Goa Gadjah (early eleventh century), Tampaksiring (middle and end of the eleventh century), Bangli (early thirteenth century), Tirta Empul, Pedjeng (1329), Yeh Pulu (fourteenth–fifteenth century), Kapal (fourteenth century), Mengwi and Besakih (close of the fourteenth century).

The material presented below will follow this rather simple classification.

Scarcely rich in architectural systems (with the exception, however, of certain unusual types like the Great Stupa of Borobudur, the Tjandi Bhima, and several others), Javanese art nevertheless displays a wealth of wall decoration and temple forms. The Borobudur bas-reliefs are strikingly beautiful. Yet the floral or animal motifs used elsewhere are with few variations all borrowed from India. The most common motifs are kala, makaras, garlands of beading, vases of abundance, sacred animals, gazelles, and geese. The rather stylized bas-reliefs of Borobudur add a lively note to the gallery walls of the Prambanan temples.

In east Java bas-reliefs seem to become conventional the more they are separated from their Hindu models and adapted to the Javanese character; persons, animals, and floral themes are treated as shadows with almost no frontality. Décor becomes important, and certain motifs, like those of caryatids supporting garlands in one of the Panataran temples (Naga), appear to have been borrowed from ancient Indian motifs found at Amaravati in the decoration of *vedika* crosspieces.

Temples erected in Central Java consist of isolated sanctuaries or edifices arranged in a symmetrical complex according to an Indian plan, formed of a square sanctuary with a single cella on a high pedestal which is reached by means of a flight of steps, or of several chapels arranged on a single base but always having a massive aspect. In the east, the tendency is to expansion: the cellas are very narrow (although also square in plan), slender, and topped by very pointed roofs. The doors are unduly high and narrow, surmounted by corbeled motifs which make them appear narrower still. A horizontal median ring separates the temple walls into two equal sections. The kala motif above the doors treated simply as a frame cannot be related to the motif that decorates the richly embellished doors of Central Javanese monuments. Whereas the tjandis of Central Java reveal extreme diversity, if not in plan at least in their architecture, those of eastern Java seem to be reduced to a single type whose perfect example is the Tjandi Singhasari.

These two art forms which create the Indo-Javanese style seem best related by the extreme emphasis of the antefixes and their increasing number. In Bali, this resulted in a real tearing apart of the covering sections, which stand out against the sky. Both in eastern and in Central Java, construction is carefully executed.

As for sculpture, it is of equal quality in eastern and Central Java. Sculpture in the round and bas-relief are also carefully executed with great concern for accurate detail.

Whereas divine or royal figures are conceived in Central Java with greater freedom, those of eastern Java reveal a certain stiffness, perhaps due to religious conventions. On the other hand, scenes of daily life are animated and seem treated in a more summary manner in which gesture is more important than detail. In eastern Java, freedom and accuracy in sculpture are retained only in representations of nature. Certain techniques of representing the lotus appear to have been inspired by those of a flower altarpiece found at Ruvanveli in Ceylon.

Incised bronzes, both statuary and ornamental objects, are of remarkably fine quality. The art of wall painting, on the other hand, was hardly popular in Java.

THE CENTRAL JAVANESE STYLE

145. CELEBES, BUDDHA. Beautifully treated, this bronze Amaravati-style Buddha, found in Celebes (Sulawesi), was brought from southern India by early Buddhist missionaries to the distant island. From the style, it would date from between the second and fifth centuries. Height: 2 feet 6 inches. *Djakarta Museum.*

146. SUMATRA, DJAMBI, STANDING BUDDHA. This life-size stone Buddha in the post-Gupta style probably belongs to Dvaravati art, for it has all its characteristics. We do not know whether this work was executed on the spot or imported. Archaeologists agree that it dates from about 750. Height: 5 feet 3³/₄ inches. *Djakarta Museum.*

147. JAVA, TEMPLES OF THE DIENG PLATEAU. At the center of the island of Java, not far from Mount Prahu, on a volcanic plateau 6500 feet high, are the foundations of a city and many temples, eight of which are still standing. The central group consists of five temples. In this photograph we can see, from

purpose; the sole exceptions are the tjandis Sumar and Bhima which, being devotional places, are open to the east. To the north of the principal group are the foundations of a large building which may have been a palace. To the left of the group can be seen many temple foundations. All these sanctuaries were surrounded by walls or railings which were probably of wood, for they have vanished, although the stone bases are still in place. Dedicated to Shiva, the mountain god, those temples were built of volcanic stone. The most ancient inscription is from 809, but these monu-

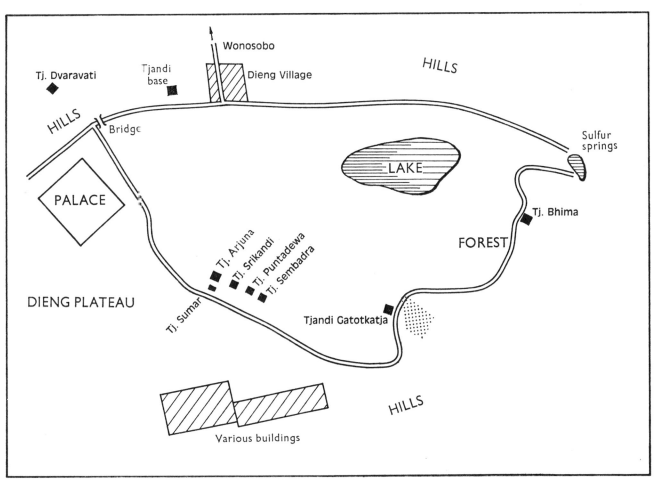

FIG. 18. TEMPLES OF THE DIENG PLATEAU

left to right, the Tjandi Arjuna with, fronting the entrance, the small Tjandi Sumar structure (open to the east), the Tjandi Srikandi, and the Tjandi Puntadewa (also known as the Tjandi Samyadji). More to the right is the Tjandi Nakula (or Sembadra). Less than a mile to the north, in the hills far in the distance, on the left of the photograph, stands the Tjandi Dvaravati. Finally, toward the south is the Tjandi Dvaravati Gatotkadjo, and, in the direction of the sulfur spring, the very strange Tjandi Bhima. All these temples are open to the west, which seems to indicate their funerary

ments were probably erected at a somewhat earlier date—750 seems more likely. This complex may have been the sanctuary capital of a small Hindu state. (See plan.)

148. JAVA, DIENG, HEAD OF A DIVINITY. A divinity or a deified king, this handsome portrait is from the principal group of the Dieng temples. Sculptured of lava stone, it probably had a stucco coating. It may have belonged to an Indian temple, since the mustache, headdress, and halo are typically Indian. Height: 10 inches. *Djakarta Museum.*

155

149. JAVA, DIENG, TJANDI ARJUNA AND TJANDI SUMAR. The Tjandi Arjuna consists of a simply decorated base, $19^1/_2$ feet square, surmounted by a cubic cella decorated with three false windows and a projecting west porch. The roof is formed of three false stories which narrow toward the top, emphasized on the corners by small constructions, and by a slightly projecting niche in the center of each side. The whole was probably topped by a similar reduced construction. A flight of steps led to the sanctuary, where a lingam probably stood, for beneath the false north window (shown here) we can see a gargoyle makara. In India, this opening was generally used for the outflow of lustral water poured on the lingam. Even the plan of this small building is typically Indian. It is about 23 feet high.

The Tjandi Sumar, which is scarcely 8 feet high, consists of a rectangular room with a door in one of the long sides and small ogival windows. It is built on a deeply molded base. The corbeled roof has curved lines which are heightened at the corners by small decorations. A flight of steps on the left connects this antechamber to the Tjandi Arjuna by a paved path.

150. JAVA, DIENG, TJANDI ARJUNA, ENTRANCE. A popular decorative element throughout Central Java is that known as kala-makara, seen here framing the entrance to the sanctuary. It consists mainly of the head of a kala (the demon Rahu?) with heavy, globular eyes, decorated with hooks and horns, but without a lower jaw (which was supposedly beneath the path of the person entering this huge mouth). From here decoration leads, on each side of the door, to a makara (mythical monster of Indian origin, represented here with the outward-facing head of a crocodile with an elephant tusk from which hang flowers or strings of beading). These kala-makaras were to decorate all the openings of almost every temple in Central Java. Makaras later disappeared in east Java, leaving merely a head of kala, which often assumed huge proportions, above the openings. In Central Java this makara, often used to decorate gargoyles, is sometimes so decorated that it disappears almost completely beneath a floral stylization. It is then adorned with very short claws (Tjandi Puntadewa). We shall see how this makara motif is used to decorate the beginning and the end of a flight of steps.

151. JAVA, DIENG, TJANDI SRIKANDI, BAS-RELIEF. This bas-relief adorns the north false window of the sanctuary. It represents Vishnu, one of whose emblems we can recognize, namely, the *chakra*, or sun disk, symbolized by a wheel. He is mounted on a pedestal on which there are a vase of flowers and an incense burner. On either side of his head a divine being is showering a rain of flowers. Seen from the front, this forms a very curious background décor. A parasol above the head of this effigy indicates its divine rank.

152. JAVA, DIENG, TJANDI SRIKANDI. Somewhat smaller than the Tjandi Arjuna, this sanctuary, conceived on the same plan, has lost its covering stories. But its walls remain decorated with handsome bas-reliefs, sculpted in the stone mass itself, as shown in the preceding photograph.

153. JAVA, DIENG, TJANDI BHIMA. This particular temple, the only example of its kind in Indonesian art, is built along the lines of a square (about 16 by $14^1/_2$ feet) with a projecting porch. It is especially remarkable for its sikhara, which seems to combine two different styles, those of the north and the south. Actually, this sikhara consists of a squared central tower, flanked on each side by a series of false windows recessed one above the other, acting as buttresses for the tower, and of reductions of this same central sikhara which become part of it on the corners and terminate in an amalaka. Although the sanctuary entrance is decorated with the kala-makara motif, the niches of the false windows follow a typically south Indian design, that of the kudu—a horseshoe opening characteristic of Indian monuments. Here, the kudus are decorated with human heads, as though a crowd perched about the summit of this monument were witnessing a ceremony taking place around the temple. Seven stories of windows were to have surmounted this sanctuary, which is open to the west in contrast to most of the other Dieng monuments. It was planned to be the principal one of the group. It stands on a height, near sulfur springs. Its low base is undecorated.

154. JAVA, DIENG, TJANDI BHIMA, KUDUS. Here we clearly see the kudus of the west side of the sikhara, alternately decorated with human heads and vases of flowers. Floral decoration reminiscent of Amaravati art adorns these niches, some of which, first and third in the center, are divided into two lobes, a new form in relation to Indian art.

155. JAVA, MAGELANG, TJANDI MENDUT. Standing not far from the Borobudur Stupa, this temple, whose upper part is missing, is oriented to the northwest. It is merely the enlargement of a more ancient brick temple whose walls were enveloped by the stones of the present edifice. Rising on a high square base, with a projection on the northwest terminating in a flight of steps, is the cubic mass forming the sanctuary, which is topped by three recessed stories (here we see only two), surrounded by small stupas. A niche derived from the kudu decorates the center of each story. On the summit of the third and last there was undoubtedly a terminal stupa, like the one on the Tjandi Pawon (plate 160). The total height was probably about 85 feet. The walls are decorated with bas-relief panels representing divinities of the Buddhist pantheon or scenes from the Jatakas. The sanctuary is a simple, windowless cella, adorned with three statues nearly 10 feet high, representing Lokeshvara on the left, Buddha in the center, and Vajrapani on the right, all seated on high bases. The ground, dropped below the bottom of the last of the entrance steps, was constantly covered with water in order to purify the officiants. In the foreground, one may see two of the small stupas which have fallen from the roof terraces. This temple may have been contemporary with the Borobudur Stupa and dates from about 800.

156. JAVA, MAGELANG, TJANDI MENDUT, BAS-RELIEF. This bas-relief, on the south wall of the interior of the entranceway, reveals a yaksha ogre converted to Buddhism, playing with children. The latter are playing and climbing a tree, while the ogre, seated above jars full of money, is looking at them in a kindly manner. If the treatment of the yaksha is still in accordance with the canon of divine representation, the children, on the contrary, are treated with greater freedom, revealing a sense of nature and freedom of observation which is characteristic of Javanese artists. Above this delightful scene two doves indicate that peace reigns in Java due to the triumph of Buddhism. Height of the panel: 3 feet 7 ¼ inches.

157. JAVA, MAGELANG, TJANDI MENDUT, BAS-RELIEF ON THE ENTRANCE RAMP. One would think that La Fontaine had found inspiration here for his fable, *The Turtle and the Two Ducks*. The theme is very old and has been borrowed from the Buddhist Jatakas. The turtle is represented simultaneously in the air, held aloft by two ducks, and on the ground, smashed to pieces, while hunters in a field of grazing buffalo are shooting at the duck with bows and arrows. The movement is lively and well expressed. Dimensions of the panel: about 3 feet 2 inches by 20 inches.

158. JAVA, MAGELANG, TJANDI MENDUT, A STATUE OF BUDDHA. We see the Buddha Shakyamuni (expression of the Ultimate Truth) with a lancet-shaped halo, seated in the Western manner in an attitude of *dharmachakra-mudra* (the gesture of Turning the Wheel of the Law). The throne back is sculptured with makaras and lions standing on elephants. The Buddha himself is shown without genitalia, firmly seated, with his robe clinging to his arms, legs, and the throne. The features are mature and serene, the right shoulder is exposed, and the feet rest on a double lotus. This is one of the finest pieces of

sculpture ever produced, ideal for bringing peace and assurance to the hearts of the faithful. In spite of the stiff pose, there is nothing ascetic about the image. And in spite of the human appearance, this is really a supernatural being. Flanking the Buddha (but not shown here), arranged against the walls, are his companions, Lokeshvara (or Avalokiteshvara or Padmapani), who symbolizes the Law, and the repentant demon, Vajrapani, who designates the *Samgha*, the Buddhist and human community. This group forms the Three Jewels of Buddhism, the *Triratna* (*Tipitaka*) which once seen can never be forgotten. Height of the Buddha: 9 feet.

159. JAVA, MAGELANG, TJANDI NGAWEN, LION ON TEMPLE II. Consisting of five sanctuaries, the Tjandi Ngawen is of Buddhist rule. Square in plan, the sanctuaries were dedicated to the five Dhyani Buddhas. Only Temple II has been restored. The corners of the terrace are adorned with rampant lions whose very humanized heads act as antefixes. The temple entrance is fronted by a small porch. Temples II and IV were slightly different from I, III, and V. These temples are contemporary with the preceding ones, dating from about 800. Height of the lion: 3 feet 4 inches.

160. JAVA, MAGELANG, TJANDI PAWON. Standing between the Tjandi Mendut and the Borobudur Stupa, this small temple is dedicated to the god of wealth, Kubera. It follows the plan of the Tjandi Mendut with the exception that it has two small decorative openings on each side. It is oriented to the northwest. The triangular head of kala that decorates the door pediment, and the two unusual makaras, form a kind of arch. The wall panels are beautifully decorated. Like the Tjandi Mendut, this small temple is related to the Srivijaya, which can still be seen at Chaiya in Thailand, and is probably of the same date (plate 141). In Indonesian Badjanalan, its ancient name was "Vajranala Mandir."

161. JAVA, MAGELANG, TJANDI PAWON, CENTRAL PANEL OF THE NORTH WALL. It represents a kinnari (mythical being, half-woman, half-bird) bringing an offering to a celestial tree (symbolizing Understanding of the Law) surrounded by vases full of gems.

162. JAVA, MAGELANG, BOROBUDUR, MODEL OF THE GREAT STUPA. Much literature, although very specialized and scarcely accessible, has been published on Borobudur since the masterly study by N.-J. Krom, which unfortunately is unavailable. Few monuments have raised so many questions, not only about its form, which has no equal, but also about the reason for its existence and the meaning of its component parts. This enormous

FIG. 19. PLAN OF THE BOROBUDUR STUPA

stone monument, standing on the top of a hill, is more than 403 feet square. It consists of six square terraces surmounted by a triple circular terrace, the whole topped by a stupa. Built about 800 by sovereigns of the Sailendra Dynasty, this structure is above all a wonderful construction of stone. It both is an image of the life of Buddha and a representation of the cosmos according to Buddhist philosophy. Its name, which has yet to be clarified, perhaps means "the monastery on the hill" (*bara* = vihara, or monastery, and *budu* = hill). Sivaramurti thinks this may be a corruption of the Sanskrit

name *Varabuddhapura*. No inscription that can be dated with certainty helps us to assign an exact date to the erection of this fabulous summary of the art and science of the period. Epigraphists, turning to a few inscriptions in old Javanese Pallava writing that were discovered on the hidden base, hesistate between 800 and 850. The Sailendra kings (*saila* = mountain, *indra* = king) belonged to Mahayana Buddhism or protected it. This Buddhist sect, which developed strongly in Asia in contrast to Theravada Buddhism (now confined to Ceylon and southeast continental Asia), developed the non-theistic philosophy of original Buddhism into a theist religion. Mahayana Buddhism recognized the historical Buddha as only one of the gods of the celestial pantheon. The world was governed in periods by Dhyani Buddhas (Meditating Buddhas), five in number and each living in a different paradise. Supreme Being, Transcendental Reality, or Pure Buddha can be seen only by those who have attained Nirvana, the final beatitude which is part of the cosmos. Mahayanism also venerates human Buddhas, including Gautama, who have come to teach men truth, and a large number of bodhisattvas, demigods of kindness whose task is to help men advance on the Right Path.

At Borobudur we find the effigies of all these Buddhas and bodhisattvas. Buddhas are distinguished only by their gestures (mudras). Adi Buddha or Vajrasattva is turning the Wheel of the Law (dharmachakra). Akshobya governs the east and is shown touching the Earth with his right hand (bhumisparsa). Ratnasambhva is making the gesture of offering (vara-mudra). His home is in the south. Amitabha, in the west, is meditating (dhyani-mudra). Amoghasiddha, in the north, is protecting (abhaya-mudra). Finally in the center is Buddha preaching the Law (vitarka-mudra). The bodhisattvas, each with a halo, are generally represented richly dressed and recognizable through certain details. The bodhisattva Lokeshvara (Avalokiteshvara) has in his headdress a small image of the Dhyani Buddha, Amitabha. Maitreya, the future Buddha, has a small stupa in his hair. All these gods and demigods are accompanied by

divine cohorts, among whom the most curious personages are kinnaris—musicians who are half-human and half-bird.

The structure of Borobudur attempts to explain the nature and composition of the cosmos. It consists of three levels: the World of Desire (*Kamadhatu*), the World of Forms (*Rupadhatu*), and finally the Formless World (*Arupadhatu*). Paul Mus has accurately translated these terms into "material worlds, ecstatic vision, and pure perception." The architectural conception of Borobudur tends in its conception to materialize these three states (see fig. 20). The first level, describing the World of Desire, or Human Actions, has been covered over (we still know neither why nor how) by an added terrace. The World of Ecstatic Vision, or World of Forms (Rupadhatu), consists of four terraces decorated with more than 1800 bas-reliefs representing the life of Gautama Buddha (first gallery), the Jatakas (second and third galleries), and the future Buddhas (fourth gallery). Finally, the Formless World, or World of Pure Perception, is represented by the last four terraces: the first is plain, the three others are simply decorated with 72 open stupas, the interior of each one containing a Dhyani Buddha. On the highest terrace, Absolute Beatitude is expressed by a stupa which is 26 feet high.

The form: Several theories have been put forward as to the origin of the general form of Borobudur. Parmentier thought that the galleries were intended to form the foundation of an enormous stupa,

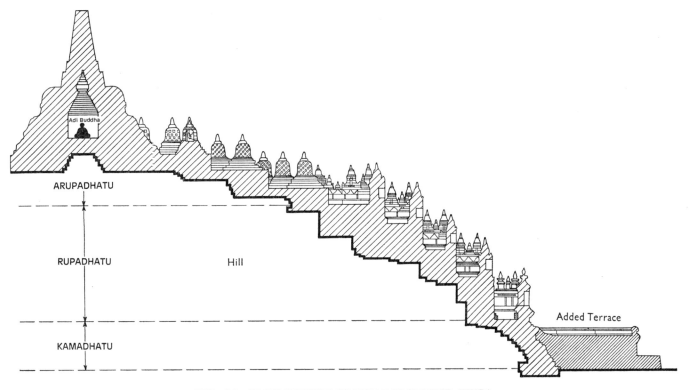

FIG. 20. CROSS SECTION OF THE BOROBUDUR STUPA

which would have replaced the circular terraces, but the project was abandoned, perhaps because of the excessive weight of the terminal stupa to be added. Van Erp believed that this stupa was a segment of a circle in two parts, all the round terraces being considered a stupa, the square terraces merely the foundation. Foucher suggested that this stupa had been "reelaborated" into successive terraces, and Hoenig that the original monument had been enlarged by successive additions, like Khmer terraces.

Moreover, the general form of Borobudur has been explained by suggesting its origin (in my opinion, this is very plausible) in the step pyramids or primitive sanctuaries found in west Java, Sumatra, Bali, and in the Polynesian Islands (maraes). A stone erected on a summit representing the spirit being honored (cf. seats of the ancestors at Bali—plate 242) may be the origin of the idea of the terminal stupa. In regard to this, at Pedjeng in Bali, there is a curious stone that consists of two square terraces on which a third stone is standing, round and sculptured. This stone is the object of great veneration and the natives call it "The Center of the World." It is very probable that Borobudur was erected on a site venerated since prehistoric times and where a stone of this type was honored. Borobudur would then be a fabulous enlargement of this cult object. Without dismissing this origin (whose certainty might be established if excavation were made beneath the monument), I believe that this monument was designed as a roof (it has all the characteristics: recessed stories, terminal stupa surrounded by small stupas) covering a sanctuary formed by the mountain itself and symbolizing not only Buddhist cosmology but also the dynasty that erected it, the Sailendras—Kings of the Mountain (summit). The natural hill of Borobudur symbolizes the Earth itself. This might partly explain the covering over of the bas-reliefs of the lower terrace (Kamadhatu): men, their actions, and their passions belong to the earth from which they are made. The Buddhist knows this but refuses to consider actions and desires: from the summit of Beatitude nothing is now distinguishable. Actions, the result of human desires, now count no more than the Earth itself of which they are an integral part. The faithful one who ascends the terrace steps must forget the earth, its passions and unhappiness; he knows they exist but he knows also that he can surmount and destroy them to reach a higher stage. The first is that exemplified by the edifying life of Gautama Buddha, which is described on the bas-reliefs of the first gallery. As the worshiper gradually ascends, he frees himself and reaches the stories where nothing can distract him. Here he can meditate on the Formless Whole, facing the Ultimate Truth, which is represented by the great terminal stupa.

The hidden base: All around the stupa base is a massive platform of crude stone without decoration. A theory has been put forward that this terrace was built afterward as an abutment surrounding the monument, but Marchal proved that as each terrace was independent, there was no valid reason to enclose the monument.

Moreover, in 1885, IJzerman discovered on the hidden base 160 bas-reliefs illustrating the Laws of Cause and Effect (*Karma*), which determine men's good and evil actions and their retribution. Some are unfinished, others have short captions, still others are workmen's graffiti. If my opinion is correct, it is normal that this should be so: actions are not always completed and the most harmless are part of the Law of Karma. Writing, not found on any other gallery, is also part of human, earthly action.

The terraces: Four flights of steps, all alike, placed at the cardinal points, lead to the upper stories of Borobudur. The principal entrance, however, seems to be on the west, for the bas-reliefs begin at this flight of steps and continue in the direction of the circumambulation (pradakshina), keeping the stupa on the right. These terraces are adorned with parapets decorated with bas-reliefs and surmounted by small stupas and niches containing Dhyani Buddhas. The terrace walls are also decorated with bas-reliefs arranged in rectangular panels on two rows. Finally, the circular terraces, without decoration, support the small, open stupas of which we have just spoken. Their repetition may suggest eternity.

The Great Stupa: Of the classic Indian type, this stupa is surmounted by an octagonal pillar which terminates abruptly. Contrary to certain architects who have attempted to place parasols (chattras) on the summit of this point (an old photograph shows these parasols added unduly), they probably never existed there. The octagonal pillar most likely represents an infinite number of superimposed parasols, no longer distinguishable one from another. Moreover, this simplified form is found on all the stupas which adorn the roofs of Javanese temples. On examining this stupa in 1842, the diplomatic resident, Hartmann, discovered that it was hollow and contained an unfinished statue of a seated Buddha. Some have thought this statue to be an image of Adi Buddha, of the Supreme, Eternal Truth, never attained, never ended, never perceived, silent. West of the monument the foundations of brick monastery buildings (vihara) with stone octagonal bases have been found. The building itself was probably made of wood, as many bronze nails have been discovered together with a bell and terra-cotta oil lamps. Somewhat west of the monastery were the kitchens and a prayer room, the site of present clumps of Bombax trees. The foundations are now almost invisible.

163. JAVA, MAGELANG, BOROBUDUR, VIEW OF THE MONUMENT FROM THE NORTHWEST. Here we see the clump of Bombax trees where certain monastery buildings once existed. The monument itself, which stands on the hilltop, is 105 feet high.

164. JAVA, MAGELANG, BOROBUDUR, EAST FLIGHT OF STEPS. A similar flight of steps in the center of each side connects the terraces. At the beginning of each flight of steps, a corbeled arch decorated with a kala-makara motif forms an entrance porch. Most of the ornamentation on these arches has disappeared, leaving holes indicating where the sculptured blocks were attached, as can be seen here at the entrance to the flight of steps of the first gallery. The arch of the third gallery (uppermost in the photograph) is the only one intact. These monsters "devouring" the pilgrims perhaps symbolize the death and resurrection of the visitor ascending the steps toward Understanding, which would confirm the monument's initiatory value.

165: A, B, C, D. JAVA, MAGELANG, BOROBUDUR, BAS-RELIEFS REPRESENTING SHIPS. These four bas-reliefs describe with much accuracy the types of ships used by the Javanese (and perhaps also by other inhabitants of Southeast Asia) about 800. The largest three have outriggers. Each vessel has two masts, a mizzen gaff, and square sails on movable yards. When there was no wind, rowers used the poles (lats). These passed through holes in the bridge which could be sealed. In fact, two of these ships, sailing on the open sea, show no oars. The fourth, reaching port, is reefing its sails and letting out oars (we can see the rowers' heads). The first ship, much smaller, does not seem to have outrigging. It has a single mast whose sail seems about to be swept away in the violent storm. A huge fish threatens the skiff. These maritime scenes have been sculpted by an artist well acquainted with the sea. The ships were often 65 feet long. Maneuvering was facilitated by ten rowers on each bank.

166. JAVA, MAGELANG, BOROBUDUR, STUPAS ON THE CIRCULAR TERRACES. Designed as three concentric circles consisting of 32, 24, and 16 units around the central stupa, these small stupas, contrary to custom, are hollow and each contains a statue of Buddha seated in the dharmachakra-mudra position. Openings purposely left in the anda of these small stupas allow us to glimpse these effigies. Thus the pilgrim could catch a glimpse of the Ultimate Reality entirely hidden in the central stupa. The mountain seen in the background is Mount Menore. According to legend, the architect who conceived Borobudur retired there to contemplate his work.

167. JAVA, MAGELANG, BOROBUDUR, GALLERY BAS-RELIEFS. The bas-reliefs of the Borobudur galleries are arranged in panels 2 feet 4 inches to almost 3 feet high and in lengths varying from 3 to 9 feet. They are separated by vertical decoration formed of ornamental foliage. Here in a palace (notice the ornaments of the roof edges of this light pavilion), two women are dancing before an audience of nobles. An old man (the dancing master?) seems to be offering advice. The attitudes of these dancers are the same admired to this day in classic Javanese dancers.

168. JAVA, MAGELANG, BOROBUDUR, GALLERY BAS-RELIEF. This represents a king and queen holding court. The king is seated in tailor position, his knee held by a strap, on a throne with a back. He is addressing his courtiers who are seated on the ground, their hands joined. A standing young woman is holding the ritual fly swatter. Beneath the throne (actually beside it but represented in smaller size because they are less important personages) are people presenting gifts. The back of the throne is adorned with makaras, and above it is a canopy. To the left, attendants and nobles have arrived by horse or elephant. The faces are calm and inexpressive, as it was unfitting for important personages to reveal their emotions. The attitudes are graceful, the details superbly rendered.

169. JAVA, MAGELANG, BOROBUDUR, GALLERY BAS-RELIEF. Part of the railing of a gallery, this bas-relief is treated as a frieze. The arrangement of the figures, juxtaposing the heads, is very clever. In fact, the attitude expresses their character better than the expression of the faces. Height of the bas-relief: about 20 inches.

170. JAVA, MAGELANG, BOROBUDUR, GALLERY BAS-RELIEF. A noble, his wife, and child distributing food to the poor. The women are kneeling, and the mustachioed men are standing. On the left, a village house is represented in great detail, and for this reason the bas-relief is of great documentary interest. Between the stone pillars supporting the wooden house, the style of which has scarcely changed to this day, a woman is seated grinding grain, while a young man appears to be courting her. On the roof, two pigeons are billing. This delightful scene has both poetry and accuracy.

171. JAVA, MAGELANG, BOROBUDUR, GALLERY BAS-RELIEF. This figure represents a hermit or a rishi (the knot of hair seems to indicate this) teaching, seated at the threshold of his cave, whose entrance is symbolized by the sculptured pillar on the right. He wears neither earrings nor jewelry, only a string of beans or seeds around his neck and simple bracelets. The band across his chest suggests this may be a brahman. Height of this detail: 16 inches.

161

172: A, B, C, D. JAVA, MAGELANG, BOROBUDUR, FOUR DHYANI BUDDHAS.

A. *Amitabha.* Ninety-two of these sculptures are in niches in the west part of Borobudur.

B. *Ratnasambhva.* Ninety-two in the niches of the south part.

C. *Akshobhya.* Situated in the 92 niches of the east part.

D. *Amoghasiddha.* Ninety-two of these images adorn the north part.

In addition, the walls of the fourth gallery are adorned with 64 Vairotchana Buddhas representing the Dhyani Buddha who governs the zenith. Half-hidden in the 72 open stupas of the three round terraces, the Buddhas belong to the Vajrasattva type, the form of the Supreme Buddha. With the Adi Buddha of the central terminal stupa, these effigies of Buddha total 505. All the sculptures are of volcanic stone. The four shown here are 5 feet high. *Djakarta Museum.*

173. CENTRAL JAVA, HEAD OF A DEVATA. This wonderful piece of sculpture shows the refinement achieved by sculptors between the ninth and tenth centuries. With its delicate smile, it is difficult to compare this head to any other. The famous "smile of Rheims," although that of an angel, remains very human. Calm and serene, this smile belongs more to a divine creature. Volcanic stone. Height: 10 inches. *Jogjakarta Museum.*

174. CENTRAL JAVA, STANDING WOMAN. Although less beautiful than the preceding one, this figure is equally attractive for its full forms and stability, which bring to mind the work of Maillol. This is really a human image of flesh and blood, which, in spite of its halo, belongs to earthly reality. Volcanic stone. Height: 2 feet 8 inches. *Djakarta Museum.*

175. JAVA, MALANG, TJANDI SANGGARITI. Situated in east Java, near Batu, this temple dedicated to Shiva adjoins hot sulfur springs with baths. The style relates it to the close of the eighth century or beginning of the ninth and to the art of central Java. It is greatly damaged. All that remains of its foundations are a few sculptures and a stone lingam. The sculpture in front of the lingam is difficult to identify. It may be an image of Vishnapaharana, one of Shiva's forms, who guards the poison that was produced by the serpent Vasuki during the Churning of the Sea of Milk. The vase at its feet leads us to think so. Absence of other detail prevents certainty. The treatment and proportions are clumsy. Height: 3 feet 4 inches.

176. JAVA, MALANG, TJANDI BADUT. This small temple has all the characteristics of the Central Javanese style: base, flight of steps, and, especially, makaras decorating the door and niches. Square in plan with a projecting porch open to the west (perhaps indicating a funerary foundation), dedicated to Shiva (proved by the lingam in the interior), it is similar to certain temples of Dieng (Arjuna) and the Tjandi Mendut. Although some authors (*e.g.,* E. B. Vogler) believe that it is later in date than the Lara Djonggrang (915), I am inclined to think that, considering its decoration, it would date, on the contrary, from the early ninth century. The north wall is adorned with a bas-relief representing Durga, while a representation of Agastya decorates the south wall. On the east, a Ganesha has disappeared.

177. JAVA, PRAMBANAN, TJANDI KALASAN. Greatly ruined, this sumptuous temple is merely the third state of the one probably founded in 778—if this temple can be linked to an inscription found not far away. Its present state therefore can be dated from about a century later, that is, from the close of the ninth century. It may have been founded by two allied princes—one from the Sailendra Dynasty, the other from the Mataram. Open to the west, it is dedicated to the Buddhist divinity, Tara. Square in plan, it is adorned with projecting porches which give it the form of a Greek cross. Its very high walls were surmounted by a series of reduced octagonal stories, crowned by a large stupa, and surrounded by miniature ones. Niches arranged between these small structures probably contained effigies of Dhyani Buddhas. The structure of the roof was rather complex, adorned with bas-reliefs in different places. The walls are decorated with twin kala-makaras (turned toward the exterior and the interior), the only such example in Indonesian art. The ornaments executed in stone are plastered with stucco. The central cella probably contained a large bronze statue which has disappeared. The temple is often known as Kali Bening.

178. JAVA, PRAMBANAN, TJANDI KALASAN, SOUTH ENTRANCE. This side, the best preserved of Kalasan, presents new aspects of decorative Indonesian art of the ninth century. The enormous head of kala directly above the door is very flamboyant, spreading out on all sides into floral decoration from which lions and celestial musicians (*gandharvas*) seem to be emerging. Above the door, surmounted by a niche containing a seated Buddha, a floral ornament replaces a kala. The makaras of the bases, whose jaws are stuffed with people, no longer delimit the door but merely frame it. False octagonal columns with gana (dwarfs) caryatids support the false arch formed by the floral decoration. On each side is a sculptured divinity, the guardians of the sanctuary. A rather steep flight of steps, since destroyed, led down to the threshold makaras similar in type to those framing the door. The massive courtyard is lightened by vertical ornamental foliage between the pilasters. A frieze of small personages runs along the upper cornice. The dimensions of this temple can be judged by the size of the children playing below the doorway.

179. JAVA, PRAMBANAN, TJANDI SARI. A very special temple, the Tjandi Sari consists of three sanctuaries connected by a corridor, having a single entrance and built upon the same platform (see plan). Obviously dating from the same time as the Tjandi Kalasan—although conceived very differently—it consists of two stories separated by a wooden floor. The three roofs corresponding to the three sections of the building are adorned with niches having kala-makaras and are each surmounted by three stupas. The spaces between the niches, the false windows, and the windows are sculpted with Buddhist divinities. A large horizontal molding adorned with antefixes marks the separation of the stories. In the interior are statues of Buddha and bodhisattvas placed on stone pedestals occupying the far end of each sanctuary. The entrance porch and most of the foundation have disappeared.

180. JAVA, PRAMBANAN, TJANDI SARI, TWO TARAS. The walls of this tjandi are adorned with 36 sculptures of divinities, both feminine (taras and kinnaris) and masculine (nagas, celestial musicians), treated with undeniable grace and skill. The legs have been lengthened in respect to preceding representations and the attitude takes into consideration the Indian tribhanga (S-curve). On the far left is a kinnari. The pilasters of the niches, with their bases and capitals in the form of a vase, are divided in the center by a molded band, like the building itself. Height of each figure: about 6 feet, 8 inches.

181. JAVA, PRAMBANAN, TJANDI LUMBUNG. Square in plan and open to the west, the Tjandi Lumbung is surrounded by 16 small temples arranged in a square. This largely ruined temple has several beautiful sculptures. They are no longer sculptured in the very blocks which form the architecture, as at Dieng, but in a separate monolithic block. The one shown here, carefully executed, lithe in movement, represents a bodhisattva, Padmapani, holding in his left hand a royal fly swatter. He is dressed in a princely manner and strangely enough wears two different earrings—one masculine, the other feminine. This personage might symbolize, like the Shiva Ardhanari, the identity of both a bodhisattva and a tara. The treatment of the folds of the girdle recalls the style of certain Nalanda sculptures. Late ninth century (?). Height: 4 feet.

182. JAVA, PRAMBANAN, TJANDI SEWU, SMALL TEMPLE OF THE ENCEINTE. Almost completely ruined, the

Tjandi Sewu presents a plan similar to that of Tjandi Kalasan but with cells projecting on each side. Only the east cell led to the central raised sanctuary, thus forming an antechamber. Each cell was surmounted by a roof, connected only to the central one, above the galleries. This temple, dedicated to Buddha, to the Dhyani Buddhas, and to their shaktis, and probably symbolizing the Mahayana pantheon, was surrounded by four rows of small temples (240 in all) of two different types: those of the first and fourth rows were fronted by porch roofs (plate 188), those of the second and third (whose reconstruction on the site is shown here) by pediment porches topped by the kala-makara motif and a lintel. They are formed of a simple cella on a low platform. The very high roof of each temple, terminating in a large stupa surrounded by 12 small ones, rested on a false story flanked by a stupa at each of the four corners. The inner walls are often adorned with niches having a kala-makara decoration and supported by a triple

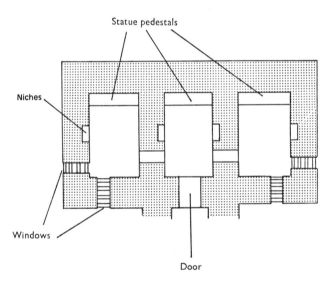

FIG. 21. PLAN OF THE TJANDI SARI, PRAMBANAN

lotus. Thirteen standing figures in bas-relief decorate the outer walls of these small temples which, like the principal temple, probably date from the first half of the ninth century.

183. JAVA, PRAMBANAN, TJANDI SEWU, MAKARA ON THE MAIN TEMPLE. The form of the head offered the artist an occasion to display great virtuosity; he transformed even the eyes and teeth into vegetal motifs. This monster has a parrot in its maw, and strings of beading hang from its horn. It is on the side of the sanctuary entrance.

184. JAVA, PRAMBANAN, TJANDI SEWU, WALL DECORATION. The decoration of this temple is both original and rich. Many niches are adorned with a pointed arch, which suggests a Moslem influence.

163

However, this is not the case and the motif is completely underivative. Here, the arcade contains a bas-relief representing the bodhisattva Padmapani flanked by a flower vase and an incense burner. Above, two grotesque beings seem to engage in combat. This decoration is found above a deep niche in the outer wall of the main temple.

185. JAVA, PRAMBANAN, TJANDI PLAOSAN, SANCTUARY WALL. The cornice which separates the two stories is adorned with antefixes (or accent pieces) decorated with heads set in arcades of a floral design which seems to be derived from a kudu. The ornaments above the windows consist of a head of a monster which is not that of a kala; in fact, we can see its lower jaw (stylized lion?). Those which surmount the statues in bas-relief consist of converging makaras on each side of a triangular motif adorned with pendants. All these sculptures are very carefully executed.

186. JAVA, PRAMBANAN, TJANDI PLAOSAN, SOUTH SANCTUARY. The principal complex consists of two similar buildings analogous in plan to that of the Tjandi Sari, separated by a wall, and surrounded by 58 stupas arranged in three rows. The latter have almost all disappeared. To the south, another complex known as Tjandi Plaosan Kidul consists of 69 stupas and 18 small temples which surround a small square temple (plate 188). The temple shown here was recently restored; it has the same characteristics as the Tjandi Sari but is open to the west. According to Bernet-Kempers, it is the work of a Sailendra princess who married a king of the Mataram Dynasty. Mid-ninth century.

187. JAVA, PRAMBANAN, TJANDI PLAOSAN, SANCTUARY BAS-RELIEF. This relief bears the image of a bodhisattva.

188. JAVA, PRAMBANAN, SMALL TEMPLE OF THE PLAOSAN KIDUL GROUP. This structure consists of a simple square cella with a projecting porch on the west, lit by means of two windows, and covered by a roof in the form of a curved porch. The entrance is decorated with a kala-makara motif. The roof is reminiscent of that of the Tjandi Pawon, but without accessory stories. Here, the latter have been replaced by a square central structure raised and surrounded by eight others. On the foundation is an inscription, "Tarumah Sri Maharajah," which would indicate that this small temple was the tomb of King Rake Pikatan, the predecessor of King Rake Kayuwangi, of the Mataram Dynasty. The temple would therefore date from the mid-ninth century.

189. JAVA, PRAMBANAN, TJANDI LARA DJONGGRANG, MODEL OF THE COMPLEX. This elaborate temple,

whose model (courtesy of the Prambanan Archaeological Service) is shown here, was probably founded by one of the first Shivaist kings of the Mataram Dynasty about the mid-ninth century (856?) and finished by his successors. It was abandoned incomplete in 928 when, for some unknown reason, King Sindok transferred the seat of the kingdom to east Java. According to Sutterheim it was perhaps King Daksha, and, according to others, King Balitung, who built this ensemble. Some archaeologists believe this to be the funerary monument of King Rake Kayuwangi. Reconstruction of the Temple of Shiva took 80 years of archaeological work. This temple consists of three principal sanctuaries dedicated to Vishnu (Temple A), Shiva (Temple B), and Brahma (Temple C), all of whose entrances face east. Opposite the Temple of Shiva (B) is a small sanctuary (E) dedicated to Nandi, Shiva's mount; to Surya, the sun god; and to Chandra, the moon god. Opposite the other temples two other sanctuaries (D and F) were probably dedicated to minor forms of Shiva, perhaps Ganesha (D) and Agastya (F). To the north and south were two other small temples, but their divinities have disappeared and we do not know to whom they were dedicated. These temples were surrounded by a square wall measuring about 360 feet per side (I) and having four entrances placed at the cardinal points. Another enceinte, 720 feet square with a projection on each side (J) enclosed, on four successive tiers, 284 small temples all alike (H), measuring 45 feet high, almost all of which have collapsed (the model shows only two tiers complete; the lower two merely show their bases). Finally, a third enceinte measuring 1279 feet per side, oriented north-northeast, probably consisted of adjacent light buildings used by brahmans and temple assistants (K). All the temples, however different in size, were built on the same model. This consisted of a high base which terminates in a gallery, determining a platform with a two-story temple separated by a horizontal entablature, the whole topped by a roof formed of successive recessed stories and decorated with stupas except on the outer temples. The pyramid was terminated by a larger stupa. Only the three large temples of Shiva, Vishnu, and Brahma are square in plan with projections on the sides. A flight of steps leads to the porch of a small temple and to the gallery. The others are square in plan and a flight of steps leads directly to the sanctuary.

190. JAVA, PRAMBANAN, LARA DJONGGRANG, TEMPLE OF SHIVA. This is the highest of the group, measuring 154 feet high, and is placed on a base 98 feet square. It consists of a central sanctuary enclosed by three very small cellas, that on the east only forming a vestibule. The statue of Shiva, which was supposed to receive the soul of the deceased king, stood in the center of the sanctuary. The king's ashes were placed on its base. The vestibule contains images of Mahakala and Nandishvara. The other cellas have representations of Shiva as Agastya (south), Ganesha (west), and Durga, Vishnu's sister and Shiva's shakti (north). The group of temples was named after this statue of Durga (Lara Djonggrang means "frail virgin"). The outer walls of the base are decorated with panels representing celestial trees with kinnaris or gazelles, alternating with niches containing seated lions. Above, on the outer side of the gallery parapet, which is surmounted by fluted stupas, niches containing divine spirits are interspersed with sculptured designs representing the 32 dances of Shiva Tandava. But the most interesting decoration of this temple is the bas-relief of the inner parapet representing the legend of *The Ramayana*. The base of the walls of the temple itself is decorated with 84 figures of the gods of the cardinal points (*lokapalas*), while the empty niches on the stories contained bronze or metal images which have since disappeared.

191. JAVA, PRAMBANAN, LARA DJONGGRANG, ENTRANCE TO THE TEMPLE OF SHIVA. Above the door, the entrance is decorated by a bas-relief surmounted by an enormous head of kala. On the right, we can see the roof of the vestibule-cella. In the foreground are the fluted stupas of the parapet and niches, each containing three sculptured divinities.

192. JAVA, PRAMBANAN, LARA DJONGGRANG, EAST STAIRCASE OF THE TEMPLE OF SHIVA. This flight of steps, massive and rather steep, is decorated with a railing terminating in a makara. The sides are delicately adorned with ornamental foliage and vegetal motifs in low relief. In the left foreground one of the niches, whose attractive kala-makara motif is framed by birds, is supported by pilasters of a special type.

193. JAVA, PRAMBANAN, LARA DJONGGRANG, TEMPLE OF SHIVA, BAS-RELIEF ON THE GALLERY. This represents a scene from *The Ramayana* showing a dancing girl armed with sword and shield. On the right, spectators are beating rhythm; the one above holds *talams*, or bronze cymbals. On the left is a group of brahmans, one of whom is holding a ritual shell in his left hand. This well-arranged, dynamic scene has been executed in an attractive manner. The realistic draperies, trees, and attitudes all reflect the sculptor's talent.

194. JAVA, PRAMBANAN, LARA DJONGGRANG, TEMPLE OF SHIVA, BAS-RELIEF ON THE GALLERY. This wonderful genre scene shows an episode in everyday life. In front of a wooden house (on the roof of which a rat seems to have frightened two roosters) is a woman who is angered by a dog that has kicked over a pot of food. Beyond her is a banana tree and in front of it a pot of flowers. On the left, in front of a tree whose leaves shelter frisking birds, a man is offering a banana to a monkey. On the tree trunk is a squirrel, and on a platform supporting the house is a portable water jar with a ladle attached made from a coconut shell. The clear detail of the clothing, tools, and house provide valuable information about Javanese life in the tenth century.

195. JAVA, PRAMBANAN, LARA DJONGGRANG, SMALL SOUTH TEMPLE. The entrance faces north. Opposite, on the other side of the platform, near the Temple of Vishnu, is a similar temple whose entrance faces south. The purpose of these temples is a mystery. Height: 55½ feet.

196. JAVA, PRAMBANAN, LARA DJONGGRANG, TEMPLE OF BRAHMA, SCENE FROM "THE RAMAYANA." The story of Rama and his wife, Sita, begins on the bas-reliefs of the gallery of the Temple of Shiva and continues along the parapet of that of the Temple of Brahma. Here we can see Kumbhakarna, the brother of the demon Ravana, ruler of Lanka (Ceylon), awakening from sleep to find himself attacked by Rama's archers and the monkeys of Hanuman's army. On the left, a brahman with the trident of Shiva urges them into battle.

197. JAVA, PRAMBANAN, LARA DJONGGRANG, TEMPLE OF VISHNU, SCENE FROM "THE KRISHNAYANA." The bas-reliefs of the gallery of the Temple of Vishnu relate the story of Krishna and of his brother, Balarama, both incarnations of Vishnu. Here, in a garden at the far end of which we can see a house, two people are in deep conversation, while a third seems to be making fun of them. The intense life that stems from the attitudes is amazingly realistic.

198. JAVA, TEGAL (NORTH COAST), STATUETTE OF SHIVA-MAHADEVA. This statuette, one of the finest in the Djakarta Museum, represents Shiva as Lord of the World. He has a third eye in his forehead, the moon and a death's-head in his headdress. Around his shoulder is a serpent. A wonderful work in its execution, this bronze, plated in places with silver (eyes, lips), came from Lowatan Adiwarna. Height: 2 feet 11½ inches. *Djakarta Museum.*

199. BORNEO, EAST COAST, HEAD OF KALA. This head of yellow sandstone, 16 inches high, was part of a building which is no longer in existence. The treatment is rather different from Javanese work of the same period. *Djakarta Museum.*

146

147

148

153

154

162

163

182

183

184

185

186

187

188

189

190

191

196

197

200. JAVA, MOUNT PENANGGUNGAN, FIGURE ADORN-ING A FOUNTAIN. Coming from Belahan or the Djalatunda Spring, this sculptured figure repre-sents a woman holding a serpent(?) which acted as the water spout of a fountain. The expression of the face is moving, the headdress wonderfully treated. This may be the image of a princess condemned to pour water as the result of a curse. Volcanic stone. Total height: 23 ¼ inches. *Djakarta Museum.*

201. JAVA, TULUNG-AGUNG, SELAMANGLENG CAVE, BAS-RELIEFS. The entrance to this small cave (19 by 13 feet by 6 feet high) hewn in the rock on the flank of the Wadjak Mountains is decorated with an enormous head of kala, now greatly damaged by the elements. It contains interesting bas-reliefs on two of its three sides which seem to date from the close of the tenth century. They were probably executed for the use of a celebrated hermit. The bas-relief shown here, on the left wall of the en-trance, represents Indra in his paradise, giving orders to his nymphs so that they will descend to earth and ask Arjuna to end his voluntary penitence on Mount Indrakila. Although Hindu, the story of Arjuna is here used for Buddhist purposes. Behind the trees, we see a Javanese-style house of the period. The bearded figure behind the nymphs could be Narada, the messenger of the gods. At the far left are musicians.

202. JAVA, DJALATUNDA, FOUNTAIN BAS-RELIEF. On Mount Penanggungan, in east Java, a lofty place sacred since prehistoric times and covered with sanctuaries, there are two baths, Djalatunda and Belahan. These baths, fed by springs, were said to contain water mixed with the Dew of Immortality, the summit of Mount Penanggungan being identi-fied with that of Mount Meru, transported here in a magical manner. This fountain was adorned with bas-reliefs relating episodes in the story of the five Pandavas brothers. Here Princess Mrigavati, married to a descendant of Arjuna named Sahasra-nika, was carried away by a *garuda* and taken into a forest where she gave birth to Udayana, the last of the Pandavas family and the namesake of this fountain.

Water flowed from a simple hole cut into the bas-reliefs. The one shown here is especially inter-esting for the different forms of light architecture it depicts. This fountain has an inscription dated 899 in the Saka era, that is, A.D. 977, and was probably dedicated by King Udayana, the father of the hero-king Airlangga. Sandstone. Height of the bas-relief: 20 inches. *Djakarta Museum.*

203. JAVA, MALANG, TJANDI KIDAL. A small, square temple typical of the east Javanese style. Built on a high base, it is a square sanctuary with a narrow door flanked by niches and surmounted by a huge head of kala. The latter supports a projecting entablature on which rises a massive pyramidal roof formed of successive stories separated by pilasters. Oriented to the west, it was erected as the funerary monument of King Anushapati of the Singhasari Dynasty, who died in 1248. Consecrated according to custom 12 years after the king's death but begun before the consecration date, this monu-ment therefore must date from about 1255. Note that the doors, still adorned with a kala—here with the jaw complete—are now treated as a mere slit and that the kala-makara combination, dear to west Java, no longer exists, the makaras having disap-peared. We will find them again, however, as ornamental motifs on flights of steps. Actual height: 39 feet.

204. JAVA, MALANG, TJANDI KIDAL, BAS-RELIEF DECORATION. On one of the sides of the temple, this bas-relief shows Garuda, the mythical bird, car-rying his mother Vinata, who has become the slave of a family of serpents. In order to ransom his mother, Garuda stole the Amrita, the Dew of Immortality, from the gods. Height: 2 feet 6 inches.

205. JAVA, MALANG, TJANDI DJAGO, WEST VIEW. Sometimes known as Tumpang (formerly Jajaghu), this temple oriented to the west is the funerary monument of King Singhasari Vishnuvardhana, who died in 1268. The monument dates therefore from the 12-year period that followed. The arrange-ment is unusual. The temple itself stands on three terraces reached by lateral flights of steps. The walls and roof have for the most part disappeared. It lies toward the east, with the terraces, being larger, toward the west. Of the roof we know nothing. This temple is decorated with many bas-reliefs and contains many statues.

206. JAVA, MALANG TJANDI DJAGO, BAS-RELIEF. This bas-relief of the lower terrace represents a scene from the story of Kundjarakarna. Height: about 10 inches.

207. JAVA, MALANG, TJANDI DJAGO, BAS-RELIEF. This bas-relief is part of the story of Arjuna. But for us it is of the greatest interest, for it represents merus—light structures with several superimposed roofs numbering as many as 12—whose type, having disappeared from Java, remains one of the charac-teristics of Balinese architecture. Is the creation of such a style due to Chinese influence? This is quite probable, for we know that China had close relations with eastern Javanese kingdoms. This opinion seems confirmed by the high roof corners, which are due to the roof line, and not to the presence of antefixes.

208. JAVA, MALANG, TJANDI KIDAL, DECORATION ON A FLIGHT OF STEPS. This bas-relief is treated as incision, like many ornaments of this temple, and introduces a new style. Here the vegetal element is preponderant.

209. JAVA, MALANG, TJANDI SINGHASARI. Erected to the memory of King Kirtanagara, who died in 1292, this mausoleum-temple appears to be unfinished. In fact, its decoration is more elaborate in the upper parts than in the lower ones. On a large, low, square platform rises what in another temple would be the base but which here contains the sanctuary, adorned with projections on four sides. Above is the main section of the temple, which consists entirely of niches. The pyramidal roof has collapsed. The architect arranged empty spaces in both the temple and its roof in order to lighten the carrying load of the cella's vault. In the center of the cella is a *yoni* which received the lustral waters flowing from outside by means of an opening (compare the Arjuna Temple at Dieng). Each base projection contained a cella and was surmounted by a pyramidal roof, which caused the entire temple to resemble Mount Meru with its five summits.

210. JAVA, MALANG, TJANDI SINGHASARI, GUARDIAN-DEMON. Two enormous statues of guardian-demons (*rakshasas*) adorn the sanctuary entrance. Their function was to frighten off evil spirits. Almost all Javanese temples had such guardians. These are 12 feet high. One of them, seen here, is still half buried.

211. JAVA, BLITAR, PANATARAN TEMPLES. About 7 miles north of Blitar, not far from a celebrated sacred spring, lies the greatest complex of east Javanese temples. It consists of three walled courts. The first contains two terraces, one having a sculptured base (on which there were probably wooden pavilions) and a small temple dated 1369. The second court also has several terraces and temples, one of which is known as "Naga" because of its decoration. A gateway leads to the last court with the main temple, surrounded by small temples and terraces. Somewhat beyond the enceinte, to the south, are baths whose sculptures are dated 1415 (see plan). Many square terraces probably supported merus (see plate 207 and the section on Bali). It seems that this arrangement of courtyards, temples, and terraces later found its way to the island of Bali, where the same type of design can be seen to this day. This complex devoted to Shiva was erected between the close of the twelfth century and the middle of the fifteenth, in the Singhasari and

Madjapahit dynasties. Only monuments from the latter period exist. This photograph was taken from the terrace of the main temple, facing northwest. On the left, we can see the 1369 temple and, on the right, the Naga Temple. Behind them are the terraces. In the foreground is a corner of the main temple's terrace.

212. JAVA, BLITAR, PANATARAN, 1369 TEMPLE. Completely rebuilt, this small temple, measuring 23 feet high, consists of a simple cella open north-northwest and having no base. Three false doors probably contained bronze sculptures, which have now disappeared. Of equal value as the lower section, the pyramidal roof terminates in a kind of ornamental cube. The date, 1291 of the Saka era (A.D. 1369), is inscribed above the cella door (on

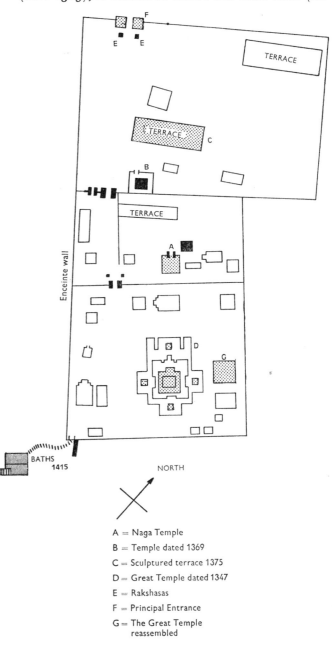

A = Naga Temple

B = Temple dated 1369

C = Sculptured terrace 1375

D = Great Temple dated 1347

E = Rakshasas

F = Principal Entrance

G = The Great Temple reassembled

FIG. 22. TEMPLES AT PANTARAN

the right of the photograph). The heads of kala, clearly separated from the door, which is simple and slender, are typical of the style.

213. JAVA, BLITAR, PANATARAN, CARYATID ON THE NAGA TEMPLE. This structure may have contained a treasure room destined to guard the god's wealth and the cult objects. On the exterior, caryatids support a serpent whose coils hang between each figure. The bodies' positions seem to have been inspired by a very ancient motif often found on the railings (vedikas) of Amaravati. At the base of each caryatid is a small scene generally containing animals (here an ox and a lion) set amid vegetal ornaments. The walls between the caryatids are decorated with sculptured *mascarons* similar to those found on the foundation walls of the main temple. This now roofless building probably never had a stone roof but only one of wood, which seems surprising if it was actually intended as a treasure house. The main section of the sanctuary of the great temple, similar in construction and adorned with very hieratic caryatids, stands on a higher level to the north of the main temple.

214. JAVA, BLITAR, PANATARAN, MAIN TEMPLE (VIEW FROM THE NORTH), THREE TERRACES. On the first terrace, reached by two lateral flights of steps, are four small chapels. The walls are decorated with scenes from *The Ramayana*. Space between the pilasters was filled by mascarons. The walls of the second terrace describe Krishna's adventures. That of the third is adorned with lions and winged serpents. The main section of the temple (which is now roofless) is decorated with female figures and serpents. It seems to have been finished between 1323 and 1347. This temple probably had meru-like roofs.

215. JAVA, BLITAR, PANATARAN, BAS-RELIEF FROM THE GREAT TEMPLE. This section of the decoration bears figures whose costume and ethnic type strangely recall those of the Aztecs. The treatment is rather crude, since the coarseness of the stone scarcely allowed for fine detail. This relief is in the Wayang style, in which the sculptured figures are reminiscent of Javanese shadow-play puppets rather than sculpture

216. JAVA, KEDIRI, MAHAMERU. This sculpture represents Mount Meru, which helped to produce the Dew of Immortality (Amrita). The base of the sculpture is a tortoise (an avatar of Vishnu), supporting devas and lokapalas (gods of the cardinal points). Wound around the base mountain (the pivot) is a serpent (the Naga king), who was instrumental in the Churning of the Sea of Milk. The sculpture probably dates from about 1360, and may have been used for the center of a fountain.

Sandstone. Height: 3 feet 4 inches. *Djakarta Museum.*

217. JAVA, PARONG, TJANDI PARI. This structure, in the Madjapahit style, dated 1236 Saka (A.D. 1341), is square in plan and is built of brick with a single cella. It includes a pyramidal vault, corbeled with layers of brick, and shows definite Cham influence. Constructed of large-size bricks, provided with a triangular pediment at the entrance and false windows on the other three sides, and standing on a high foundation, this 65-foot-high temple seems to have been designed for a funerary purpose. (This is indicated by its entrance, which faces west.) It is one of the first monuments of the Madjapahit Dynasty, whose capital was the present village of Trawulan, near the city of Madjakerta.

218. JAVA, PARE, TJANDI TIGAWANGI, BAS-RELIEF. Built about 1365 by the Prince of Matahun, the temple was never finished. All that remains is its high base, richly decorated with friezes representing the story of Sudamala. The sculpture is of rather good quality. Here we see Shiva's sister Uma (who has been transformed into a demon by her brother) and a nymph, surrounded by a delightful decoration containing many details drawn from everyday life. On the right, we see a woman following a man. Note the clouds stylized in the Chinese manner.

219. JAVA, TRAWULAN, BADJANG RATU. This small temple acted as a gate in the enceinte surrounding the city of Madjapahit. Forty-eight feet high, built entirely of brick, it is complete with roof. This photograph illustrates the type of monument which in the fourteenth century began to taper toward the top in imitation of wooden merus.

220. JAVA, TRAWULAN, TJANDI TIKUS. Situated somewhat beyond the walls of Madjapahit, toward the southeast, these baths were reached by means of a flight of steps on their northern side. Like many monuments of the Madjapahit Dynasty, they were built of large-size bricks. A small temple symbolizing Mount Meru stood on the extreme south, where spring water flowed, and a small statue of Shiva has been found on the site. At the entrance to these baths stood a split gate, which has now disappeared. Mid-fourteenth century.

221. JAVA, TRAWULAN, TJANDI BRAHU. This temple, whose entrance has entirely collapsed, was built of brick and has a square cella on a very high base. The walls and roof are decorated with many projections (here the upper part is missing). The base was largely destroyed.

222. JAVA, TRAWULAN, WRINING-LAWANG. This brick split gate, northeast of Madjapahit, led to a

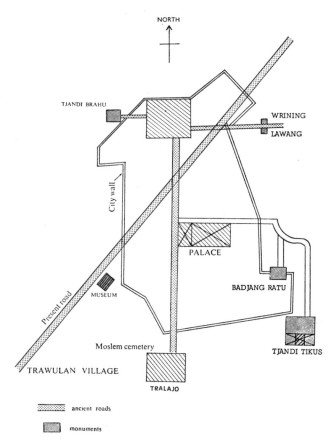

TJANDI BRAHU

WRINING
LAWANG

City wall

PALACE

Present road

MUSEUM

BADJANG RATU

Moslem cemetery

TRAWULAN VILLAGE

TJANDI TIKUS

TRALAJO

ancient roads

monuments

FIG. 23. RECONSTRUCTED PLAN OF THE ANCIENT
CAPITAL OF MADJAPAHIT AT TRAWULAN

route toward a harbor not far away. Almost totally lacking in decoration, it appears to be a tjandi broken in two, as though both halves were separated to allow passage. In Bali this type became one of the architectural characteristics of temple gates.

223. JAVA, KEDIRI, JAVANESE KING. Yellow limestone statuette dating from the close of the fourteenth century and the beginning of the fifteenth. It may have decorated a funerary monument. Height: 3 feet. *Djakarta Museum.*

224. JAVA, SURABAYA, A DIVINITY. This fine statue, sculpted from rather coarse tufa, belongs to the late Madjapahit Dynasty. It is difficult, however, to assign it an exact date. Early fifteenth century? Height: 22 inches. *Djakarta Museum.*

225. JAVA, KEDIRI, TJANDI SURAWANA. Used for a funerary purpose, this ruined temple has lost all but its very high base (more than 14½ feet) and is wonderfully decorated with scenes from Indian legends. A steep flight of steps led to the sanctuary,

which was probably square in plan. On the foundation plinth, small panels with erotic scenes (which are rare in Indonesian art) separate the axes of the corners decorated with ganas. This may have been the temple erected for a member of the royal Rajasanagara family who had died in 1388. It is similar in type to the Tjandi Tigawangi (plate 218).

226. JAVA, KEDIRI, TJANDI SURAWANA, BAS-RELIEF. Scene from the *Arjuna Vivaha*. Arjuna and a nymph leave the nymphs of Indra's paradise. The figures here are treated like Javanese Wayang shadow-play puppets: very long arms, stereotyped heads, posed in the stiff and broken attitudes of articulated dolls. Amid a rich vegetal decoration, we can also see tjandis and a meru (on the right). Each scene is separated from the other by vertical ornamental foliage.

227. JAVA, KEDIRI, TJANDI SURAWANA, BAS-RELIEF FRAGMENT. Detail from the base of the temple.

228. JAVA, BLITAR, PANATARAN, CORNER OF THE BATHS. These baths are very small, and lie somewhat south of the temples. The inner walls are sculpted with bas-reliefs, dated 1337 Saka (A.D. 1415), which show birds billing and animals nuzzling one another in the midst of curious symbols and figures. The water is luminously transparent.

229. JAVA, TULUNG AGUNG, PORTRAIT OF A QUEEN. This wonderfully decorated statue, one of the most beautiful of east Javanese art, probably represents Queen Suhita of the Madjapahit Dynasty. The date is uncertain. Sculpted of very hard stone able to take a fine polish, the statue stands on a double lotus base. The back of the statue has a lotus whose motif and treatment seem to have been inspired by those adorning the base of a flower altarpiece in Ceylon. It dates perhaps from about 1450. Height: 5 feet 3¾ inches. *Djakarta Museum.*

230. JAVA, PENANGGUNGAN, STATUE. Probably representing a child (Raden Damarwulan?) dressed like present-day Balinese, this charming, lifelike statuette is perched on a base on which we can read the date 1334 Saka (A.D. 1412). Sandstone. Height: 23¾ inches. *Djakarta Museum.*

231. EAST JAVA, ORNAMENTAL BRONZE. This small bronze of uncertain origin probably dates from the fifteenth century. Length: 8 inches. *Djakarta Museum.*

203   204

205

206

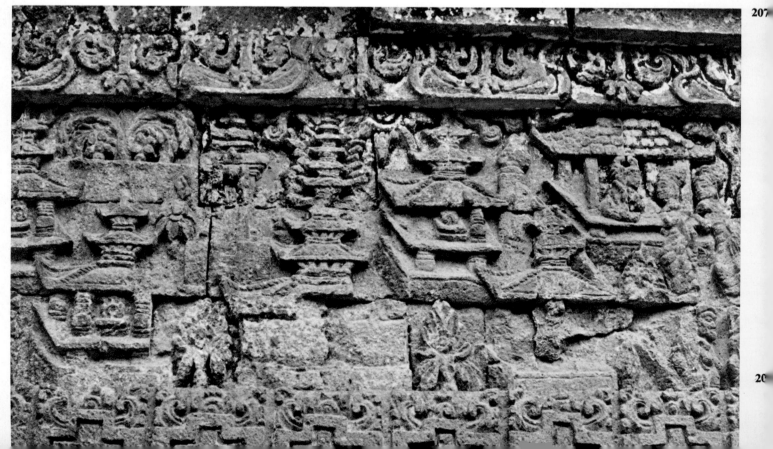

207

214

215

217

218

222 223

224

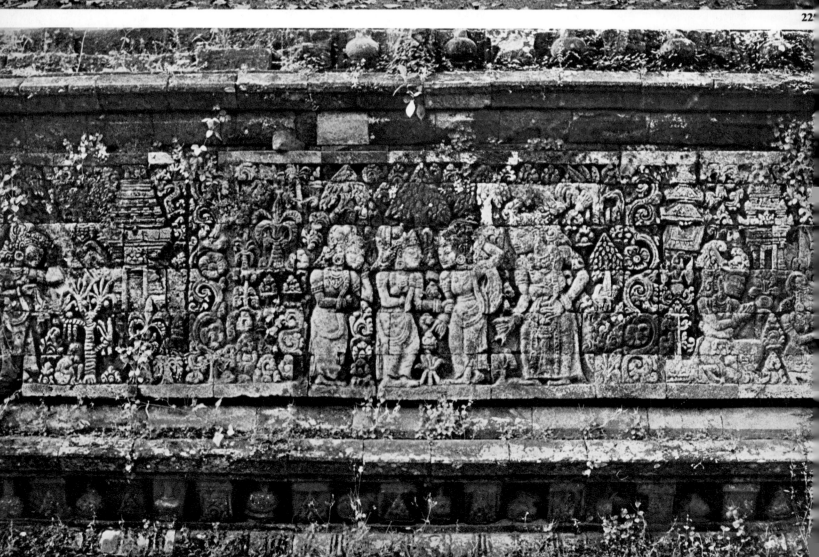

228

229

232. BALI, GOA GADJAH, THE CAVE. Also known as the Elephant's Cave (Lwa—or Air—Gadjah), this cave is adorned with a monstrous head of kala or of Rangda (?) above the entrance. It seems to have been consecrated to Shiva. In fact, the interior contains a triple lingam in a niche on the right, and, opposite, a statue of Ganesha. However, no one can explain the presence of fragments of a statue of a Buddha discovered in the central niche. This cave may well be older than the inscription found on it. Not far away there have been found fragments of a stupa with triple parasol as well as stone Buddhas which can be dated from the eighth–ninth century. The cave may have been sculpted by Buddhists, then reused by Shiva's followers, who consecrated it by engraving the inscription. The later occupants may well be responsible for the façade decoration. This question has yet to be settled, however. At the entrance, toward the south, a Shivaist inscription enables us to date the execution of this curious sanctuary from before the eleventh century. Height of the entrance: 6½ feet.

233. BALI, GOA GADJAH, THE BATHS. Recently discovered, these baths have been partly restored and are functioning again. Six fountains, each consisting of a woman standing and holding a jug from which water flows, feed the very low basins. The arrangement of these baths is rather similar to that of Belahan on Mount Penanggungan. Eleventh century(?).

234. BALI, GOA GADJAH, FOUNTAINS OF THE BATHS. Each statue measures about 6½ feet high.

235. BALI, TAMPAKSIRING, GUNUNG KAWI. On each side of the Pakerisan torrent, sandwiched between high rocky hills, hewn in the rock, are niches 23 feet high containing representations of tjandis. The bases of these tjandis have holes in which boxes, which were probably meant to contain ashes, were discovered. A series of tombs (those shown here) consist of four tjandis—cells hewn from the rock and stone platforms which we assume supported wooden pavilions, perhaps similar to those seen here. The rock to the right has been curiously cut into steps. The opposite group (plate 236) consists of the representations of five tjandis. Water probably flowed from holes made in the edge of a drain sculpted at the base of the group. Several of

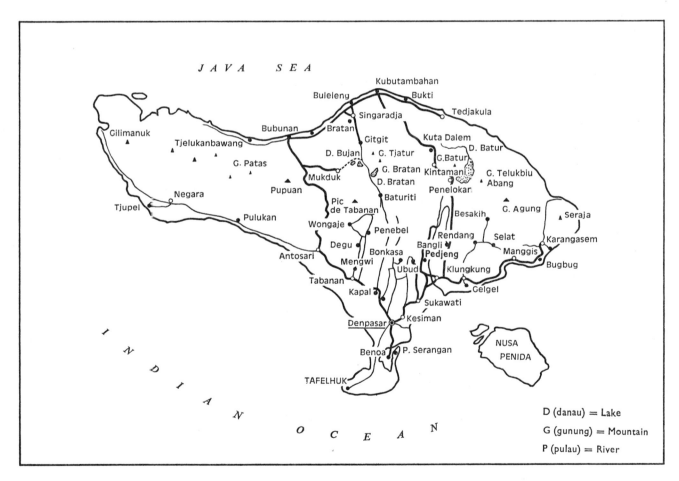

FIG. 24. THE ISLAND OF BALI

these tombs have inscriptions on the upper part of the false doors (studied especially by Louis-Charles Damais), which prove to be chronograms relating events that took place at the close of the eleventh century and dating, one of them at least, from 1001 of the Saka era (A.D. 1079). Thus they well could have been commissioned by King Anak Wungsu, the younger brother of the hero-king Airlangga. These reliefs were covered with very hard "diamond stucco," which has partly resisted erosion.

236. BALI, TAMPAKSIRING, GUNUNG KAWI. Partial view of the group of five tombs. We can see the largely obliterated inscriptions on the lintels of the false doors. The deciphered chronograms belong to the two tombs which lie to their left. A tenth tomb is situated not far away.

237. BALI, TAMPAKSIRING, GUNUNG KAWI, MONASTERY. Around the royal tombs were various caves which were used by hermits, and a monastery where this curious monolithic monument stands in the center of a courtyard. The walls of the courtyard are hewn with large niches. These caves (others are found along the bank upstream for almost a mile) have yet to be studied, for they were recently discovered. The caves and monasteries were probably hewn about the same period as the royal tombs.

238. BALI, PEDJENG, PURA PASAR ING DJAGAT, MONOLITHIC VASE. Hewn from a single block of lava stone, this vase, according to its decoration, was used to contain holy water. The entire surface is decorated with a mountain range, whose base is in water, and which is encircled by a serpent. These symbols represent Mount Meru, the divine churn that was instrumental in condensing Amrita. Eight gods support the serpent. Here we can see two of them, and above the tail of the serpent another seated divinity who may be Indra. On the rim of this 30-inch-high vase or bowl is an incised chronogram which specialists have dated 1329.

239. BALI, PEDJENG, KABU EDEN, PEDESTAL FOR A STATUE. Sculpted with skulls and garlands, this pedestal probably supported a seated statue of Bhairava (?), the terrible aspect of Shiva. Date uncertain (fifteenth century?). Diameter: 3 feet 4 inches.

240. BALI, PEDJENG, KABU EDEN, SCULPTED FOUNTAIN. This group, which has recently been discovered and is known by the Balinese as Arjuna, has yet to be properly identified. Moreover, it is very likely that the two sculptures in front of the group are of a more recent date and belong to another monument. The exact site of the spring or water source itself is unknown. Fifteenth century(?).

241. BALI, KAPAL, KAPAL TEMPLE, BRICK MERU. Of very ancient conception but certainly rebuilt at a relatively recent date, this meru is typical of east Javanese sanctuaries of the fourteenth and fifteenth centuries. The decoration is recent.

242. BALI, MENGWI, MERUS. These small and very slender sanctuaries are built of wood and thatch. Their bases, which consist of brick and sculptured tufa stone, are modern. In the foreground are seats (or thrones) of the ancestors.

243. BALI, KAPAL, SADA TEMPLE, ENTRANCE. This is a fine example of a Balinese split gate whose style dates from the fifteenth century. The present structure, however, is more recent. To the left, we can see the brick meru shown in plate 241.

244. BALI, BESAKIH, MERUS. During volcanic eruptions, these light structures were unharmed by showers of red-hot stones (lapilli), since the roofing of smooth thatch allowed the lapilli to bounce off harmlessly. These merus have 9 or 11 stories. Although of a very ancient type, they are, however, of modern construction.

245. BALI, BESAKIH, ENTRANCE TO THE GREAT TEMPLE. Standing on the slopes of the Agung Gunung volcano, this mountain sanctuary consists entirely of terraces. It dates from the fourteenth century, but its structures have often been rebuilt. This photograph was taken only seven days after a terrible volcanic eruption caused much destruction throughout the entire region. The ground is still covered with a thick layer of lapilli and ash.

246. BALI, BEDHULU, BAS-RELIEFS AT YEH PULU. Along the entire cliff, at the entrance to a small sanctuary hewn from the rock, is a frieze of figures forming a line 82 feet long and seemingly heading toward a statue of Ganesha. Measuring 6½ feet high and of an uncertain style, this frieze appears to be related to a small drainage basin in front. Yeh Pulu means "water pot." Although some authors date these reliefs from the fourteenth or fifteenth century, I believe they are more recent.

247. BALI, HEAD OF BARONG. This relief in soft tufa is modern. It represents the Spirit of Good (Barong) who is eternally opposed to the Spirit of Evil (Rangda). Often restricting themselves to the baroque and producing marvelous stylizations, Balinese artists enjoy decorating their monuments and temples with traditional motifs where excess is *de rigueur*. Height: 20 inches. *Jogjakarta Museum.*

232

238

239

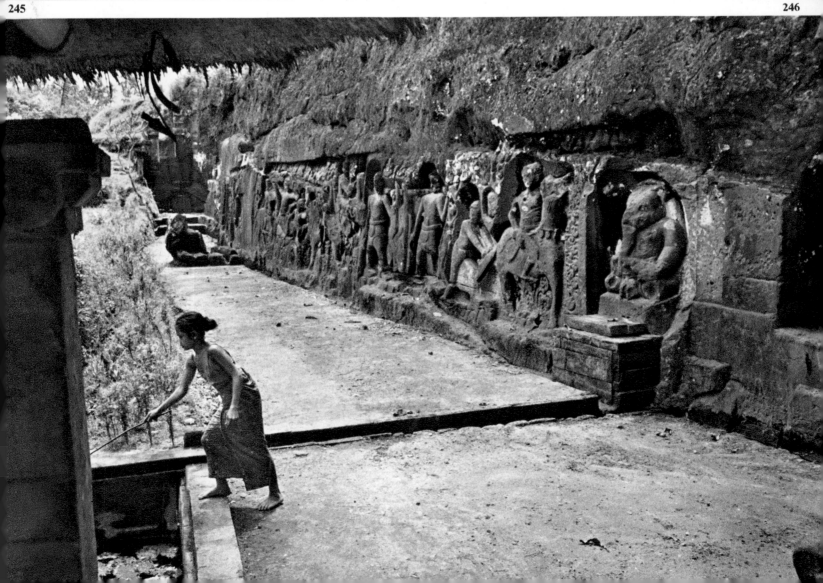

VI. THE ORIENTAL KINGDOMS

1. FUNAN AND SRI DEB (First–Seventh Century)

ONE of the first kingdoms founded in Southeast Asia by emigrant Hindus was situated in the Mekong Delta, on the territory now partly in Cambodia and partly in South Vietnam. No inscription reveals the true name of this kingdom which, nevertheless, has left many vestiges and it is designated by the name the Chinese gave it, Funan, a phonetic transcription of an old Khmer word meaning "King of the Mountain" which probably applied to the sovereign of the country. What was the extent of this kingdom? We do not know exactly, but at its zenith it extended as far as the Menam (Chao Phraya) River in Thailand and the Malay Peninsula on the one hand, and toward central Vietnam on the other, including the entire middle course of the Mekong River. An empire rather than a kingdom, Funan was the origin of the great states of the Indochinese Peninsula and their art forms. According to legend, the country's founder was an Indian (?) named Kaudinya who, after arriving by sea on the coast of Funan (the legend does not state exactly where) and after many adventures, married Soma, the daughter of the king of the Nagas (underworld spirits), and founded a dynasty. The time this took place was about the first century after Christ. As early as the third century, Chinese chronicles mention the Funan Empire and describe it as a great maritime power whose suzerainty was already established over the neighboring territories. There are few extant artistic examples from this period: a handful of jewels, including a Sassanid one and Roman bracteae (thin plates of precious metal), one bearing the effigy of Antoninus Pius (A.D. 150). This certainly resulted from maritime trading in southern India and relations with the Roman Empire. Fu Chan, one of the most famous kings of this period, whose conquests are recorded in history, sent the first ambassadors to India and China in 243. Chinese murals show that the cities of Funan were surrounded by walls. Vyadhapura (Phnom Da) seems to have been one of the most important, if not the capital. The simple inhabitants (farmers, talented goldsmiths) employed a writing of Indian origin. With the exception of the reign of a foreign sovereign at Funan, perhaps of Indo-Scythian origin, no further mention is made of this kingdom until the fifth century, when a second Hinduization, this time more complete, took place in the "King of the Mountain's" country. Emissaries to China increased, and a great building program was undertaken; the temples containing splendid sandstone statues dedicated principally to the cult of Shiva. But from the same Chinese sources, we know also that Hinayana Buddhism flourished, that the greatly developed cities were enclosed by wooden palisades, the king's palace had a single story, and the inhabitants built ships more than 80 feet long and cast bronze images "with four faces and eight arms." The kings took the imperial Hindu title of Varman, and from the fifth to the seventh century the most common writing was Sanskrit. There are no architectural remains from this period with the exception of brick foundations (and perhaps also the Ashram Maha Rosei of Phnom Da). But judging from certain vestiges found especially at Oc Eo, the system of roofing the buildings was probably similar to that in India, that is, recessed corbeled stories adorned with niches, or kudus, decorated with heads. It would be reasonable to think that after the collapse of the Funan Empire and its conquest by Chen La, certain groups left for Java. The monuments of the Dieng Plateau on that island, especially the Tjandi Bhima, could well be related to the architectural styles then flourishing in Funan. Made of perishable material, they have disappeared. However the case may be, it is certain that the architectural styles of Chen La and of the Champa Empire, which we will shortly discuss, were greatly indebted to Funan influence. In sculpture, the representations of gods are related, insofar as the Buddhas are concerned, to the Gupta styles in India, and insofar as the Brahmanic statues—Shiva, Hari-Hara (a combined form of both Shiva and Vishnu), Vishnu, Surya—are concerned, to those sensuous works found in southern India during the Pallava and Chalukyan dynasties. However, the style of these statues, examples of which have been found not only in south Cambodia but also as far as Sri Deb in central Thailand, reveals a masterful execution which earns them a choice place in Southeast Asian art. These statues are especially distinctive for being set against a stele or a stone arch, and are thus classified as halfway between high relief and sculpture in the round. They are also extremely elegant, since by the sixth century Funan sculpture had probably reached its full development.

248. VIETNAM, CONG-NGUYEN, BUDDHA. Although few vestiges of wooden architecture of the Funan period have survived, certain statues have been conserved, thanks to the quality of their material, which has resisted dampness and the elements. This very Indian-style standing Buddha is of *calophyllum insophyllum* wood, known as *Mu-u* in Vietnamese. Carved from a tree trunk (including the base), this sculpture not only has great plastic quality but also is a typical example of the Funan style. Standing in a slightly swaying position, Buddha appears to be making an appeasing gesture with his right hand. Held by the left arm, his cloak falls in a double fold and clings to the body, one of the characteristics of the Gupta style. Fourth century (?). Life-size. *National Museum, Saigon.*

249. VIETNAM, PHUOC CO'TU, NUI SAM, TERRA-COTTA ORNAMENT. Inspired by the south Indian kudu, this motif, representing a person peering from a dormer, is flanked on each side by a motif that resembles a makara. It was probably used to adorn the edge of a roof. Terra cotta with recent polychrome. Height: 10 inches. *National Museum, Saigon.*

250. VIETNAM, OC EO, STANDING BUDDHA. This small, fine bronze was discovered during excavation in the vestiges of Oc Eo harbor. Gandharian in style, this bronze may have been brought into the country from north India or executed on the spot from another model. The second opinion seems preferable—certain details of the robe seem, in fact, rather clumsily executed, as though the sculptor had not understood his model. Height: 5 inches. *National Museum, Saigon.*

251. CAMBODIA, ANGKOR BOREI, PHNOM DA, ASHRAM MAHA ROSEI. Oriented to the north, this small temple is probably not the most ancient of those known to us in Cambodia, but is perhaps the only

building in the Funan style to have remained intact. Built of gray basalt, the interior consists of a windowless cella (the false wooden ceiling has disappeared), measuring about $9^1/_2$ feet square, surrounded by a narrow corridor lit by means of eight dormers arranged in the heavy outer wall. The outer door is flanked by round slender columns supporting a lintel with double arch (plate 252) adorned with garlands. Above the door is a large horseshoe-arch pediment which probably supported a sculpture, now no longer in place—the attachment hole is still visible. Formed of three stories, two of which are false, the roof is decorated with an amalaka on a thin stem. Decoration of vegetal and geometrical motifs consists generally of kudus and paneled reduced edifices. The door frames are of sandstone. A fine pink-gray basalt stone leads to the first entrance step. This structure, which is shown here from the southwest, probably dates from the close of the seventh century and was carefully executed.

252. CAMBODIA, ANGKOR BOREI, PHNOM DA, ASHRAM MAHA ROSEI, PEDIMENT ABOVE THE ENTRANCE.

253. CAMBODIA, ANGKOR BOREI, PHNOM DA, PARASURAMA. In contrast to Indian sculpture, which was seldom able to free itself completely from the stone, we see here one of the most successful ensembles of Eastern sculpture liberated from the mass. Although the talent of this artist can be advantageously compared with that of the greatest Western sculptors, he still shows a certain timidity toward the material. Accustomed to wood, it appears that he does not consider his new medium to be very strong and feels the need to support his work. The box which the figure is holding in his right hand is extended to the ground (the hand therefore rests on a bracket or support) and the loincloth itself is also supported. These artifices, however, do not affect the graceful quality of the work, the subtle interpretation of volumes, and the wonderful treatment of the detail—hands, head, and feet. Sandstone. Height: 5 feet 10¹/₂ inches. *National Museum, Phnom Penh.*

254. CAMBODIA, ANGKOR BOREI, PHNOM DA, ENTRANCE TO CAVE I. A natural cave on the hillside of Phnom Da, this sanctuary was embellished with an entrance made of blocks of cut sandstone. Kudu motifs form a frieze on each side of the door. The paintings we see are modern. The sanctuary itself is bare, formed by the rock walls. Opposite the entrance is a curious portico consisting of two blocks of schistic sandstone set on end and supporting a third. This cave, the first of a series of four, lies to the north of the hill; the openings of all the caves are toward the south. The sanctuaries probably contained statues set against the wall or supported by low arches, like those now in the National Museum of Phnom Penh. Fifth–sixth century.

255. CAMBODIA, ANGKOR BOREI, PHNOM DA, HEAD OF PARASURAMA. This handsome, sensitive profile with its almost Buddhist smile and long nose is still embellished with long hair treated in tight, overlapping curls, which fall gracefully down the neck (see plate 253 for the entire figure). The stylized ear has an enlarged lobe from wearing heavy jewelry. A small chignon, perhaps reminiscent of the Buddhist ushnisha, gives this Brahmanic statue an aesthetic quality which relates it to Buddhist philosophy rather than to that of the Brahmans.

256. CAMBODIA, ANGKOR BOREI, PHNOM DA, STATUE OF VISHNU. This image of the supreme god Vishnu, facing his assistants Balarama and Rama (which is quite unusual) combines attributes of both Vishnu and Shiva. His four right arms hold the spiritual flame (Shiva), a stick (?), a goatskin (Shiva), and a box (?), while the four left arms support two attributes which are missing, an ax (?) or the simplification of a *dameru* (?), and a pot (the one that contained Vasuki's poison produced during the Churning of the Sea of Milk?), while the cylindrical miter is Vishnuist. This might be Hari-Hara. The style of this statue is hieratic and contrasts with the lithe aspect of its assistants. A horseshoe arch and brackets support the weight of the arms (this type of arch remained in Khmer art until the Koulen style—ninth century). Although the body of this divinity is treated more crudely than that of Parasurama (plates 253 and 255), the details are nevertheless carefully executed—the hands, for example, seem very feminine. The loincloth with its regular folds evidently represents a common piece of clothing, and the very tight pleats suggest an extremely fine material. Sixth century. Schistic sandstone. Height: 9 feet. *National Museum, Phnom Penh.*

257. CAMBODIA, ANGKOR BOREI, PHNOM DA, DETAIL OF VISHNU'S HANDS. In the foreground, the lower right hand holds a round box which some authors recognize as a club handle. But on examining the manner in which this handle is attached to the body of the club (actually a bracket), we find a solution of continuity. The very fine hand, with its long, slender fingers and well-defined nails, hardly seems to be holding the box. In the background, we see the hand holding the vestiges of a goatskin (symbolizing the *Virabhadra* aspect of Shiva?).

258. CAMBODIA, TAKEO, VAT KO, KRISHNA RAISING MOUNT GOVARDHANA. This powerful work in the Phnom Da style, dating from the early sixth century, is sculpted high relief against a slab of sandstone. The bearing is dynamic, the attitude well observed; the garment, held by a low belt, falls from each side and appears to be in motion. The finely curled hair seems more suitable for a Buddha than for a deity of the Hindu pantheon, even though curious protuberances adorn the head (strands held by a ring?). But is this really a portrait of Krishna? As we are scarcely familiar with the beliefs of the Funan people, this statue may very well be a kind of caryatid supporting an entablature. Sandstone. Height: 5 feet 3³/₄ inches. *National Museum, Phnom Penh.*

259. CAMBODIA, ANGKOR BOREI, VAT KOMPONG LUONG, MALE TORSO. Another example of the sixth-century Funan style, but the dedication is unknown. Divinity? Portrait? The supporting arch along with the arms and head have disappeared. Yet the perfect modeling of this body shows how great Funan artists were in representing the human figure. Sandstone. Height: 2 feet 9¹/₄ inches. *National Museum, Phnom Penh.*

260. CAMBODIA, ANGKOR BOREI, RECLINING BUDDHA. More than 9¹/₂ feet long and unfortunately in fragments, this statue represents the Sage reclining "on his right side like a lion" and retains all the characteristics of the late Phnom Da style. The figure appears to be sleeping. The full features, the sensitivity of sculpture, and the calm expression lend this damaged work a relation to Greek statuary. Early seventh century. Sandstone. *National Museum, Phnom Penh.*

261. THAILAND, SRI DEB, STATUE OF VISHNU. While Funan reached maturity, other Indian-inspired schools of sculpture developed in different parts of the Malay Peninsula and in central Thailand, especially at Sri Deb. In the seventh century the Indochinese Peninsula seems to have been divided by well-defined influences: Dvaravati, Funan—which perhaps extended as far as Sri Deb and Malaysia—Chen La in north Cambodia, and the nascent Cham Empire in present Annam. Sri Deb may have been one of the most northern cities of the Funan Empire, which was nothing more than a group of rather autonomous states. This city may have been part of Chen La of the Land, which in the early eighth century separated from the Chen La of King Isanavarman. In the latter case, Sri Deb sculptures would at least date from the eighth century.

This four-armed Vishnu has a less Indian-like face than the sculptures of Angkor Borei and perhaps reveals an ethnic type closer to that of the Dvaravati Kingdom. Yet the elegance and slenderness of the body, although not typical of the Sri Deb style, relate it to Funan art. Like all divine representations of Southeast Asia, this sexless statue is wearing only a clinging loincloth. The statue may have had a supporting arch. Sandstone. Height: 6 feet 8 inches. *National Museum, Bangkok.*

262. THAILAND, SRI DEB, BUST OF SURYA (?). This mitered god, in a slightly hieratic pose and with a halo, perhaps represents Surya, the sun god. The head, with its full features, adorned with heavy earrings, seems to belong to an aboriginal race. The necklace and decoration on the miter are unusual. Unfortunately, this greatly damaged statue offers us little information. It can be dated somewhere between the sixth and the eighth century. Sandstone. Height of head and miter: 11 inches. *National Museum, Bangkok.*

248

251

252

254

253

257

256

58

259

60

261   262

2. CHEN LA (Seventh Century–802)

One of Funan's vassal states, long established on the middle course of the Mekong, in the Bassac region, had established its capital at the foot of Mount Vat Phu, which had been venerated since time immemorial. At the close of the sixth century, this state was sufficiently strong to revolt against the Funan rulers and begin to conquer the lower country. The marriage of a Bassac princess and a Funan prince served as pretext. The conquest of Funan was completed by King Isanavarman (616?–35?), whose name then disappeared from the chronicles, and he transferred his capital from Vat Phu to Isanapura (Sambor Prei Kuk), not far from Tonle Sap (the Great Lake). He erected many brick temples of a special style (isolated towers with stone door frames) which may have been influenced by Funan and Champa styles while still retaining a strong similarity to the style of certain Indian temples. Sandstone began to be used for construction and sculpture. Rich, vigorous forms of feminine statues and harmonious proportions of divinities (Hari-Hara seems to have been the supreme divinity) are among the finest achievements of human genius. But this splendid period lasted only a short time. In the early eighth century (about 710–15) the empire, unified by Isanavarman, separated into two kingdoms: Chen La of the Land, which comprised the territories of lower Laos (Bassac) and Siamese Laos, and Chen La of the Water, which seems to have succeeded Funan on its territories. Of the very isolated Chen La of the Land we know little, and equally little of its art. It may have influenced late Koh Ker art or continued, at Sri Deb and Ubol in Thailand, the style already inaugurated in these regions by that of Funan. It may also have been the territory of Bhavapura. Chen La of the Water continued the tradition of unified Chen La. But internal disorder led to its separation into several small states. Political decadence was such that about the close of the eighth century, the Sailendra sovereigns of Java (or even sovereigns related to the Chams—certain etymologists finding a relationship between the names "Java" and "Cham," and between "Funan" and "Sailendra") did not hesitate to conquer it. The brief passage of these conquerors contributed new elements to the Khmer civilization which enabled them to develop a new style.

Unified Chen La saw the erection of its greatest monuments, but because of disorder in the eighth century, the sovereigns were unable to undertake great works. At the very most, the site of Sambor Prei Kuk was increased by several temples and south Cambodia witnessed the creation of isolated sanctuaries. Sculpture had a certain stiffness and a tendency toward frontality which were later to develop in Angkorian arts. At first restrained and of distinctively Indian inspiration, decoration developed toward excess, borrowing mainly from vegetal themes. Many steles with inscriptions in poetic Sanskrit or archaic Khmer inform us of the political life of the Chen La sovereigns and their religious beliefs. Buddhism appears to have been gradually eliminated, to the benefit of the Hari-Hara cult and Brahmanic mythologies, whose rich iconography progressively furnished artists with themes.

263. CAMBODIA, KOMPONG THOM, SAMBOR PREI KUK, NORTH GROUP, TEMPLE 17. Floral decoration on the south pillar of the east façade. Sandstone.

264. CAMBODIA, KOMPONG THOM, SAMBOR PREI KUK, NORTH GROUP, TEMPLE 17. Although the Funan Empire, at least in its south Cambodian part, was conquered by Isnavarman, king of Chen La, in the early eighth century, the new art apparently did not prevent the inhabitants of Funan from producing their own works. (Chen La certainly took its own inspiration from some of them.) It is even possible that Funan architects settled in the new capital, Isanapura (Sambor Prei Kuk), where they

left several monuments whose style, still closely related to that of India, was nevertheless different from the one inaugurated in its capital by the conqueror. Witness this small structure, standing beyond the walls northeast of the north group of the Isanapura temples. Built entirely of large slabs of sandstone embedded between massive pillars and roofed by a single slab, it is cubic in form and is entered by means of a single opening in the east fronted by a small flight of steps. Although this is a simple sanctuary, the decoration is nevertheless remarkable. The edge of the slab-roof is adorned with kudus, four on each side, and symmetrical in relationship to small niches with figures decorating the foundation of the structure. Pillars at each corner and columns at the opening are adorned with delicate ornamental foliage; the base and the top of the walls are decorated with balustrades in bas-relief. The building is about 8 feet high. Some authors believe this to be a *garba-griha* (inner sanctuary) whose brick mandapa has disappeared, but the entirely enclosed aspect of this structure leads us to think that no temple was ever erected around it, although Parmentier has discovered traces of foundations which may be part of the same structure.

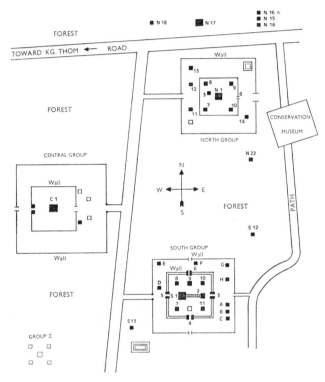

FIG. 25. THE GROUPS OF TEMPLES AT SAMBOR PREI KUK

265. CAMBODIA, KOMPONG THOM, SAMBOR PREI KUK, TEMPLE 22, NORTH GROUP, NORTH VIEW. Entirely covered by jungle, the site of the ancient city of Isanapura has revealed not only isolated small temples but also three large groups of sanctuaries surrounded by walls, and a small subsidiary group (Z). The best preserved temples are those of the south group. The central group, a more recent one, dates from the early ninth century. These temples are usually designated by letters corresponding to their group, N, S, C, Z, also an order number (see plan). The north group is dedicated to Gambhireshvara, one of the many aspects of Shiva. The temple shown here, N22, lies somewhat south of the outer enceinte of the north group. Built of brick, like all the temples of Sambor Prei Kuk except N17, it consists of a sandstone door frame, lintel, and slender columns. The roof is formed of multiple false stories. Three false brick doors decorate the south, west, and north walls. The stucco decoration

has completely disappeared. The temple is square in plan. Nothing remains of the interior. The beautiful sculpture of Brahma which occupied the place of honor is now in the National Museum at Phnom Penh.

266. CAMBODIA, KOMPONG THOM, SAMBOR PREI KUK, NORTH GROUP, TEMPLE 22, LINTEL OF THE EAST DOOR. This sandstone lintel imitates the wooden *toranas* in India. Garlands hang from two arches connected by an ornament composed of tight little coils. At each end similar ornaments surmount the round, slender column, adorned with rings and joined to the lintel by a mortised joint. Sandstone.

267. CAMBODIA, KOMPONG THOM, SAMBOR PREI KUK, NORTH GROUP, TEMPLE 7. This octagonal sanctuary has a single projecting entrance with a sandstone door frame. The decoration of the sculptured brick walls, once coated with stucco, is remarkable. Its seven rows of superimposed, intersecting small receding terraces were probably adorned by now-vanished kudus on their projecting edges. The bricks were laid with a vegetable cement mixed with brick dust, which gave the very thick walls an exceptional cohesive strength that enabled them to resist both dampness and destruction by encroaching vegetation. This temple is the only one in the north group to have an octagonal plan. All the others are built on a square plan.

268. CAMBODIA, KOMPONG THOM, SAMBOR PREI KUK, NORTH GROUP, TEMPLE 7, RIGHT ENTRANCE WALL. This typically Indian decoration displays a flying palace. Figures are shown at the windows which are separated by slender columns. Above this, a round kudu window framed with figures is supported by diverging makaras. Between these two stories is a low arch formed by two diverging makaras ridden by small figures and connected at the apex by their tails, which form a coiled rosette. The slightly projecting balcony is supported by a small frieze formed of kinnaras, horses, and winged bulls acting as caryatids (plate 269). The excellent-quality brick is very delicately sculpted. Coating can be seen in places, for these decorations were probably polychromed. This may well depict the wooden architecture in use during the period.

269. CAMBODIA, KOMPONG THOM, SAMBOR PREI KUK, NORTH GROUP, TEMPLE 7, FRIEZE BENEATH A BALCONY. Here we see how carefully animals were depicted. The horse is well observed and seems copied from one decorating a bas-relief at Amaravati representing the "Great Departure" (British Museum). The winged bull, a motif borrowed from Achaemenid Persia, is rarely found in Indian art. It is occasionally seen at Amaravati and Sanchi where it also decorates friezes, especially one

250

adorning a vedika railing (Madras Museum). This detail is from a largely ruined central temple of the north group (N1) which has four open entrances and probably contained a lingam. This sanctuary is built on a platform reached by means of four axial flights of steps.

270. CAMBODIA, KOMPONG THOM, SAMBOR PREI KUK, SOUTH GROUP, TEMPLES 2 AND 10, SEEN FROM THE SOUTHWEST. The small temple S2, square in plan, with pyramidal roof, open to the east and west, is dedicated to a statue of Nandi, the bull mount of Shiva. Its interior consists of a sandstone canopy supported by four square, sandstone pillars, wonderfully decorated with human-headed kudus and floral motifs directly sculpted in the sandstone, as in Temple N17 which we have just seen. An elevated walk built on laterite posts connected this small temple to the principal one of group S1 (plate 271). On the left of this photograph is one of the small octagonal temples which surrounded the central sanctuary. The site was completely overgrown by the jungle, but is now being cleared.

271. CAMBODIA, KOMPONG THOM, SAMBOR PREI KUK, SOUTH GROUP, TEMPLE 1, EAST FAÇADE. Situated in the center of the south group, this temple contained the principal divinity, a smiling Shiva (or a gold lingam) which has disappeared. Erected on a small terrace and connected to the small Nandi temple (S2) opposite by means of a walk (the posts of which are visible here), this rectangular temple has a false door on each side. Four sandstone steps lead up to the entrance. The terrace is also reached by four flights of four steps each. The door frame, lintels, and slender flanking columns, which are topped by bulbous capitals, are of sandstone and are finely executed. There is a single step on the threshold, so that one steps up and down upon entering. The interior of the building is paved with sandstone, and illumination was originally dim as the only light source was the door. The pyramidal roof consists of slightly recessed stories. The walls hold projecting niches which probably contained sculptures, but are now empty. A pyramidal pediment, which reproduced a model of the entire temple, stood above the door. Of majestic proportions, this temple is the finest one at Sambor.

272. CAMBODIA, KOMPONG THOM, SAMBOR PREI KUK, SOUTH GROUP, TEMPLE 1, INNER VAULT. Vertical view of the temple interior looking up. Here we can see how layers of brick have been corbeled. Vertical sections corresponding to outer false stories made it possible to attenuate the pyramidal structure. A false roof separated this once-blind vault from the sanctuary proper. Since the top of the temple roof has caved in, light entering the sanctuary made this striking photograph possible. The sanctuary walls were adorned with slightly projecting pilasters ending in a groove which probably supported a false wooden ceiling. Stone hooks attached to the corners were doubtless meant to support an awning. An inner bench extended along the base of the walls.

273. CAMBODIA, KOMPONG THOM, SAMBOR PREI KUK, SOUTH GROUP, SOUTH WALL, MEDALLION. This medallion, which appears unfinished, adorned the inside of the first enceinte wall of the south group. This is one of the rare medallions not left in the rough. It depicts a crouching monkey making an offering to a woman. On the right is a figure difficult to identify. Although this decoration is in a deplorable state, we can nevertheless still judge its very simple, almost classic, composition. The enceinte wall of laterite and brick is faced with sandstone on the exterior. Oblong *gopuras* also adorned with sculptured medallions commanded the entrances. The corners of the enceinte are decorated with false structures of solid brick. The south group consists of two concentric enceintes.

274. CAMBODIA, KOMPONG THOM, SAMBOR PREI KUK, SOUTH GROUP, DETAIL OF A LINTEL. Strings of beading are separated by round ornaments holding emerging torsos. On each end of the lintel the beading is "swallowed" by a makara ridden by a man. In a dynamic position, its body covered with scales, with a horn over its eye, and curled tail, this makara seems to stem from Amaravati art, as does the figure riding it. However, the surrounding decoration here is quite different.

275. CAMBODIA, KOMPONG THOM, SAMBOR PREI KUK, SOUTH GROUP, TEMPLE 11, DETAIL OF A FIGURE ON THE NORTH WALL. Because of his emphasized features and headdress, this anonymous figure greatly resembles an ethnic type of Kui now living around Sambor. Observe how carefully the bricks have been assembled, enabling the sculptor to produce a fine work. Height of the head: 6 inches.

276. CAMBODIA, KOMPONG THOM, SAMBOR PREI KUK, CENTRAL GROUP, TEMPLE 1, LION ON THE SIDE WALL OF THE SOUTH STAIRCASE. This roaring, crouching lion, carved out of the sandstone base, decorated the side wall of the south staircase of Temple 1. According to Philippe Stern, it is of a later date than the other structures, perhaps early ninth century, which would mean that this temple is not in the Sambor style but in that of Koulen. It is a poorly observed lion with its mane of sausage curls and shows the decline of genius at Sambor. The sanctuary itself appears unfinished. Entirely of sandstone, the false doors have very handsome lintels also of the same material. The lintel of the east entrance was abandoned before being finished.

277. CAMBODIA, KOMPONG CHAM, KOH KRIENG, FEMALE DIVINITY. Lacking hands or attributes, this statue can only be defined as the "Lady of Koh Krieng." This pure effigy may perhaps symbolize Lakshmi, a shakti, or even a devi. The statue is replete with rich forms: full breasts and pronounced hips. The clothing consists only of a skirt held by a low belt, and the body shows no movement. The texture of the skin is so perfectly rendered in sandstone (in other words, it does not imitate flesh as such) that all sensuality is absent. The face is round, no longer young, and reveals a serene maturity. An impression of sovereignty emanates from the powerful features, which are plainly treated as volumes to allow a free play of light and shadow. The high, simple chignon with carefully arranged curls, generally associated with Lakshmi, Vishnu's shakti, or a devi, makes the face seem longer. If it were otherwise it would lack a certain elegance. Beginning of middle of the seventh century. Sandstone. Total height: 3 feet 10 inches. *National Museum, Phnom Penh.*

278. THAILAND, ARANYA PRATHET REGION, TORSO OF A FEMALE DIVINITY. This attractive headless sculpture, found far from any city, doubtless represents a young woman, perhaps Uma. The full body, the frontality of the attitude, and the folds of the robe relate this statue to the Sambor style. Jean Boisselier, who has made a careful study of the piece, dates it between 620 and 640 and considers it a transitional work between the Sambor style proper and those of Prei Khmeng and Kompong Preah, which follow chronologically. Sandstone. Height: 2 feet 11¾ inches. *Collection H.R.H. Princess Chumbhot, Bangkok.*

279. CAMBODIA, KOMPONG THOM, PRASAT PHUM PRASAT. This brick structure, 32 feet high, is consecrated to Hari-Hara. This is indicated by a five-line inscription on the door jamb. The temple stands not far from the road, midway between Phnom Penh and Siem Reap (about 88 miles from the latter). It had a foresection in the form of a long cross, a space now occupied by a modern temple. The sandstone east door is adorned with ringed, slender columns with decorative small flowers and a handsome, well-preserved lintel. The square, recessed tower is vaulted with a series of drums, and terminates in an enormous stone. The three false doors are higher than the entrance; their columns are decorated with bands of vegetal motifs sculpted in brick and coated with stucco. This sanctuary, dated 706, is attributed to the Kompong Preah style.

280. CAMBODIA, KOMPONG THOM, PRASAT PHUM PRASAT, LINTEL OVER THE EAST DOOR. With a completely vegetal décor, the arch is here replaced by a garland raised at each end. Garlands which in the Sambor style fall from the arch are replaced here by a motif of scalloped leaves. The round, slender columns are encircled by rings decorated with small flowers or beading. The door frame is undecorated.

281. CAMBODIA, KOMPONG THOM, PRASAT ANDET, HARI-HARA. A supreme divinity uniting Shiva and Vishnu, Hari-Hara was greatly venerated at Chen La during the seventh century. The miter's right section (Shiva) consists of the stylized curls of the ascetic chignon and the forehead has Shiva's third eye (but only one half of it). The left half of the face belongs to Vishnu. A crude head, wonderfully treated, with heavy, thick lips adorned for the first time in Khmer statuary with a mustache—it is related to a new ethnic group rather than to an aboriginal one. This may be the portrait of the first Khmer. The body is long and thin, slightly swaying but very lithe and with an astonishingly accurate anatomical structure. Four arms supporting a stone arch complete this statue. The clothing, also in a new style, is the forerunner of the later Khmer loincloth adorned with a pocket on one side. The garment is held up by a fine, slender chain passed around the hips. Prasat Andet style (or Prei Khmeng). Sandstone. Height: about 6 feet 5 inches. *National Museum, Phnom Penh.*

282. CAMBODIA, TAKEO, PHNOM BAYANG, PRASAT ANG TUL. This is a square brick *prasat* (sanctuary-tower) with a single entrance facing west. The interior is vaulted with a series of drums and shows traces of a ceiling about 13 feet high. Total height: 39 feet. Inner dimensions about 8 feet square. At the left is the summit of Phnom Bayang and its sanctuary (eighth century). To the left, not far from the Prasat Ang Tul is a second brick tower known as Prasat Ang Tuk (not shown in this picture). It is 65 feet high and its entrance faces east. The interior of this sanctuary, whose vault is identical with that of Prasat Ang Tul, is floored with sandstone. The walls show traces of stuccowork and paintings with dominant red tones (dark cadmium-red). Inner dimensions of the sanctuary: 14 feet square. Thickness of the walls: 2 feet 4 inches. The east wall is 4 feet 4 inches thick. In the interior, above the east door, the architect has carved a very high relieving triangle in reserve on the sandstone lintel. Framed by sandstone, the door frame is undecorated but is adorned on each side by vertical bands of floral decoration sculpted in brick. A thin, plain lintel is supported by slender brick columns. The west, north, and south walls are adorned with brick false doors. These two sanctuaries probably date from the ninth century. They lie on the side of a small hill about 2600 feet as the crow flies northwest of the summit of Phnom Bayang.

263

264

265

266

268

269

270

271

276   277

279

280

281   282

3. THE NORTHERN CHAMS (Seventh–Tenth Century)

In order to describe the art of the most eastern part of the Indochinese Peninsula, or Cham art, we must go back in time again. Chinese texts give the year 192 for the official union of a group of tribes who refused to submit to China, known as Lin-Yi, situated to the north of Funan, on the Annam Coast. These "barbarians" were probably Indonesians, later known as Chams from the ancient name of their country, Champa. It is very likely that emigrants from India or Funan soon attempted to Hinduize the Cham tribes but with little success, as they were busy with dynastic quarrels and the establishment of their kingdom, which seems to have been unified by a sovereign named Fu Wen, who died in 349. Henceforth, its frontiers were recognized by China. The king's son, Bhadravarman, erected a sanctuary in the form of a lingam and dedicated to Shiva on the site of Mi-Son, not far from the capital (Tra-Kieu?). Inscriptions found at Tra-Kieu in the Cham language and in Sanskrit characters are the most ancient evidence we have of the Chams. Buddhism and Shivaism were shared by the faithful, but it appears that the latter was practiced especially by the ruling class. During the entire fifth and sixth centuries, the Chams quarreled and took to piracy and were constantly at war against Tonkin, sometimes allied with China, or sometimes independent—a confused history often marked by the success of Chinese troops, who pillaged the Cham capital several times. However, about the mid-seventh century, the original sanctuary of Mi-Son was re-erected by Prakasadharma (653–86), together with new constructions which constitute for us the first evidence of Cham art. The Cham Empire seems then to have extended very far to the west, including the famous sanctuary of Vat Phu, in Bassac, and was in constant contact with the Chen La kingdoms. But about the mid-eighth century Tonkinese advances forced the dynasty to fall back more to the south, in the Nha Trang region. Prosperity returned, but this time the Chams had to defend themselves against another formidable enemy, the Javanese, who incessantly pillaged the Annam coasts.

In spite of such troubles and wars, Champa continued its relations with Funan, then with Chen La. Reciprocal influences were numerous and enable us to determine the styles of Cham art in relation to pre-Khmer ones. The most ancient style is the one commonly known as Mi-Son E1, which shows great affinities with the Prei Khmeng style of Chen La. This is the first tower built of brick (the most ancient ones, probably of wood, have vanished) and is very similar to post-Gupta Indian models, of which little remains, with the exception of a sandstone lingam pedestal wonderfully decorated with small porticos containing figures and dancers, as well as a pediment adorned with a reclining Vishnu. Buddhist art of the period is represented by several stone or bronze statues of Avalokiteshvara in a style that is also very Indian.

Monuments closely follow the ancient style; Cham architects appear to lack imagination. A Koulen monument, the Prasat Damrei Krap, northeast of Angkor, could be attributed to them (802), proving existing relations between Cham and Khmer sovereigns. At Mi-Son many monuments were erected which, with the towers of Hoa Lai, form the Hoa Lai style. Bricks, remarkably well laid and held together by a kind of vegetable cement, lent themselves to sculpture and decoration. As at Chen La, stone was carefully used. Doors were framed by slender octagonal columns adorned with heavy rings and had no lintel, a projecting ornamental arcade acting as such. Decoration consisted chiefly of vegetal motifs framed by pilasters decorated with vertical bands. Sculpture reveals a decided ethnic type, and the figures are covered with jewelry.

Toward the close of the ninth century, a new dynasty seems to have conquered the northern part of the country and settled at Indrapura, in Quang Nam province. Indravarman II, the first sovereign of this dynasty, then founded a great Buddhist monastery of Mahayana rule at Dong-Duong, southeast of Mi-Son, the first evidence of this sect in Champa.

The style is rather similar to that of the preceding century: towers on each story and walls adorned with pilasters. But the décor becomes increasingly involved and vermiculated, covering the entire surface, sometimes revealing certain Chinese aspects, which is not at all surprising

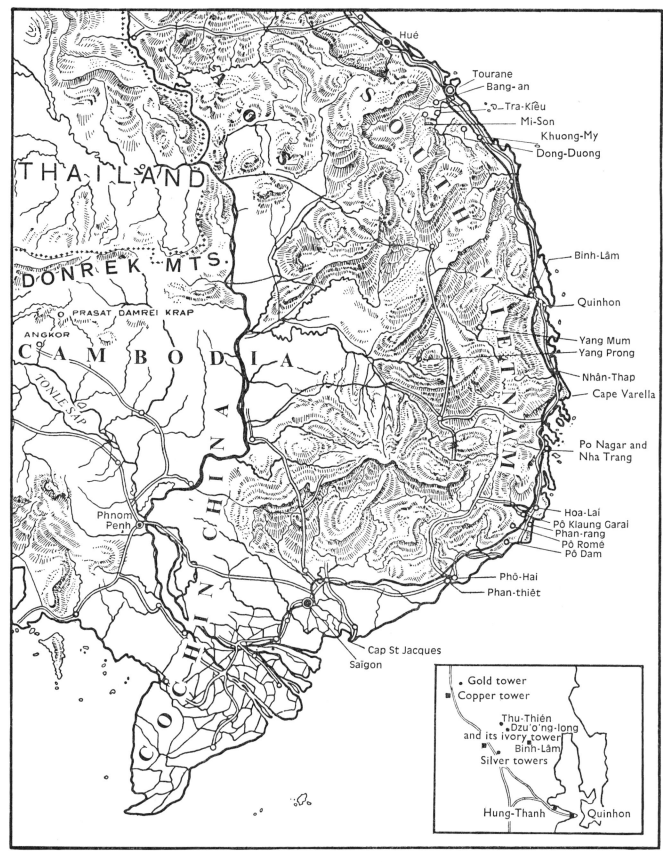

FIG. 26. THE INDOCHINESE PENINSULA (*After Parmentier and Maspéro*)

since relations existed between the two peoples. Abundant sculpture attests the heights reached by Cham art. Faces with emphasized features, connecting eyebrow ridges, and heavy lips with mustaches contrast with relatively graceful, lithe bodies. Divinities were not the only themes that inspired sculptors; animals, door guardians, dancers, and demons are treated in a lively manner, often with a Javanese spirit. But as the style ended there was a rapid decline of forms and decoration.

However, in the early tenth century, Cham art was revived from Khmer and Javanese sources, influenced by Indravarman III (918–?). This is the Mi-Son AI style. Towers became taller and the somewhat unbridled Dong-Duong style is emphasized, acquires discipline, and orders itself into balanced compositions. Engaged slender columns, like those at Dong-Duong, are separated into two balusters divided by a ring. Accent pieces abound in the shape of flames, a motif imported from Java. The kala-makara motif is found on the ornamental arcades. Statuary is humanized, the faces become softer, and the poses more graceful. Those on the pedestal of Tra-Kieu are among the most famous and most beautiful in the style, although still of distinctively Indian influence. This style was to continue throughout the entire tenth century. In the eleventh century, however, it became weaker and inspiration was poverty-stricken. No further construction took place because of constant wars fought by the Chams against the Vietnamese and the Khmers, and the Chams were finally vanquished. They retreated and established their capital more to the south, at Vijaya (Binh Dinh).

283. VIETNAM, ORIGIN UNKNOWN, APSARA. An architectural ornament, this sculpture might be a devata rather than an apsara (hands joined). It wears a necklace and earrings as well as a kind of Hindu-inspired diadem. These ornaments later became very popular among the Khmers. Seventh–eighth century. Sandstone. Height: 22 inches. *National Museum, Saigon.*

284. VIETNAM, TRA-KIEU, ELEPHANT. The lion and the elephant, symbols of force and power, are regularly used in Cham art. Whereas lions are often treated with great fantasy—the artist working without a model—elephants, on the other hand, are always well observed and their attitudes well described. In contrast to the Khmers, the Chams were rarely able to liberate themselves from the frontality of the subjects they treated and, like their Indian masters, remained with bas-relief; with almost rare exception did they free the subject from the block from which it was sculptured. Here the sculptor, who worked in high relief, was fortunately able to represent a full-face head, ears shown and stylized, on a profile body. This piece was probably used as a metope. Seventh–eighth century. Sandstone. Height: 2 feet 1¾ inches. *National Museum, Saigon.*

285. VIETNAM, TRA-KIEU, PEDIMENT GARUDA AND NAGAS. This curious work, which probably adorned the top of a pediment, shows many peculiarities which reveal the originality of Cham art in its translation of foreign themes. The presence of breasts on this garuda relates it to a kind of kinnari

monster. On the other hand, the nagas, in contrast to those of the Khmer country, are distinctively separated and do not seem to possess a hood. Their heads recall demons rather than serpents, which would indicate the diabolic nature of this mythical animal, whereas in all other Indian arts it played a protective role (Buddha's naga, Mucilinda). This is difficult to understand if we admit that the chief subject of this pediment is a garuda who, in all Indian mythology, was the enemy of serpents. Sixth–seventh century. Sandstone. Height: 3 feet 4 inches. *National Museum, Saigon.*

286. VIETNAM, DONG-DUONG, HAND OF A STANDING BUDDHA. Detail of a sculpture 3 feet 4 inches high, this hand shows great realism, a quality rarely found in Cham art. The care the artist took to define volumes with a new sense of figuration and to accurately delineate the lines of the hand makes it rather difficult to determine the origin of this sculpture, which has characteristics both of the Indian post-Gupta and the southern Chinese styles. This may even be an imported sculpture. Late ninth century. Bronze. *National Museum, Saigon.*

287. VIETNAM, TRA-KIEU, DANCING SINGHA. This lion-demon is treated in a very special style and is remarkable for the rhythm of its forms. Represented in a human manner, the head recalls, from the arrangement of its features (especially the eye horn), certain Javanese monsters. Posed in a threatening attitude (seeming at the same time to be dancing), the demon's mane has become a double collar. Sandstone. Height: 2 feet 1¾ inches. *National Museum, Bangkok.*

288. VIETNAM, THAP-MAM (BINH DINH), RISHI. This relief is an example of conventional Cham sculpture. Treated with a certain facility, which is in contrast to older productions, the subject also shows the hieratic attitudes and the stylization known to Cham art at the time when the capital, under Vietnamese pressure, had to be transferred to Vijaya (Binh Dinh), in the south. Tra-Kieu style. Tenth–eleventh century. Sandstone. *National Museum, Saigon.*

289. VIETNAM, HOAI NHON (BINH DINH), AVALO-KITESHVARA. This extremely rare work of unusual execution was recently discovered by a peasant in a field near Binh Dinh. We can easily recognize Avalokiteshvara from the Amida Buddha in his headdress and the attributes in three of his four hands: bottle, lotus flower, *mala*. The long, narrow torso, the absolute frontality, and the soft expression correspond to Indo-Javanese traditions of Mahayana representations. This divinity is decked with ornaments of the same origin: gold diadem adorned with small flowers, heavy earrings, high chignon in three sections, and a decorated belt and buckle. The narrow robe, with a short pleated section, is treated without litheness; the folds are clumsily rendered, the belt sash is poorly held by lateral sections. The chignon (*jatamukuta*) has no resemblance whatever to reality, and its stylization shows that the artist has copied a pre-existing model without endeavoring to understand it. Both in style and treatment, this statue is related to another Avalokiteshvara found in central Vietnam (Hanoi Museum). Jean Boisselier, in an article in *Arts Asiatiques* (Vol. IV), dates it from about the mid-ninth century. Images of Avalokiteshvara disappeared at Champa as early as the beginning of the tenth century. Light-green bronze. Total height: 2 feet 7½ inches. *Historic Institute, Saigon.*

290. VIETNAM, HOAI NHON (BINH DINH), AVALOKITE-SHVARA. This detail shows that this Avalokiteshvara has Shiva's eye in the middle of his forehead. His hair is also arranged into a chignon like the ascetic Shiva. The head is crowned by a diadem with three cabochons in the form of a flower. This motif was certainly inspired by those which adorn certain Javanese bronzes. Moreover, it is quite possible that the statue is a work imported from that island.

283

284

286

285

287

288

290

289

4. THE KHMERS (802–1406)

The inhabitants of Funan had an abundant water supply, the sea was not far away, and the lower Mekong provided alluvial deposits and irrigation necessary for rice cultivation and also facilitated Funan's many contacts with other maritime nations. Chen La, on the other hand, lying in a region covered with jungle, had to provide its own irrigation. The inhabitants of Funan had drained the marshes and feared floods. Taking advantage of a natural slope which brought water from the Great Lake (which at that time covered a far greater area than now), the Khmers of Chen La were concerned with the problem of a reserve supply. This resulted in the creation of huge reservoir-moats around the cultivable area that could be replenished during the rainy season. Only a nation led by a strong ruler could achieve the task of irrigating dry land. Like the pharaohs of Egypt 3000 years earlier, the Khmer sovereigns, basing their power on judicious irrigation of their country, formed a wealthy and powerful kingdom. Following Chen La's example and inspired by the former's sovereigns, these Asiatic pharaohs covered the country with canals and created one of the greatest empires ever known in Asia.

THE KOULEN STYLE

We have discussed how the Javanese Sailendras succeeded in establishing their sovereignty over declining Chen La. In 790 a Javanese or Cambodian prince returned to Chen La and began to reunite the country. Following the progress of his conquests, he successively founded several capitals and finally settled on the Koulen Plateau, northeast of Angkor, where according to Funan and Javanese customs he called himself "King of the Mountain." In 802 he erected a royal lingam dedicated to Shiva and began proceedings that were destined to free him from the Javanese yoke and consecrate him "Universal King." He then took the title Jayavarman II. Khmer unity was thus established and the Kambuja country now had a ruler invested with divine power, representing the supreme god on earth. As the climate of the Koulen Plateau was unhealthy, the king returned to Hariharalaya (Roluos), near the north banks of the Great Lake, in the center of the country. He erected brick towers at Koulen, Sambor Prei Kuk, and Prei Prasat, in a style similar to that of Chen La. But it is very likely that he inaugurated a type of architecture destined to remind people of the sacred mountain, Mount Meru. This type was the mountain-temple inspired perhaps by Borobudur. One example may be the Ak Yom sanctuary, which probably stood in the center of the city of Amarapura (west of West Baray at Angkor) but has since disappeared. We have discussed how Cham artists erected a sanctuary at Koulen; Jayavarman II may have been eager to acquire Champa in his liberating enterprise. If the architecture scarcely offers anything new, the decoration on the other hand seems to have regained its vigor. Sandstone lintels bear decorations (makaras disgorging deer or beading, kalas) borrowed from the Cham or Javanese styles. Horsemen emerge from ornamental foliage. Slender polygonal columns are adorned with both rings and fillets having leaf decorations on each side. Inspired by Cham art, pediments with a central figure foreshadow the historiated pediments which were wonderfully developed during the entire course of Khmer art.

Sculpture again needed a supporting arch. Statues had full faces, mustaches, and eyebrows connected in a straight line. They were crowned by cylindrical miters, then gold diadems—a motif that later became quite common.

THE PRAH KOH STYLE

From the practical viewpoint, Jayavarman II hardly improved the system of irrigation used during the Chen La period. This was to be one of the glories of Indravarman (877–89), who greatly improved the land around Hariharalaya (Roluos). He organized a system of irrigation by means of canals perfectly adapted to the land and the rivers that drained it. The Lolei Baray, a huge artificial lake measuring 2½ miles long by almost 1 mile wide, into which flowed the waters of Stung Roluos, fed the moats of temple and city, and during the dry season irrigated all the rice fields between the city and the Great Lake (which ultimately received its waters). However, these moats and canals had another purpose: they provided the routes for conveying men and material, especially those necessary to build temples. Earth excavated from moats and canals was employed to create platforms for monuments. The king thus gave life to the earth, erected sanctuaries to divinities, and ordered the rhythm of life to the image of the god he represented: the Khmer State was founded. As in Java, the king, once dead, was identified with the god he had worshiped. Thus he became the object of a funerary cult, and the late sovereign was venerated under a posthumous name. His temples then became funerary monuments.

Indravarman was, therefore, a builder. In 879 he erected the Prah Koh towers in homage to his parents, then in 881 his own mountain-temple, Bakong, in the center of the city in the Roluos plain, an artificial sandstone hill with five square terraces superimposed to form a pyramid, representing the worlds that form the universe. Small towers contained secondary divinities and stone elephants adorned the terraces. Around this mountain were brick sanctuaries and a series of stone enceintes. Here for the first time we see naga railings which later flowered at Angkor.

During Indravarman's reign, sculpture freed itself completely from supporting arches and became pure sculpture in the round; no longer static, although slightly heavy and stylized, it became dynamic. Great care was lavished on the upper part of the body and the legs became mere supports.

Heads, with features similar to those seen on Koulen sculpture, have very short beards and are crowned by diadems. Clothing is simple with stylized pleats, the triangular part of which is invariably folded on the left thigh. Narrative stone bas-relief also begins to decorate brick sanctuaries or temple terraces, revealing great skill in the art of movement, and foreshadowing the marvelous bas-reliefs which marked the height of Angkorean art.

THE BAKHENG STYLE

In 889 Yashovarman succeeded his father Indravarman to the throne. After founding the Lolei Temple at Roluos, he considered the city too small and that the land beyond it could not be properly irrigated. He therefore decided to transfer his capital and began to create the East Baray, a huge artificial lake almost 4 miles long and 1 ½ miles wide, fed by the Stung Siem Reap. The new city of Angkor was bordered by moats more than 4 miles long on each side. In the center of this cultivable area, he erected his own mountain-temple on a natural hill, the Phnom Bakheng, at the summit of which five towers arranged in quincunx formed the principal sanctuary. Adjacent towers on the terraces and their bases brought the total to 800, the sacred number, arranged around the central tower or meru. Its position made it a true lunisolar calendar. This mountain-temple was completed by two other sanctuaries erected on nearby hills, the Phnom Bok and the Phnom Krom. Sculpture now shows hieratic stiffness. Calm faces (emphasized by the striking, continuous line of the eyebrows) no longer smile, and diadems encircle a thick tuft of almost cylindrical hair. The section of the garment falling in front of the legs is doubled and the material pleated. Female statues wear a skirt falling from the belt. Decoration is like that of the Prah Koh of Roluos, but instead of being stucco it is now sculpted directly in sandstone. Technique develops with material, becoming more flexible, and the entire wall surface is covered with an almost lacelike design. On each side of the sanctuary doors are female divinities (*tevodas*) or guardians (*dvarapalas*), placed in niches and sculpted in high relief. The buildings are rather squat and their pediments quite high, almost forming a square with a central figure emerging from ornamental foliage.

Another mountain-temple, the Baksei Chamkrong, was built directly on the plain near Phnom Bakheng. It was consecrated to Yashovarman's son, Harshavarman I (900–23). Of modest proportions, it consists of a single sanctuary on the summit of the final terrace, and lacks the additional small temples. Baksei Chamkrong is a masterpiece of simplicity.

Harshavarman's reign was also marked by the erection of the Prasat Kravanh Towers (921), whose fine bas-reliefs, sculpted directly in brick on the outer walls, reveal an unsurpassed delicacy of execution. The Angkorean style had now come into its own and continued to develop, adapting in a more and more personal manner Javanese and Cham influences.

THE KOH KER STYLE

In 928 a political split caused one of Harshavarman I's uncles to flee from Angkor, and he founded another capital, Koh Ker, about 60 miles northeast. Assuming the title Jayavarman IV (928–41), he erected sumptuous sanctuaries adorned with sculpture whose very dynamic style was in great contrast to the hieratic style of the previous reigns. This particular style, part of the

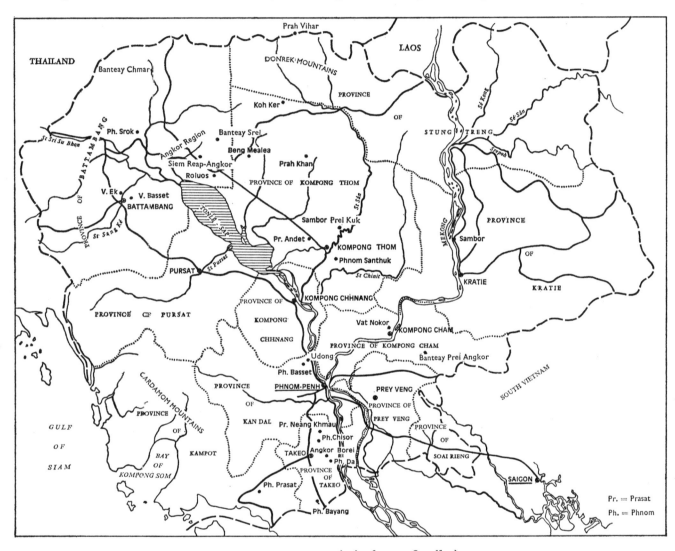

FIG. 27. CAMBODIA (1 inch = 56 miles)

natural development of Khmer art, ended with the return to Angkor by the rightful sovereign, Rajendravarman (944–68). The style was especially characterized by a tendency to gigantic forms: the tower of the mountain-temple is more than 115 feet high and the sculptures decorating the different temples were often colossal. The lintels are among the finest in Khmer art. In the center of each is a god mounted on a mythical animal emerging from a vegetal décor. Pediments become triangular, copying more and more closely the wooden structures which occupied the space between the temple and the enceinte wall.

At Angkor, Rajendravarman continued the Koh Ker style, although with slight modifications.

The East Mebon erected in 952 and the Pre Rup (961) show a desire for simplification and grandeur. These mountain-temples now have only three terraces, the third being crowded with five sanctuary-towers in quincunx. The proportions are gigantic. But the originality of these monuments lies especially in the presence of long rooms replacing the adjoining square sanctuaries on the two first steps of the pyramid. Later, these rooms developed into continuous galleries.

THE BANTEAY SREI STYLE

In 967, during the close of Rajendravarman's reign and the early years of the reign of his successor, a Brahman of royal blood named Yajnavaraha erected his own small temple—a rare event in Khmer annals—some 13 miles northeast of the capital. In so doing, he created a very particular and unparalleled style which was not only an innovation but also, since it made use of every artistic resource, he created a structure that was a real jewel of proportion and delicacy. Although quite small, the Banteay Srei is, I think, the finest building at Angkor. Standing in the center of several concentric laterite enceintes, it consists of three small towers (prasats) aligned on a high terrace. Fronting the central prasat, which is dedicated to Shiva, is a projecting room with brick vaulting. The usual buildings—libraries, gopuras, gateways—which comprise every sanctuary, are here arranged somewhat apart from one another. The central tower is only 32 feet high. Yet thanks to a skillful play of perspective, the group appears more imposing than its dimensions lead us to think. Architecturally speaking, the sanctuary offers no new elements with the possible exception of the door antefixes which imitate the beams of a wooden roof, a style found again at Prah Vihar. Decoration is sumptuous, and the fine-grained pink sandstone enabled sculptors to achieve wonders of delicacy and detail. Walls are entirely covered with reliefs of vegetal motifs scattered with figures and mythical animals. But it is the treatment of historiated pediments that gives nobility to the Banteay Srei style. Empty spaces emphasize the figures who are part of the narrative, forming a pleasant part of the composition (where we again find certain Javanese elements). The library pediments are real masterpieces, and sculpture is also refined. The treatment of tevodas which adorn the prasat walls, the animals sculpted in the round (which, on the wall of a flight of steps, guard the entrances to the sanctuary), and the charming small group of Shiva and Uma in the Phnom Penh Museum, impress one by their delicate modeling, restraint, and alluring freshness. Here there is no desire for effect or ostentation; it is the work of a man of impeccably refined taste. Unfortunately, the same cannot always be said of the gigantic temples that have made Angkor world famous. In spite of their classification, distinction, and acceptance, their enormous size often alienates any human contact and consequently loses much beauty. The gigantic equilibrium of a temple destined for the gods will never be as handsome as a simple structure of human dimensions. Architecture cannot be beautiful without intimate contact with man.

THE STYLE OF THE KLEANGS

In the early eleventh century a usurper forced his way to the throne. Claiming kinship to the sun, he proclaimed himself "King of the Mountain" under the name of Suryavarman I, after vanquishing Jayavarman V's successors in 1011. Coming from the south, where Mahayana Buddhism was still strong, this sovereign was more inclined to tolerance. His reign marked the beginning of a religious syncretism and finally witnessed the triumph of Buddhism. In fact, Buddhism was more in accordance with the popular spirit. It is very likely that Hinduism, a state religion necessary to royal prestige, was never largely followed by the people, who certainly remained faithful to either animistic practices in use before the introduction of Hinduism, or to a Funan Buddhism still practiced in south Cambodia.

An energetic sovereign, Suryavarman launched into a series of conquests which made the Khmer Kingdom into a vast empire. Foundations of the Khmer style typical of his period are found in Thailand at Lopuri (Lavo), Ligor, and at Laos. In Cambodia he erected the three fine sanctuaries of Vat Ek, Vat Baset, and Phnom Chisor, and embellished the temple of Prah Vihar in the Donrek Mountains. At Angkor, he restored and finished the Phimeanakas and the Ta Keo. The style that marked this glorious reign differs considerably from the preceding styles; it is actually their outcome. Proof of this is the unfinished pyramid of Ta Keo. Here, the mountain-temple found its perfect expression. Consisting of five tiers faced with sandstone, of colossal dimensions (328 by 416 feet at its base), surmounted by five sanctuary-towers, this 150-foot-high pyramid dominates the plain. The oblong sanctuaries of Pre Rup have been replaced by enclosed galleries completed by corner towers and gopuras in the center of each side. The name of this style comes from that of two buildings, Prasat Kleang North and Prasat Kleang South (their purpose is still a mystery), which stood opposite the royal palace of Angkor. Their exquisite decoration typifies the style used during Suryavarman's early reign. Chau Srei Vibol, a small temple standing somewhat beyond the city, was the forerunner of the next style. What little sculpture there is during this period shows the influence of the Banteay Srei style. The faces are soft and smiling, and the attitudes less hieratic. Pediments and slender columns, however, are heavy with decoration, especially vegetal; that on the lintel has little new to offer. This style is important mainly for its architecture.

THE LOPBURI STYLE OR STYLE OF THE SIAMESE KHMERS

For more than 250 years, from about the year 1000 to 1250, the Khmers extended their empire to the west over almost all of Siam. Great builders, they left examples of their art in every important city of this country. If, from the architectural point of view, they kept their methods and styles intact—not having encountered any solid architecture in Siam capable of influencing their art of building—the same did not hold true of their sculpture. For the decoration of their temples the Khmers turned to aboriginal artists who—having broken away from executing statues in a perfectly defined style, namely, the Dvaravati—left their mark on Khmer treatment. The style that remained (known as Lopburi from the name of the city—Lavo—where the Khmers had established a vice-regency) became stabilized and enjoyed great favor in Siam long after Khmer troops were forced to leave by the northern Thais. It is often difficult to distinguish between Lopburi architecture and that of Cambodia of the same period if we disregard the decoration, which in Siam is often of Buddhist inspiration. The principal monument, now greatly ruined, is that of Pimai, near Nakhon Ratchasima (Khorat). Erected in the early thirteenth century, it reveals all the characteristics of the Angkorean Khmer style. At Lopburi itself there is another sanctuary consisting of three towers built of blocks of laterite, each *prang* (tower) adorned with four porches to form an emphasized projection. Scattered throughout Thailand are many other examples of Khmer architecture, the most important being at Lopburi, at Sawankalok (Sri Satchanali), where the northernmost Khmer temple, Vat Chao-Chao was built, at Pecchaburi (Vat Kampang Leng, the last Khmer monument in Siam), and at Phitsanulok. After the invaders had gone, the Thai used certain elements from Khmer temples, especially the prasat, which they modified (into the prang) according to their own style. The Siamese were past masters in the art of metal casting, and they made countless images, especially of Buddha standing or seated on the coils of the Naga king, Mucilinda. The faces are rather square, the features clearly indicated (reworked in bronze after casting). Some sculptures with somewhat heavier forms often have less ornament. But in general, like architecture, the style of Lopburi statuary adapted to the Khmer one (there is little more than a local variation) influenced later forms and types of Thai sculpture, and furnished the latter with elements for its full development.

THE BAPHUON STYLE

Despite his short reign (1050–66), Udayadityavarman II, Suryavarman's son, built a new capital at Angkor itself, centered around a wonderful mountain-temple, the Baphuon. To provide a greater cultivable area, a gigantic artificial lake almost 5 miles long and 1¼ miles wide

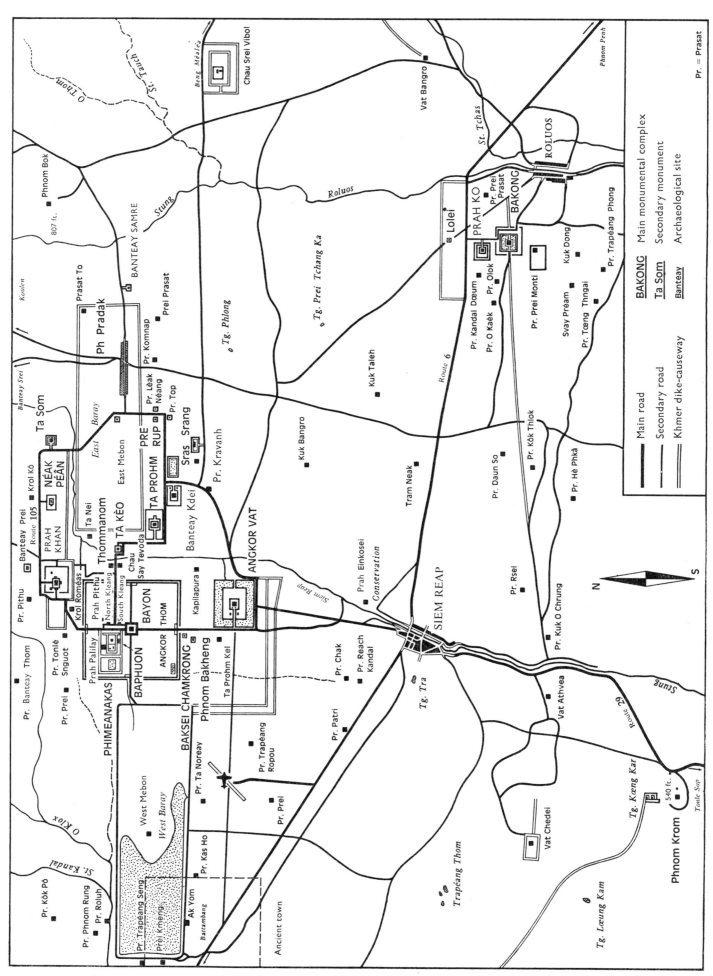

FIG. 28. ARCHAEOLOGICAL SITES OF THE ANGKOR GROUP AND SURROUNDINGS (1 inch = 1⅞ miles)

was excavated west of the city. This was West Baray, which covered the greater part of the ancient city of Amarapura where the small mountain-temple of Ak Yom probably marked its center. Harshavarman II succeeded his brother, but his reign was troubled by warlike raids from the Chams, who managed to reach Sambor Prei Kuk which they pillaged and burned. The glory of the dynasty of the sun was soon dimmed. But evidence of its splendid architecture and sculpture remains, above all the Baphuon mountain-temple whose grandeur at Angkor is eclipsed only by Angkor Vat. The Baphuon fell heir to all that was achieved at Ta Keo. But the quality of its construction is uneven. The stone, sandstone or laterite, used as facing and treated as wood, was unable to support heavy weight and parts of it collapsed.

Architects often committed great errors, like reinforcing stone walls with wooden beams. It is surprising that some of these rafters are still in place, although the stone has fallen in. Vaulting by means of rows of corbeling scarcely permitted the construction of anything but small sanctuaries or narrow galleries, thus diminishing the possibilities of innovation. On the other hand, the decoration of the Baphuon is outstanding for its restraint; it does not encroach upon the architecture and limits itself to its proper role. The historiated panels, illustrated pediments, and vegetal-decorated lintels are perfect examples of moderation and harmony. The return to sculptured decoration benefited the bas-reliefs, which are treated as small panels with much grace and fantasy; these contain some of the finest examples of animal depiction in Khmer art. Statues are smiling and slender, draped in a finely stylized garment with the front section in the form of a fishtail. One of the most beautiful sculptures of this period is the recently found gigantic reclining Vishnu from the West Mebon. It came from a small temple (which has disappeared) built on an island in the center of the reservoir. Made of bronze and more than 13 feet long, this statue is a superb example of Khmer foundry skill.

THE ANGKOR VAT STYLE

In 1080 a provincial governor forced his way to power, was crowned Jayavarman VI, and founded a new dynasty. One of his successors, Suryavarman II, is famous for having created the style that is often called classic. Suryavarman II was ambitious; he annexed Champa, went as far as Annam in the west, and conquered as far as the Malay Peninsula. But in 1149 the Chams regained their freedom and inflicted crushing defeats on the Khmer armies. Shortly afterward the king died and was succeeded by his cousin, Dharanindravarman II, who was the first Buddhist sovereign of Angkor. After some dynastic disorder, the throne was ascended by Jayavarman VII. But wars had impoverished the country and in 1177 the Chams, again returning up the Mekong, invaded, pillaged, and set fire to Angkor. These reigns, however, both glorious and miserable, witnessed the construction of many temples, the greatest and most famous of which gave its name to the style of this period: Angkor Vat.

Angkor Vat, Suryavarman II's sacred mountain, was founded about 1122 in a style that was really the result and logical development of that of the Baphuon. Suryavarman's predecessor had already erected several temples, especially at Pimai, in Thailand, where we find the first Khmer Buddhist sanctuary, while monuments dedicated to Shiva were built at Vat Phu and Prah Vihar, exemplifying the religious syncretism of the period. Surrounded by moats which form a rectangle 5000 by 8000 feet, Angkor Vat is connected to its outer portion by causeways bordered with wonderful naga railings. The building itself, a masterpiece of order and symmetry, has a façade almost 787 feet long. The whole is surrounded by a columned gallery open on its outer face, containing bas-reliefs relating the life of the king. The chief characteristic of the architecture is the handling of perspective, which gives the visitor the impression of grandeur and balance. The center of each terrace is displaced toward the west and the height of each foundation increases as one ascends the steps to the five towers which crown the ensemble in a splendid manner. Here, mountain-temple architecture has achieved perfect proportions and a total mastery of its art.

Other gigantic temples in the same style were erected at Angkor. That of Beng Mealea, 43 miles east of the royal city, is a square version of the great temple. Although smaller, Banteay Samre, Thommanon, and Chausay Tevoda reveal a slight degeneration in style.

Decoration at Angkor Vat is weaker and, turning clumsily to themes exploited earlier with more success, is no longer concerned with emphasizing the architecture. Walls are carved with motifs (some of which are reminiscent of Chinese drapery) in rather low relief depicting a series of apsaras posed with affected gestures and wearing complicated headdresses. They are all somewhat stereotyped in spite of being treated differently and with imagination. The decoration of this vast ensemble is especially striking in the sumptuous bas-reliefs of the outer galleries which cover more than 7000 square feet. There are endless scenes from *The Mahabharata*, *The Ramayana*, the story of Krishna, wars, and the judgment of the dead. The figures are expressed in a very lively manner, but the whole often appears dull from the repetition of figures and especially from their low relief. The low carving is scarcely emphasized, almost like a fresco, and scenes follow one another and are juxtaposed with no rest for the eye. Some parts of these reliefs may originally have been heightened by color. In spite of undeniable design and spirit, taken as a whole it now appears monotonous. Here, the gigantism detracts from the quality. The same is true, moreover, of sculpture in the round which seems decadent in comparison with that of previous styles. The symmetry of the bodies and faces robs them of all life and expression. The bodies are static and the treatment of clothing is heavy to the point of excess. The bronzes, however, show much skill and spirit, revealing great inspiration in their form and decoration.

THE BAYON STYLE

The Buddhist sovereign, Jayavarman VII, continued to build. In 1180 he destroyed the Cham fleet and annexed their country. Angkor was reborn after being brought to ruins in catastrophic raids. From conquest to conquest, Jayavarman VII extended his domain as far as the Burmese frontier, constantly recruiting new troops to invade Annam. At Angkor itself, he erected his own mountain-temple, with towers decorated with the characteristic faces, which he dedicated to the bodhisattva Avalokiteshvara. He redesigned the city, surrounding it with huge moats and walls, the latter pierced with gigantic gates reached by means of causeways bordered by railings decorated with nagas and giants. No temple escaped his zeal. Few failed to reveal his imprint, either in the form of additions or sculpture. During a reign that lasted fewer than 40 years (he died in 1219), he erected more monuments than all his predecessors. In addition, he created artificial lakes (Prah Kahn, Srah Srang) and reorganized the irrigation system. Proving himself a real genius for organization, Jayavarman VII revitalized not only the architecture of his period but also the art of sculpture and decoration by introducing new Buddhist themes combined with a subtlety and vigor which the followers of these themes had long since lost—qualities probably borrowed from the Dvaravati style. But this vast effort to build so great a number of monuments in so short a time was unfortunately achieved at the cost of quality; material was often poorly chosen and almost always badly assembled. Moreover, we know that the Khmers never used cement for their buildings, which were really nothing more than an assemblage of squared and cut blocks, like children's toys, held in place only by gravity. If a stone became displaced or if one of the reinforcement beams began to rot, the entire balance was affected. Cut sandstone was often set on nothing more than the uneven ground. Rain water would cause the stone to split and thus destroy the building forever. This explains why few of the many monuments erected during the king's reign have remained intact. Yet we can admire the forms, thanks to the constant effort expended since the last century by the archaeologists of the École française d'Extrême Orient, who with much skill have used and continue to use all the resources of modern science to restore these Khmer monuments. Since the Bayon buildings were erected slapdash, this has presented an enormous task.

The Bayon style is divided into four very separate phases.

Style I. This style is represented especially by the Ta Prohm (1186), Banteay Kdei (1181), and Prah Khan (1191) sanctuaries at Angkor, and to the north, near the present Khmer-Thai frontier, the huge Banteay Chmar temple. Still faithful in plan to earlier buildings, the architecture is of poor quality. Although plentiful, the sculpture suffers from hasty execution. Yet pediments with Buddhist scenes are wonderfully executed and reveal great compositional skill.

Style II. This style witnessed the foundation of new Angkor and the erection of its 10-mile walls inside the moats, its huge gates, and colossal statues of devas and asuras holding the serpent Vasuki for the Churning of the Sea of Milk. But here, Mount Meru, the Churn, is no longer a mountain but a Buddhist-inspired temple based on a mountain-temple and a stupa. Jayavarman VII inaugurated his own style of face-towers erected on the Bayon terraces like a forest of enigmatic smiles. In contrast to both the Bayon and the huge Ta Som sanctuary is the unusual small fountain-temple of Neak Pean, a masterpiece of grace and proportion. Sculpture is heavy, almost frozen, and all the heads on these face-towers resemble one another, as though the architect wanted to reproduce in stone the famous miracle of Sravasti, when Buddha rising in the air appeared multiplied 10,000 times.

Style III. Perhaps for aesthetic reasons and with a desire to approach a symbolic truth, the sovereign remodeled his great work by adding a huge circular mass in the center of the Bayon and countless bas-reliefs on its outer gallery walls. Although executed with less delicacy than those of Angkor Vat, they nevertheless fascinate and move us to a greater degree. Here, detail excels the whole and the most symbolic of scenes are amazingly accessible to the visitor. They are rich in common observations: war scenes against the Chams, naval battles, soldiers marching, scenes of palace life pleasantly balanced by picturesque scenes of daily life. Sculpture tends to develop toward an attractive naturalism, and is not lacking in strength. However, again, haste prevented their careful execution. Moreover, decoration became more restrained and we note a strange detail destined to make the sculptor's work easier: the false windows with slender columns are half-closed by a curtain drawn back toward the bottom, revealing only a part of the railings. In monuments executed for Jayavarman VII, this system was very popular with decorators, as it avoided much work. Sculpture in the round produced astonishingly strong yet serene faces, with wonderfully composed volumes. The bodies, however, are treated in a more summary manner. Also new are the creation of adorned Buddhas seated on the coils of the Naga king, Mucilinda, and representations of Hevadrja, a new Buddhist divinity in Khmer iconography. Goldsmiths' work was as luxurious as ever and proved that the art of metalworking was far from becoming decadent.

Style IV. At the close of Jayavarman VII's reign, huge terraces, probably built to support wooden pavilions, were erected in front of the Royal Palace of Angkor Thom. One is sculpted with elephants, the other with mythological scenes. The latter appears to have been remodeled, for excavation has revealed a second façade which is wonderfully sculptured but obscured by the enlargement of the terrace. Here the reliefs are more delicately executed and show greater care. Meanwhile the sovereign finished—rather hastily, it seems—the Bayon reliefs and had others sculpted on the walls of Banteay Chmar. Every temple had votive statues with the sovereign's image or that of his family, all with the same smiling grace. Standing Buddhas imitated from the Dvaravati style (Dvaravati standing Buddhas had been brought from Thailand) began to appear at Angkor, showing the influence of Hinayana Buddhism, which at last completely replaced Mahayana Buddhism in Cambodia.

THE END OF THE KHMERS

Jayavarman VII's effort to erect monuments and recruit armies exhausted the country. After his death not a single important building was created. The people embraced Hinayana Buddhism, which frowned upon excessive pictorial representation. Subsequent sovereigns continued to lead a luxurious life, but none cared to continue the great work undertaken by Jayavarman VII.

Gradually the poorly maintained irrigation system fell into disrepair and weakened the fields. Once deserted, Brahmanic temples began to collapse, conquered by the terrible strength of the tropical jungle.

In the early fourteenth century, Sanskrit in royal inscriptions was abandoned in favor of Pali, used in Theravada Buddhism. The Thai often raided Cambodia, pillaging and destroying as they went. In 1353, 1385, and 1431 they captured, pillaged, and set fire to Angkor, carrying off scholars, writers, artists, and even dancers from the royal palace. Decimated by malaria, Angkor was abandoned and the jungle soon covered the glorious city with verdure and moss.

Art, however, did not disappear. Stone, too difficult to work, was replaced by wood. The temple of Angkor Vat, where monks had settled, preserved several examples of this late Khmer wood sculpture which was much influenced by that of the Thai. At the close of the sixteenth century, the Khmers returned for a short time to Angkor and raised their hopes for a new period of splendor, but they were again driven out by the Thai. The sovereigns fled and settled at Udong—their ancient capital, Lovek, having also been destroyed—where several slender stupas are the sole evidence of their existence. Khmer art had come to an end.

291. CAMBODIA, KOULEN, PRASAT DAMREI KRAP, SOUTH PEDIMENT, *Koulen Style*. The style directly succeeding that of Sambor Prei Kuk, inaugurated by Jayavarman II, did not mark an important step in the field of architecture, unless an exception is made for the first mountain-temple of Ak Yom, west of Angkor. On the tropical, unwholesome Koulen Plateau whose rivers watered Angkor and Roluos, a series of temples was built during Jayavarman II's reign as early as 802 to symbolize his power as the representative of Indra, the supreme lord reigning on Mount Meru. Generally these were simple brick towers, square in plan, whose style was related to that of Champa. Jayavarman II may well have introduced architects and artists from that country to inspire artists from Sambor. According to Philippe Stern, the temple shown here marks the transition from the Cham style of Mi-Son E1 and that of Hoa Lai. Brick was sculpted directly, then coated with stucco. A single door, which is surmounted by a sandstone lintel with a pediment sculpted in the brick mass, leads to the sanctuary. The others have false doors also surmounted by pediments. The lintels show some originality. They are adorned with makaras at the far end, whose mouths disgorge strings of beading or deer, and kalas in the center (reminiscent of Jayavarman II and in imitation of Sambor?). Ornamental foliage includes figures and horsemen. This pediment, which was part of the central tower of a triple sanctuary, has been treated in an obvious Cham style. A central seated figure is sculpted in the brick, but the stucco coating has disappeared. All the abandoned temples of Koulen are covered by vegetation, which will eventually destroy them.

292. CAMBODIA, KOULEN, PRASAT DAMREI KRAP, VISHNU. During the early Koulen style, sculptures still influenced by previous styles bore a supporting arch. About the middle of the period only a club supported the statue. With the exception of legs, always ignored in Khmer art, the body is well observed and still shows a slight hip movement. The austere head—mustache, eyebrows almost touching —is crowned by an undecorated miter. Adorned diadems did not appear until the final phase of the style. Pink sandstone. Height: 4 feet 8 inches. *National Museum, Phnom Penh.*

293. CAMBODIA, ROLUOS, PRAH KOH TEMPLE, VIEW FROM THE EAST, *Prah Koh Style*. Really a funerary monument erected in 879 by Indravarman (877– 89) on the site of his capital, Hariharalaya, in memory of Jayavarman II and of his parents, this monument consists of six towers, three on the east dedicated to Shiva and his mount, after whom the temple is named ("Koh" in Cambodian means "ox"), and three on the west dedicated to his wife, Ghauri. They stand on a single terrace in the center of an enceinte 196 feet square. Many adjacent buildings, including libraries, occupied the spaces between the enceintes; they are now in ruins (see plan).

294. CAMBODIA, ROLUOS, PRAH KOH TEMPLE, SOUTH TOWER OF THE EAST GROUP. The six towers of the group are identical in size, if not in form. The sandstone door frames are mitered. The lintels decorated with foliage have a garland turned up at each end, adorned with a fantastic animal. In the center of the composition is a lion's head. Scattered among the foliage are mounted horses. Restrained, slender octagonal columns frame the door and seem to support the lintel by a mortise joint in imitation of wooden architecture. The very high pediment still shows Cham characteristics but is cut in two horizontally by a molding which seems to support a three-sectioned decoration. The

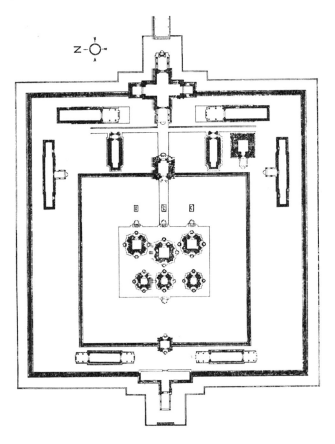

FIG. 29. PLAN OF THE PRAH KOH TEMPLE AT ROLUOS
(*After Glaize*) (1 inch = 110 feet)

façade is embellished with dvarapalas sculpted in sandstone and arranged on each side of the door. The roof is formed of recessed stories with projections of false doors. Flanking these are sandstone metopes representing divinities in niches. The buttresses in the form of reduced prasats have disappeared. Access to the main base is effected by means of a sandstone flight of steps flanked by seated lions.

295. CAMBODIA, ROLUOS, PRAH KOH TEMPLE, STATUE OF AN ASCETIC. Here we see one of the first examples of sculpture in the round without a supporting arch, a style already inaugurated at Koulen. The achievement of such freedom of expression in sculpture is one of the principal merits of Khmer art—which managed to break away from Indian origins in which sculpture was unable to free itself from the mass. Here, a seated ascetic is represented in meditation, knees held up by a belt, eyes closed, with a serene and determined expression. He has a long beard and his hair is pulled into a chignon. The lower parts of the legs are not sculpted and a decorative motif replaces their detail. This statue embellished one of the stories of the Prah Koh sanctuary and acted as an antefix. A pleasant, balanced composition, this marked a step toward the freedom which was to be fully exploited by Khmer

classicism. Sandstone. Height: 2 feet. *National Museum, Phnom Penh.*

296. CAMBODIA, ROLUOS, BAKONG TEMPLE, HEAD OF SHIVA. Prah Koh faces have not only a mustache, but also a scarcely indicated short beard. The diadem encircles a stylized, cylindrical chignon. The neck is encircled by incised lines and the joined eyebrows are in low relief. The entire impression is of a noble, powerful, and restrained art. The body is rather heavy, and the legs roughly blocked out. We recognize Shiva by his third eye and the crescent moon which adorns his chignon. Sandstone. Total height: 6 feet 2¾ inches. *National Museum, Phnom Penh.*

297. CAMBODIA, ROLUOS, BAKONG TEMPLE, EAST VIEW. Bakong, the first mountain-temple worthy of the name, was erected in the center of the city of Hariharalaya and made Indravarman famous. The king was probably tempted to equal, if possible, Borobudur—the wonderful work of the Sailendra sovereigns of Java. The imitation is obvious and inescapable: a series of square terraces, axial flights of steps, corner pavilions, and pediment doors. Consecrated in 881, this sandstone mountain-temple, built in the image of Mount Meru, has five terraces 45 feet high. The lower one forms a square

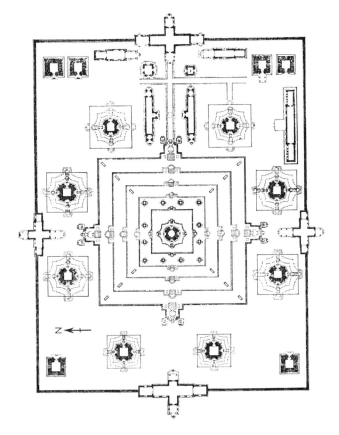

FIG. 30. PLAN OF THE BAKONG TEMPLE AT ROLUOS
(*After Glaize*) (1 inch = 130 feet)

283

about 213 feet per side. The corners of the three lower terraces are adorned with elephants. The fourth supports 12 small sanctuaries. The uppermost terrace has a single sanctuary containing the royal lingam. The one shown in this photograph was rebuilt in the twelfth century, in the style of that of the close of the ninth. The wall of the uppermost terrace was adorned with bas-reliefs (in imitation of Javanese art?) in a continuous frieze of which unfortunately only a few sections remain. At ground level, surrounding the temple, were eight brick towers, now in ruins, whose doors were hewn from single sandstone blocks. The ensemble was surrounded by concentric enceintes (which became the rule during the classic period), walls, and moats, thus completing the temple's identity with Mount Meru (see plan).

298. CAMBODIA, ROLUOS, LOLEI TEMPLE, EAST LINTEL OF THE NORTHWEST TOWER. This lentel from Lolei (893) is decorated with a garland sprouting a head of kala. This garland, which bends, and then curves at the ends (which are treated as scrolls), is characteristic of the late Prah Koh style. Horsemen and small figures emerge from ornamental foliage. Above the lintel, there is a fine frieze carved with alternating ascetics and dancers which seems to support the brick entablature.

Standing not far from the two other temples of the Roluos group, this sanctuary consists of four towers erected on a double terrace built in the center of a now-drained artificial lake. It was dedicated by Yashovarman to the memory of his father, Indravarman. Open to the east, the doors of these towers are hewn from solid blocks of sandstone, like those of Bakong.

299. CAMBODIA, ANGKOR, MOUNTAIN-TEMPLE OF BAKHENG, EAST FLIGHT OF STEPS, *Bakheng Style.* Indravarman's son Yashovarman, who had succeeded his father in 889, transferred his capital somewhat to the west of Hariharalaya where he ran a canal from the Stung Siem Reap in order to create a huge artificial lake (presently known as East Baray and now drained) and to provide irrigation for new cultivable land. In 893, he utilized a natural hill to build his mountain-temple which became the center of a new city, Yashodarapura, surrounded by moats almost 4 miles on each side. This temple imitated the Bakong, but with improvements. Its five squat terraces (250 feet square at the base and 42 feet high) are connected by axial flights of steps (without gates). The terraces contain 60 sandstone pavilions, all alike, and act as a pedestal to a group of five sandstone towers arranged in quincunx which represent the five peaks of Mount Meru. Around the base of this imposing pyramid were 44 towers, also of sandstone; the number of sanctuaries enclosing the central

temple total 108, the sacred lunar number. This temple, therefore, is not only a mythological image but also a calendar (see plan). The decoration is related to the Prah Koh style, although less exuberant, and is adapted to the sandstone medium. The temple walls are decorated with ornamental foliage and friezes sculpted directly in sandstone. The sculpture has become stiff; the curves of the eyebrows are straightened and the silhouettes become thinner and more rigid, lacking

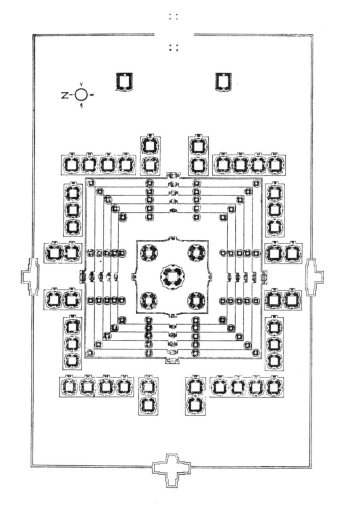

FIG. 31. PLAN OF THE BAKHENG TEMPLE AT ANGKOR
(1 inch = 136 feet)

all sense of litheness. Here, Khmer art stiffens into immobility, as though no developments had taken place since Yashovarman's reign.

300. CAMBODIA, ANGKOR, MOUNTAIN-TEMPLE OF BAKHENG, UPPER TERRACES. The terraces are entirely faced with sandstone, and are reached by flights of steps whose side walls are flanked with seated lions. The sides are sculpted with decorative motifs in which figures emerge from interlacing vegetal forms. From the upper platform there is a view of the forest, beyond which are seen the hills of

Phnom Krom and Phnom Bok, where there are other sanctuaries built by Yashovarman. These temples acted as sentinels guarding the newly founded city of Angkor, the roads to the Great Lake, and the Koulen Plateau. After Roluos had been abandoned, Khmer history was henceforth to center around Phnom Bakheng.

301. CAMBODIA, ANGKOR, MOUNTAIN-TEMPLE OF BAKSEI CHAMKRONG. Standing some 100 feet northeast of the mountain-temple of Bakheng, this simple pyramid, founded by Harshavarman in the first quarter of the tenth century, forms, together with Prasat Kravanh, a transition from the Bakheng style to that of Koh Ker. Of modest dimensions, this hill-temple oriented to the east is only 88 feet square. Its sole tower, built of brick, is 78 feet high. Its four terraces are built of plain laterite, and decoration seems to have been purposely omitted in order to achieve an absolute purity of line. The result—a perfect equilateral pyramid—does not fail to impress one.

302. CAMBODIA, ANGKOR, PRASAT KRAVANH TEMPLE, EAST VIEW. Erected almost at the same time (921) as Baksei Chamkrong, this temple belongs to the same transitional style. Consisting of four brick towers standing on a single platform, it seems to embody such former techniques as a longitudinal plan and brick sculpture. This is not a royal temple but one for important personages. It is dedicated to Shiva and to his wives. This photograph shows workmen of the Conservation Department (directed by Bernard Groslier) restoring the sanctuaries which are in peril of destruction.

303. CAMBODIA, ANGKOR, PRASAT KRAVANH, LAKSHMI TEMPLE. Whereas the group's principal tower is adorned in the interior as well as on the exterior with bas-reliefs devoted to Shiva, this one (on the extreme right of plate 302) is devoted exclusively to representations of Lakshmi. On the wall panels brick has been sculpted in reserve: the noses extending beyond the plane of the wall have been added. The style is hieratic, the lines are strong. These bas-reliefs probably had a coating and were painted. The brick is of excellent quality, the construction carefully executed. Here we can see Lakshmi on the south wall of the sanctuary interior, which is now roofless.

304. CAMBODIA, KOH KER, PRASAT AN, BATTLE OF SUGRIVA AND VALIN. In 921 one of Harshavarman's uncles revolted, took the name Jayavarman IV, and founded his own capital about 60 miles northeast of Angkor, at Koh Ker. Why he chose this site is not known. However, like the other Khmer sovereigns, he felt it was his duty to undertake the irrigation of the land around his mountain-temple.

Built of laterite, this temple was composed of seven stories and was 111 feet high. Jayavarman inaugurated a style in which movement dominated, at least so far as the non-divine personages were concerned. Huge groups of marching garudas and battling monkeys decorated the temple courtyards. One of these groups is shown here. It is a fine composition representing the battle between Sugriva and Valin, the two kings of the hero-monkeys in *The Ramayana*, a theme often used in Khmer art. Sandstone. Height: 5 feet. *National Museum, Phnom Penh.*

305. CAMBODIA, KOH KER, SHIVA'S LEFT HAND. With the exception of the groups of monsters adorning the sides of the sanctuary, nothing but fragments have survived of gigantic statuary in the Koh Ker style. Here we see Shiva's left hand; another hand has also been found, along with several small fragments. Judging from the size of the hand (17 inches), the statue probably measured 13 feet. The palm is gracefully set against the club, the two raised fingers symbolizing the horns of the bull Nandi or those of the gazelle, the god's attributes. The ornamentation of the club imitates that of slender columns. As almost always in early Khmer art, the execution is very delicate. Found in many fragments, this hand has been restored. Sandstone. *National Museum, Phnom Penh.*

306. CAMBODIA, TAKEO, PRASAT NEANG KHMAU, THE BLACK VIRGIN. The sanctuary has been named after this massive statue (now only a torso) of a feminine divinity. The sanctuary consists of brick towers dated 938. The stucco interior is decorated with Vishnuist frescoes which, though in regrettably poor condition, are the only surviving examples of this fragile art. Executed in very fine dark-green sandstone, this statue marks the height of Bakheng statuary at the time when Jayavarman IV ran off to Koh Ker—frontality, stiffness, rich forms, pleated garments, beautiful undulations of the stylized breasts in parallel lines. The patina of this stone has earned it the name the "Black Virgin." For the common people it represented Kali, Shiva's shakti, but we really do not know which divinity it was supposed to represent (Lakshmi?). Total height: 3 feet 6¾ inches.

307. CAMBODIA, ANGKOR, EAST MEBON TEMPLE, AERIAL VIEW. This mountain-temple is seen here from the northeast. Originally built on an island in the center of the East Baray, a huge reservoir-lake about 4 miles long and 1¼ miles wide which utilized the waters of the Stung Siem Reap, oriented east–west lengthwise, the temple now lies in the midst of thick forest vegetation; the water has long since been replaced by trees. The Koh Ker interlude was not destined to last, for the Angkor region was much richer. As a result, no sooner had Rajendravarman become sovereign (944–68) than he returned to Yashodarapura. His first concern was to erect a temple in memory of his ancestors, and this became East Mebon. This mountain-temple has five terraces, the last three placed westward, with the result that the ensemble looks like an irregular pyramid. The two concentric enceintes forming the first two terraces had laterite gates (*gopuras*) which were also used as landing stages. Like Bakheng, the upper terrace holds five towers built of brick and coated. Eight small towers, facing east and containing lingams, stand on the second terrace which has four libraries as well.

The first tier contains several long rooms. The ensemble measures 426 feet square at the base and took six years to build (947–52). (Photograph by Claude Guioneaud.)

308. CAMBODIA, ANGKOR, EAST MEBON TEMPLE, EAST ENTRANCE. Here we can see the laterite steps of the east landing stage, the massive base of the first gopura with the usual lions on the side walls of the staircase, the remains of the long rooms with their attractive balustraded windows, and, finally, at the back, the towers. The latter have walls studded with round holes used to hold the sculptured coating which, in spite of this precaution, has completely disappeared. The temple is in rather a pitiful state, for its materials seem to have been carried off to be employed for other purposes.

309. CAMBODIA, ANGKOR, EAST MEBON TEMPLE, LINTEL OF THE NORTHEAST CHAPEL. This lintel's garland is adorned in the center with a standing lion and two figures at the far ends. Above this fine ornamental motif is a frieze of praying figures deeply incised in the sandstone. This lintel seems to mark the transition from those of the Koh Ker style and the later ones of the Banteay Srei. Octagonal slender columns and mitered door frames support this heavy stone. 947–52.

310. CAMBODIA, ANGKOR, MOUNTAIN-TEMPLE OF PRE RUP, EAST VIEW. Comparable in plan to that of East Mebon, Pre Rup also has its three upper stories placed slightly to the west. The central tower stands 11½ feet above two small square, recessed terraces which are decorated with moldings and adorned with a seated lion on each corner. Access to all the terraces is gained by means of axial staircases. The third terrace has brick towers; the second, long rooms parallel to the sides of the terraces and two libraries whose entrances face west; the lower tier facing east has six brick towers with huge sandstone doorways 12 feet 6 inches by 5 feet 8 inches, with very large unfinished lintels. One of the towers is missing. The three other sides

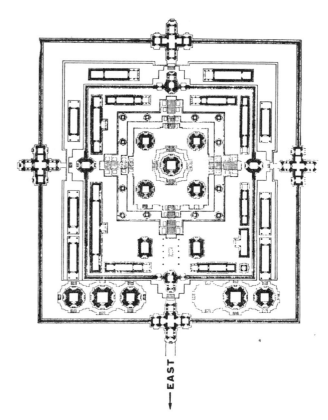

FIG. 32. PLAN OF THE PRE RUP TEMPLE AT ANGKOR (*After Glaize*) (1 inch = 150 feet)

of this first terrace have long rooms. Destined for the deification of its founder, Rajendravarman, this mountain-temple was finished in 961 (see plan).

311. CAMBODIA, ANGKOR, BANTEAY SREI TEMPLE, SOUTHEAST VIEW. This ensemble is one of the most interesting masterpieces of Khmer art. It was erected in 967 by a Brahman of royal blood named Yajnavaraha, a tax collector for Rajendravarman, and then for his successor Jayavarman V (968–1001). The Banteay Srei lacks the impressive dimensions of royal mountain-temples—in fact, it is even *too* small. The main tower is less than 32 feet high; to enter the doors leading to the sanctuaries, the visitor has to lower his head. But this temple has a quality too often lacking, due to Khmer pride: it is very human. The love of right proportions, the concern for careful detail, the quality of the material, and the color of the stone create a work which cannot fail to impress the beholder. We can be affected by Bayon, dazzled by Angkor Vat, filled with admiration at the sight of mountain-temples; but walking along the parvis of Banteay Srei, we are deeply moved. The photograph is incapable of showing, except in detail, the fine arrangement of the buildings, the measured balance of the masses, and the incomparable harmony of the ornamentation. This is an unparalleled work created by a man of great taste and fine sensitivity.

Tribhuvanamahesvara was the name given to this temple, now called Banteay Srei, the "Citadel of the Lord." (Some have translated this name into "Citadel of Women," but although "Srei" means "woman" in Cambodian, the word comes from the Sanskrit "Sri," which means "Lord.") In this shrine, Shiva is represented as a human being and the ideal of humanity. He is no longer the royal Shiva enthroned on top of the mountain Bhadreshvara, but a god who is above all an artist, close to men's hearts, teaching them beauty.

Containing borrowings from earlier styles and also new decorative motifs, Banteay Srei is in a style of its own. The beautiful and very intelligent reconstruction of this ensemble by H. Marchal (former curator of the Angkor group and the École française d'Extrême-Orient) who undertook the work in 1923–25, gives a clear and exact idea of the state of a Khmer temple seen as a complete entity. It consists of three towers, fronted by a room, standing on a single foundation. Eight flights of steps lead to the entrance, the side walls of which contain kneeling figures. Two fine libraries complete the arrangement, surrounded by several successive, concentric enceintes, with gopura doors facing east and west. Between the second and third enceintes are traces of a moat. In this photograph, on the far right, we can see the south extremity of the east gopura of the first enceinte (an extremely flattened gopura) and, on the left, the east part of the south library and, finally, at the far end, the south tower and the central one fronted by the so-called square room. The greatly reduced dimensions of the ensemble made it difficult to obtain a general view in which the elements would be detached (see plan). This temple is situated about 12 miles northeast of the principal Angkor group, at a place once known as Isvarapura. The surrounding forest and quiet setting of this isolated spot add to the charm of the sanctuary.

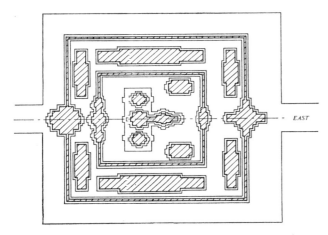

FIG. 33. PLAN OF THE CENTRAL PART OF BANTEAY SREI (*Courtesy Angkor Conservation Department*)

312. CAMBODIA, ANGKOR, BATEAY SREI, EAST GATE OF THE SECOND ENCEINTE. These gates are probably not an innovation. Similar types already existed but, having been built of wood, they have not survived. Here, translated into sandstone, we have an idea of how tenth-century wooden edifices were roofed: double, sloping tiled roofs slightly raised along the edges, and pediments of carved wood probably similar to those found later in Thai art, which seems to have taken most of its architectural inspiration from the Khmers. The acroterium motif in the form of flames perhaps comes from Java; we have already noted that similar ornamentation often surmounted the heads of kalas. The corner antefixes are perhaps also derived from diverging makaras, but stylized to the point where the subject disappears. These improved antefixes, often in the shape of a dragon, were greatly modified in Thai art. Seated lions adorn the main base.

313. CAMBODIA, ANGKOR, BANTEAY SREI, DVARAPALA ON THE SOUTH DOOR OF THE CENTRAL SANCTUARY. At Banteay Srei the coated stucco ornamentation has vanished. The decoration in solid sandstone on the walls and terraces of Bakheng had reached a peak of perfection, and the artists were in full control of the medium. Here, the hard sandstone seems to have been sculpted as though it were merely a piece of wood. This slightly swaying figure holds a spear delicately in one hand and a blue lotus in the other: it is a guard of honor rather than a ferocious warrior. The niche holding the figure is rather like a sentry box. The wonderfully designed ornamentation consists of decorative foliage which springs from the lower legs of a lion. The rampant lions supporting the niche, the moldings, and finally the flying spirits are all exquisitely rendered. Pink and purple sandstone. Height of the dvarapala: about 2 feet 8 inches.

314. CAMBODIA, ANGKOR, BANTEAY SREI, GUARDIAN OF THE EAST FLIGHT OF STEPS OF THE NORTH TOWER. This sculptured garuda (for unknown reasons also called a parrot) is holding a broken sword in its right hand; it forms a happy combination of human and animal elements. Treated in a powerful and restrained manner, its function was to frighten off evil spirits. The bulging eyes and determined pose give it the appearance of a human being wearing a mask. These guardians are placed in pairs on the side walls of the stairway. They represent either garudas, as here, or human yakshas, monkeys, or even lions. Sandstone. Height: approximately 3 feet 4 inches.

315. CAMBODIA, ANGKOR, BANTEAY SREI, CENTRAL SECTION OF THE LINTEL OF THE WEST DOOR OF THE CENTRAL SANCTUARY. In the center of the usual garland we see a small group representing a demon carrying off a woman (Ravana carrying off Sita?) and brandishing a spear. The movement, carried over from the Koh Ker style, is rapid; the pose is a dancing one. Below the group is a head of kala with small bells hanging from its mouth. The horns are curiously carved in the shape of a bull's head. On either side of kala, flamelike leaves emerge from lions' jaws. Balance and dynamism are the principal characteristics of the high reliefs of deeply cut sandstone on the Banteay Srei lintels.

316. CAMBODIA, ANGKOR, BANTEAY SREI, EAST PEDIMENT OF THE SOUTH LIBRARY. Architects and artists who worked at Banteay Srei contributed a new form in the historiated pediment. Here, above a comparatively plain lintel, we see Ravana, the demon-king of Lanka, with 10 heads and 20 arms, trying to shake the mountain on which the god Shiva is enthroned. The god is holding Parvati (or Uma) seated on his knees, to the consternation of spirits, ascetics, and forest animals on the slopes. The mountain (Kailasha) is here treated as mountain-temple architecture and is unrelated to reality. The gable-like triple arches above the scene are pleasantly set above one another, providing empty spaces to rest the eye. Ornamental arcades spring either from monsters disgorging lions, or from nagas.

317. CAMBODIA, ANGKOR, BANTEAY SREI, TEVODA. This delightful figure of a female divinity (shown here life-size) sculpted in sandstone, stands on the west jamb of the north door of the north sanctuary dedicated to Vishnu. Virginal and sensual grace, rich forms, and a lithe attitude make these tevodas (a Cambodian distortion of the Sanskrit word "devata") real masterpieces whose charm is unforgettable. This temple alone justifies the trip to Angkor.

318. CAMBODIA, ANGKOR, MOUNTAIN-TEMPLE OF TA KEO, EAST VIEW, *Kleang Style*. On becoming king, Jayavarman V (968–1001), anxious to continue the tradition established by his predecessors, began to build a superb mountain-temple which he was unable to finish. Yet it reveals the result of all the research undertaken before him to establish the material foundation of the Shivaist kingdom. Consisting of five successive terraces leading to a quintuple sanctuary on the summit, this pyramid, built entirely of sandstone, is colossal at the base (328 by 393 feet). But it differs greatly from all the others because the long rooms on the terraces have been replaced by continuous galleries decorated with false windows on the exterior and adorned with railings and blind windows in the interior. Continuing thus uninterruptedly, the horizontal lines of the terraces (broken only in the center of each side of the pyramid by gopuras on flights of steps) help to give the ensemble a majestic balance.

This is strengthened even more by the central tower which rests on a foundation 19½ feet high. The sanctuaries are square but have projections on each side, thus creating a Greek cross plan; all the doors are practicable and each projection also consists of lateral bays. Only the face of this pyramid has been decorated with carvings, many of which are incomplete.

This unfinished temple is often attributed to one of Jayavarman V's successors, and was probably begun about the close of the tenth century and the beginning of the eleventh. The Kleang style takes its name from two buildings standing on the east part of the central square of Angkor Thom. Now largely in ruins, they were perhaps used as dwellings.

319. CAMBODIA, ANGKOR, PHIMEANAKAS, EAST FLIGHT OF STEPS, *Kleang Style*. A royal pyramid standing in the heart of the Royal Palace, the Phimeanakas (Vimana Akasha or "Celestial Palace") is perhaps the work of Jayavarman V. Bernard Groslier thinks that its foundation dates slightly before that of Ta Keo, which would probably mean from the early reign of Suryavarman I, who founded the Angkor solar dynasty, or one of the two successors of Jayavarman V, thus between 1001 and 1010. This modest pyramid is composed of three high tiers and is built of laterite. The side walls of the axial stairways are adorned with handsome stone lions, while the upper platform is enclosed by a very narrow sandstone gallery 3 feet 4 inches high. On a cruciform foundation in the center of the upper platform there was probably a sanctuary built of light material covered with gold, for the Chinese pilgrim Ch'ou Ta Kouan who saw it called it the "Tower of Gold." Dimensions at the base: 115 by 92 feet.

320. CAMBODIA, ANGKOR, EAST DOOR OF THE ROYAL PALACE, NORTHEAST VIEW, *Kleang Style*. This gopura leading to the Royal Palace has an individual architectural style: a central square tower is flanked by two long rooms (with openings for passages) covered with brick and terminating in gables. Inscriptions dated 1011 attribute it to the early reign of Suryavarman I.

321. CAMBODIA, BATTEMBANG, PRASAT SNUNG SREI, LINTEL OVER THE EAST DOOR. This very handsome lintel representing the Churning of the Sea of Milk seems to mark a transition from the Kleang style to that of the Baphuon. The frieze is related to the ornamentation on the lintel and forms its upper row, while the garland is replaced by the serpent used for turning Mount Meru (here shown in the form of a huge lingam) resting on a turtle. The composition is clear and has great rhythm, and the forms are delicately executed.

This is the first appearance of the illustrated lintel in Khmer art since its abandonment in the eighth century. The form will reach its full development at the beginning of the Bayon style. First half of the eleventh century. Reign of Suryavarman I. Sandstone.

322. CAMBODIA, ANGKOR, THE BAPHUON MOUNTAIN-TEMPLE, NORTHEAST VIEW, *Baphuon Style*. In spite of its ruined state, the mountain-temple of Udayadityavarman II (1050–66) is one of the greatest monuments in the world. This five-story pyramid, 82 feet high and 393 feet square, is built entirely of blocks of laterite and sandstone. Each terrace is surrounded by a gallery interrupted by gopuras and corner towers. The final story has a very high cruciform sanctuary which is reached by four flights of steps. This monument is so ruined that it is difficult to gain an idea of how it originally looked. Khmer architects had so little confidence in stone that they often helped support their stucture by inserting squared tree trunks between the sandstone blocks, as was done here. The wood gradually rotted, leaving empty spaces which caused the monuments to collapse. Thanks to the restoration now being done by Groslier (equivalent to rebuilding the entire pyramid), we realize that Khmer architects, if they were the builders of these structures, were wretched engineers. A combination of wood and stone, heavy roofing supported by nothing but corbeling, unstable rubble filling, ignorance of stone resistance, insufficient water drainage, blocks of stone often badly cut—these are the characteristic building features which caused the deterioration of many Khmer monuments.

323. CAMBODIA, ANGKOR, THE BAPHUON, TOWER ON THE SECOND TERRACE.

324. CAMBODIA, ANGKOR, THE BAPHUON, DECORATION ON THE EAST JAMB OF THE NORTH GOPURA ON THE SECOND TERRACE, *Baphuon Style*. Treated as bas-relief, the Baphuon's decoration is one of the most restrained in Khmer art, since it is restricted to its principal role of emphasizing the architecture. The ornamentation of pilasters consists of decorative foliage containing small figures or animals (seen here at the left). Between the decorative strips are many scenes which create the same delight as small paintings. From top to bottom we see the demon Ravana in his chariot, attacked by Rama and Hanuman; the leader of the monkey army throws Ravana off his chariot; the struggle between Rama and an enemy monkey; and the victorious Rama on his chariot. In addition to these Vishnuist-inspired scenes, there are many small genre scenes on the walls of the Baphuon galleries depicting butter-churning, artisans at work, and carriers at work. Charming, somewhat naïve, but always

eloquent, the décor of the Baphuon is a perfect example of its kind.

325. CAMBODIA, SIEM REAP, PRASAT TRAPEAN, LAKSHMI, *Baphuon Style*. The statuary from which came this graceful statuette is of a refined and almost precious elegance. The bodies in this style are now slim and no longer stiff, and the gestures are both full and lithe. The clothing is treated with restraint. The garments worn by men and women, folded and held by an elaborate belt beneath the navel, rise on the hips. The fold of the pleated skirt tied in a flat knot falls in the form of a fishtail, a typical style of this period (late eleventh century). Green sandstone. Height: 3 feet 2 inches. *National Museum, Phnom Penh*.

326. CAMBODIA, ANGKOR, EAST MEBON, RECLINING VISHNU, *Baphuon Style*. A wonderful work, cast in bronze by the lost-wax process, this head belonged to a reclining Vishnu 13 feet long, which had water flowing from its navel. According to the texts, it stood in the center of an artificial lake on an island in the middle of West Baray (an artificial lake almost 5 miles long and 1 ¼ miles wide holding 39,238,500 cubic yards of water and created by Udayadityavarman to replace East Baray, which had dried up). The bust, head, and arms of this gigantic statue were found at the bottom of an octagonal well in the middle of the island. The eyes, eyebrows, and mustache were once inset with precious metals and enamel which were stolen by looters. This wonderful bronze is an unparalleled work not only for its plastic beauty but also for its casting and dimensions. Mid-eleventh century. Bronze with green patina. Height of the head: 2 feet 1 ¾ inches. *National Museum, Phnom Penh*.

327. THAILAND, PECCHABURI, VAT KAMPANG LENG, PRASAT. In the eleventh century the Khmers, who had conquered almost all of south Siam (Laos) and continued as far as Luangprabang, built many temples and religious establishments in the conquered countries. The style of these monuments is similar to that of contemporaneous works on Khmer territory, although the almost constant use of laterite often limited the decoration which at Pecchaburi, like Phra Prang Sam Yot at Lopburi, was of stucco. Built by Siamese under the direction of Khmer architects, these temples were generally small and many were consecrated to Buddha. The reduced prasats adorning the Khmer prasats (Siamese prangs) are now often replaced by accent pieces representing nagas.

328. THAILAND, LOPBURI, HEAD OF SHIVA. It is difficult to differentiate between the Khmer style known as Lopburi and that used during the same period in Cambodia. Presumably representing

289

Shiva, this head could well have been sculpted by the same artists who worked on the Baphuon at Angkor. Sandstone. Height: 22 ½ inches. *National Museum, Bangkok.*

329. THAILAND, LOPBURI, PHRA PRANG SAM YOT. Consisting of three laterite towers (or prangs), this sanctuary is an imitation of the prasats of Angkor Vat and displays rudimentary decoration. Since laterite hardly lent itself to sculpture, Thai architects had to resort to stucco, a process long abandoned by the Khmers. Accent pieces and mortised garreting of the prang stories are of sandstone. Blocks of laterite are crudely cemented. These monuments probably date from the close of the twelfth century. Thai countries were scattered with other monuments such as the Vat Maha That (Vat Phra Prang) at Sawankalok, Vat Phra Pai Luang at Sukhothai, Vat Sulamani near Phitsanulok, and the Prasat Hin Pimai near Khorat, which was begun by Dharanindravarman I and finished by Jayavarman VII. Khmer art was based on Thai art, but the Khmers created a happy blend of Dvaravati styles with truly Thai (of Lan Na) and Burmese influences.

330. BURMA, MANDALAY, ARAKAN PAGODA, HEAD OF SHIVA. Almost totally unknown, this wonderful head was part of a group of six large bronzes (two male divinities, three lions, and one representing Airavata, Indra's three-headed elephant mount) brought from Mrohaung in 1784 by the son of King Bodawpaya, who vanquished the Arakanese. These statues may have been stolen from Siam by the Burmese, brought to Arakan after a pillaging raid, and finally recovered during the war of 1784. Of the finest quality bronze and in a wonderful style, the statues probably date from the close of the eleventh century. Collars, diadems, eyes, ears, eyebrows, mustaches, and beards were probably inset with jewels and precious metal, which have since been stolen. The Burmese of Mandalay have the highest respect for these statues which are said to heal stomach disorders if the patient's navel is rubbed against them. In fact, constant rubbing has worn a hole into one of them. It is quite regrettable that these beautiful and rare pieces are left in the care of the monks, who mean well, of course, but who scarcely realize the value of these works. Height of this statue: 6 feet 8 inches. Courtyard of the Arakan Pagoda, Mandalay.

331. CAMBODIA, PRAH VIHAR, NORTH ENTRANCE, *Angkor Vat Style.* Lying on a rocky spur in the region of the Donrek mountain chain on the Khmer-Thai frontier, 158 miles north of Kompong Thom, this hard-to-reach temple was founded by Yashovarman about the close of the ninth century and dedicated to Sikhareshvara, "Lord of the Summit" (Shiva). It

was remodeled several times, especially by Suryavarman I about 1018. The present structures probably date from the early Angkor Vat style, that is, toward the close of the eleventh century (Jayavarman VI's reign) and from the time of Suryavarman II (second quarter of the twelfth century). Because of the topography, this temple is oriented to the north. It is surrounded by a single enceinte fronted by five gopuras. Two libraries and two long rooms complete the arrangement which is reached by means of a gigantic ramp and flight of steps 1312 feet long. This photograph was taken on January 4, 1963, the day Cambodia regained possession of the temple which had been held by Thailand since 1954 and returned to the Khmer people by a decision of the International Court of Justice at The Hague on June 15, 1962. (Photograph by the Service of the Cambodian Ministry of Information.)

332. CAMBODIA, BENG MEALEA, GREAT TEMPLE, FALSE DOOR. Jayavarman VI died in 1107 and left the throne to his brothers, but in 1113 his grandnephew seized power. His reign was marked by the construction of an impressive series of monuments which concealed the decadence which already threatened the huge and overambitious Khmer Empire. Twenty-five miles west of Angkor, he erected a great flat temple in memory of his ancestors: Beng Mealea. Vishnuist and Buddhist themes seem to mingle in the decorations, anticipating the great religious syncretism of the following reigns. The central sanctuary, surrounded by concentric galleries, has the same arrangement later used at Angkor Vat. Decoration is the same— historiated pediments and lintels surrounded by nagas, and railings with nagas, all founded on the rich heritage of previous accomplishments. Early twelfth century.

333. CAMBODIA, ANGKOR, THE PRAH PALILAY, CENTRAL TOWER. Of a rather special style, the sanctuary of Prah Palilay is situated a little apart, north of the Royal Palace, and surrounded by large trees. It lies in the center of a laterite enceinte 164 feet square with a gopura with three entrances on the east. The central tower shown here is built on a high, 23-foot, four-tiered base. The chimney-shaped roof has obviously lost its facing stones, which may have been removed at a later date along with other material for re-use elsewhere. Built in the form of a Greek cross, the sanctuary was probably consecrated to Buddha, as evidenced by the handsome pediments (now standing on the ground) containing Buddhist scenes. Early twelfth century. Sandstone.

334. CAMBODIA, ANGKOR, THOMMANON TEMPLE, SOUTH VIEW, *Angkor Vat Style.* This modest temple consists merely of a sanctuary tower fronted on the east by a rectangular room, the whole standing on a platform. This structure is one of the most graceful examples of works built during the reign of Suryavarman II. Surrounded by a now-destroyed 196- by 131-foot enceinte, the temple is only 72 feet long, and possesses only one library, which may be seen at right. It is decorated with ornamental foliage, apsaras, and female figures, all of great delicacy. These features, as well as the beautiful illustrated lintels and pediments (especially those over the doors of the projecting room, depicting scenes from *The Ramayana*) are typical examples of this style dating from the late twelfth century. The temple was probably dedicated to Vishnu. About 65 feet south of this temple, and similar to it, lies the Chausay Tevoda sanctuary. The latter structure was probably designed by the same architect, although its conception is somewhat different, relating it more to the Angkor Vat temple. Overgrown with jungle growth and trees, the Chausay Tevoda is in a bad state of preservation, but it will be restored to its original state once the restoration of the Thommanon is complete.

335. CAMBODIA, ANGKOR THOM, MIRROR SUPPORT, *Angkor Vat Style*. This delightful statuette representing a woman with both arms raised, was probably the support for a round mirror. It is one of the few extant pieces of Khmer bronze art, the rare examples of which reveal great quality and delicacy. The Khmers excelled in casting large statues (many of which are unfortunately lost) and utilitarian objects such as the ends of a palanquin, poles, rings, portable altars, cult objects, or merely domestic items such as this one. Here we find the same balance and symmetry, the same powerful and majestic serenity that characterize the beautiful Khmer temples. Bronze. Height: 12¾ inches. *National Museum, Phnom Penh.*

336. CAMBODIA, ANGKOR, BANTEAY SAMRE TEMPLE, NAGAS ON THE INNER BALUSTRADE, *Angkor Vat Style*. This sanctuary is situated somewhat beyond Angkor on the path leading to the Koulen Plateau, and was entirely rebuilt by M. Glaize and the Ecole française d'Extrême-Orient. It is characterized by its small size and the constriction of its component parts. The temple itself (ignoring the concentric enceintes added at a much later date) is composed of a sandstone tower with four projecting porches. It is fronted on the east by a rectangular room which is enclosed by two libraries. Framing this is a terrace running along the first enceinte wall and surrounding the entire sanctuary. It is adorned with naga balustrades whose multiple heads rise at each corner and at the beginning of each flight of steps. Despite the buildings' constriction, the curious feature is that they are elevated on a very high molded platform, which reaches the top of the

naga-adorned terrace and delimits a very deep courtyard (over 6½ feet) which has no direct access to the exterior other than flights of steps. On visiting this temple, I had the clear impression of finding myself at an island-temple surrounded by water. In fact, it is very possible that this entire inner courtyard was once filled with water, which would justify the naga railings, as this type is also found on the edge of the water level at Srah Srang. The water may have served to both isolate the sanctuary and feed an ablution basin. Banteay Samre's pediment motifs are difficult to interpret, but it may have been a Vishnuist temple, a surmise arising from the position of the sanctuary surrounded by water. Its construction shows great care. For lack of inscription, the style of its decoration dates this temple as contemporaneous with Angkor Vat.

337. CAMBODIA, ANGKOR, TEMPLE OF ANGKOR VAT, AERIAL VIEW FROM THE SOUTHEAST. Angkor Vat is the perfect and logical result of the mountain-temple. It was erected about the middle of the twelfth century by King Suryavarman II Paravishnuloka (1113–52), and is the greatest of all Khmer constructions. Its perfectly symmetrical plan, concentric galleried enceintes, and corner towers enclosing the meru of its very high sanctuary, created an architectural masterpiece of the final flowering of Khmer art. This temple is oriented to the west, but whether this was because its entrance was meant to face the road leading to Angkor Thom or because it was intended to indicate more clearly its funerary purpose is difficult to say. The huge enceinte surrounded by moats (shown in the upper part of the photograph) almost 4 miles long, with inner parapets entirely fitted with tiers, probably surrounded the palace of Suryavarman II, artificial lakes, and many light dwellings which have since disappeared. In modern times a Buddhist temple was installed here among trees (upper right). The laterite west gate of the first enceinte (almost 2½ miles long and reached by a sandstone and laterite walk 720 feet long bordered by sandstone nagas and giants) is separated from the temple entrance by a paved avenue leading to a cruciform platform facing the main door. The west gopura of the enceinte is an exact reproduction of the façade of the temple itself. The effect in perspective is striking. (Photograph by Claude Guioneaud.)

338. CAMBODIA, ANGKOR, TEMPLE OF ANGKOR VAT, WEST ENTRANCE. The platform (A in fig. 34), fronted by two artificial lakes (B in fig. 34), shown here in full view, is adorned with lions and fine naga railings. It leads to the raised platform which forms the main foundation of the temple. Entrance is gained by means of a porch with three superimposed pediments situated in the center of a long

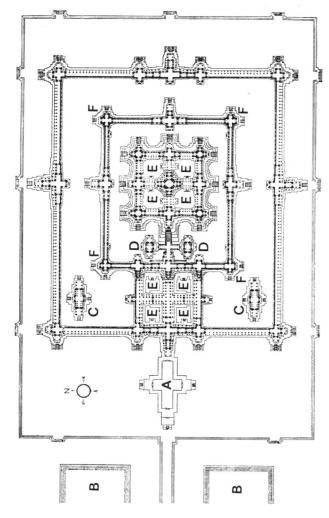

FIG. 34. PLAN OF THE CENTRAL PART OF THE
TEMPLE OF ANGKOR VAT
(*After Glaize*) (1 inch = 270 feet)

cross with the first and thus forming a cruciform, columned room. With the galleries, this room is divided into four sunken courtyards which are reached only by flights of steps (E, at lower part of fig. 34). As at Banteay Samre, I had the impression that these courtyards were once filled with water and formed artificial lakes. Two libraries occupy the northwest and southwest corners of this terrace (C in fig. 34). Also enclosed by galleries (open toward the interior this time), the second terrace is adorned with prasat towers on each corner (F in fig. 34) and pavilions on the axes, the only openings leading to the first terrace below. Two small library buildings (D in fig. 34) are joined by a raised passage leading to the foot of the west axial flight of steps, then up to the final terrace which is completely occupied by the five sanctuary towers. The public probably had access only to the first terrace, where bas-reliefs, statues, and galleries served to divert and instruct. The second terrace was reserved for priests and officiants. Finally, the last terrace formed the holy of holies. This is a high, massive block, 196 feet square and 42 feet high, supporting five towers the highest of which—that in the center, raised more than the others—stands 213 feet above the walks. The corner towers are connected by galleries, and their axial pavilions are connected with the central tower by raised covered walks delimiting four courtyards which were also probably filled with water (E in fig. 34), like the artificial lakes of the four sunken courtyards of the first terrace. This arrangement is logical if we remember that this temple was dedicated to Vishnu, Lord of the World, who resided in the center of the primordial ocean. The four sides of this last story are all similar, with only the flight of steps at a 45-degree angle leading to the west axial pavilion being featured more importantly.

339. CAMBODIA, ANGKOR, TEMPLE OF ANGKOR VAT, COLUMN. This type of column is a rare element in Khmer art, where slender columns on entrance doors, pilasters, and railings are more common. In the galleries of Angkor Vat, the pillars are square and the columns are of a special type: base and capital are almost similar, delimiting a round shaft which is fluted and plainly decorated with floral motifs above and below. These monolithic columns are about 9½ feet high and support certain corners of the gallery roofs, which are covered with corbeled slabs of sandstone sculpted in imitation of tile. The galleries are pierced with openings for seven balustrades of polished sandstone often having vertical grooves. The square pillars and spaces between the windows are decorated with devatas (tevodas) and apsaras.

340. CAMBODIA, ANGKOR, TEMPLE OF ANGKOR VAT, BAS-RELIEFS OF THE WEST WING OF THE SOUTH

room with stepped roofs—the beginning of the enclosed gallery open on the exterior and entirely embellished with beautifully executed bas-reliefs. The central porch is adorned with lateral doors surmounted by half pediments (the long room of the Phnom Chisor temple has the same arrangement) forming a flying buttress. The tiered arrangement of the roofs, their gradual descent toward the galleries which extend to the right and left, give a horizontality to the ensemble which leads the eye automatically toward the sanctuary towers. There is not the slightest error of taste in this severe alignment and majestic design, which by its very mass seems to defy time and man. The general plan (fig. 34) follows that used by former Khmer sovereigns. The center of the monument is slightly to the east. This is a three-story pyramid which is entirely surrounded by a gallery adorned with bas-reliefs. The first terrace communicates with the base of the second, on the west, by means of a triple covered passage leading to the entrances whose galleries are connected by an open walk, forming a

GALLERY. The stone for the inner walls of the galleries was selected from a fine-grade sandstone, and the slabs were set in place with great precision. More than 2624 feet of wall were faced in this fashion and the reliefs were sculpted on its 9½-foot-high surface. The character or style of the execution is more or less evidenced by the varied talents of the artists who created the scenes represented. These are carved on the walls of the galleries that lie between the corner pavilions and the pavilions on the axes. Each panel is either 3 feet 4 inches, 2 feet 4 inches, or 2 feet 1¼ inches wide. Scenes succeed one another without interruption, changes in subject-matter or décor being indicated by flat bands or rows which are superposed, and are often connected by shapes and designs on an inclined plane. The sculpture is rendered in very low relief in a kind of accentuated engraving, and many details (embroidery, clothing, etc.) merely indicated by incised lines. Everything that would seem impossible or uncongenial to express in the medium of stone sculpture—such as airy veils floating on the breeze, poses or attitudes, and numerous accessories and details—is here conceived in a design that often rises to very high quality. Detailed examination of these reliefs provides a harvest of information regarding twelfth-century Khmer dress, vestments, weapons, ornamentation, and décor. The incidents depicted are either mythological (the battle of the Pandavas and Kauravas), legendary (scenes from *The Mahabharata* and Vishnu's heroic exploits), historic (episodes glorifying the reign and the armies of Suryavarman II and of his Siamese cohorts), or genre and domestic scenes. The slabs on which they are sculpted are often no more than ½ inch thick and it is logical to believe they were colored and heightened with gold. In this illustration we see parading Khmer archers wearing curious, crested helmets adorned with the heads of animals. They are wearing light jerkins embroidered with small flowers and filmy flowing skirts, and are armed with different types of bows and arrows. On the far left we see a javelin thrower holding a round shield. These soldiers marching in perfect order seem to belong to a well-disciplined army. Gray-black sandstone.

341. CAMBODIA, ANGKOR, TEMPLE OF ANGKOR VAT, AN APSARA. A recurrent yet always varied motif at Angkor Vat, the apsaras depicted on the temple are always different, fresh, and new, rivaling one another in charm, jeweled sumptuousness, and grace. They cannot all be described here—nor can all the other elements which ornament this temple. The lively figure shown here dances for us on one of the library walls. She is wearing an elaborate headdress and flourishes a Chinese-like fan in one hand while the other hand sweeps back one of her tresses which has become unwound in the heat of the dance. These apsaras are divine creatures, born of the dreams of Khmer sculptors. Numberless and impersonal, they dance eternally on the temple walls to the joy of the beholder. Grace personified, they are the highest expression of femininity ever conceived by the human mind. Gray sandstone.

342. CAMBODIA, ANGKOR, TEMPLE OF ANGKOR VAT, AN APSARA. With their wealth of rich costumes and jewels, delicate movements, and perfect female bodies, the apsaras also reveal a discreet sensuality belonging only to the kingdom of the gods. Dark-gray sandstone.

343. CAMBODIA, ANGKOR, MONASTERY TEMPLE OF BANTEAY KDEI, FALSE WINDOW, *Bayon Style*. After being held as vassals by the Khmers, the Chams regained their freedom in 1177. At the head of an imposing fleet, they sailed up the Mekong, crossed the Great Lake, and took Angkor by surprise, setting fire to the buildings and pillaging everything. They slew the usurper king Tribhuvanaditya, who seized the throne in 1165 from the legitimate sovereign Yashovarman II, successor to the Buddhist king Dharanindravarman II, and cousin of the sovereign who built Angkor Vat. The great catastrophe weakened the country, which seemed unable to rise again. But one of Dharanindravarman's sons, who was born around 1125, fought a naval battle against the Chams, emerged victorious, liberated the country, and in 1181 proclaimed himself King Jayavarman VII. Like his father, the prince was Buddhist. He rebuilt Angkor from its ruins and, as better protection, surrounded the city with walls and moats. During his reign an unbelievable number of monuments, temples, religious establishments, roads, and hospitals were built, all inspired by Buddhism. No sovereign equaled this number of buildings, the quality of which, however, was not of the highest. Their style followed that of Angkor Vat with little improvement, at least in the beginning. A few clever innovations were introduced such as false windows two-thirds closed by a curtain with incised ornamentation. The design of the temples was square, always included concentric galleries, and was enlarged by the addition of numerous other galleries plus additional pavilions used to house the monks. Buddhist statues replaced the Brahmanic images. But the décor remained much the same as in the temples of the previous style.

344. CAMBODIA, ANGKOR, BANTEAY KDEI, HEVADJRA. Of Tibetan influence, this wonderful statuette represents a divinity of the Mahayana pantheon, a Buddhist version of the Brahmanic god, Shiva Nataraja. Like the latter, Hevadjra is dancing on a human body. But this divinity has eight heads, each adorned with a frontal eye, and sixteen arms. The photograph does not show its four legs which have been tightly joined side by side, and there are generally two corpses beneath the four legs of this type of divinity. The balance is harmonious and the pose bold and aggressive. A part of the garment reinforces the single supporting foot. Late twelfth century. Bronze. Height: 12 inches. *National Museum, Phnom Penh.*

345. CAMBODIA, ANGKOR, TA PROHM TEMPLE, SMALL SANCTUARY TO THE EAST, *Bayon I Style.* Erected in 1186, this sanctuary is now mostly in ruins and so overgrown by vegetation that it is difficult to guess at its original plan. But we can already perceive the defects which were to be the attributes of the Bayon styles. Somewhat spared from the encroaching jungle, this small sanctuary stands in one of the courtyards east of the main temple. Historiated pediments and lintels, small false windows with half-railings (a time-saving operation), a very high five-story roof, engaged slender columns on the door jambs, and all surfaces covered with elaborate ornamentation—these are the chief characteristics of the temples of this period, whose unusual plans add to their complexity. According to writings, this monastery had 2740 priests, 18 high priests, and 2232 assistants, including 615 dancing girls.

346. CAMBODIA, ANGKOR, PRA KHAN TEMPLE, COLUMNED LIBRARY, *Bayon I Style,* The Pra Khan Temple is one of the most spacious of the Angkor group and its plan is also one of the most complex. Surrounded by a high laterite enceinte almost 2 miles in circumference, and by a wide moat once filled with water and crossed by four walks bordered by nagas and giants, the temple consists of many buildings. Some of them, like this library which is raised on round columns and which does not have a single flight of stone steps, differ from the usual Khmer design, many aspects of which were quite limited. A wooden flight of steps led to the first story of this (restored) building. Despite its being designated a library, the structure's actual function remains a mystery. The pillars of the upper story are ornamented with the usual decorations along with the addition of apsaras and dancers, and the lower columns, formed of superposed stone blocks, are undecorated.

347. CAMBODIA, ANGKOR, PRA KHAN TEMPLE, GARUDA ON THE NORTH WALL, *Bayon I Style.* On the outer façade of the temple's laterite walls are huge sandstone garudas supporting a niche which, like those found at the base of the walls, probably contained a Buddha. The style is heavy and conventional. Nagas with five heads emerge from either side of this giant. Height: 10 feet.

348. CAMBODIA, ANGKOR, PRA KHAN TEMPLE, GIANT HOLDING A NAGA, *Bayon II Style.* Forming the end of a railing along a walk, this giant demon with many heads and arms is supporting a naga with seven wonderfully treated lion-like heads. Sandstone. Total height: about 10 feet.

349. CAMBODIA, ANGKOR, BANTEAY KDEI TEMPLE, EAST GOPURA, *Bayon II Style.* Added to the temple itself about the close of the twelfth century, this gopura (enceinte gate) is a typical example of the style invented by Jayavarman VII and known as a face-tower. Some believe this to be the image of both the sovereign and the bodhisattva Lokeshvara, and it is repeated, not only on the sanctuary of the Bayon, but on the gates of Angkor Thom as well. The blocks are poorly cut, the corners and alignments irregular, the décor crude. Only the heads show a certain care, but they are far from attaining the expressivity later found at the Bayon itself.

350. CAMBODIA, ANGKOR, NEAK PEAN ARTIFICAL LAKE, *Bayon II Style.* Not far from Pra Khan and some of its outbuildings is a 210-foot-square artificial lake, abutted by four secondary ones connected to the main lake by means of small, delicately adorned pavilions. The center of the main lake contains a round sandstone island, 45 feet in diameter, on which has been built a very small temple dedicated to Lokeshvara. The margins of the lake and central island are sculpted in tiers. Four sculptural groups (only the east one has been restored) seem to emerge from the water at the four cardinal points of the island. Cruciform in plan, the temple itself consists of a single tower. It stands on a lotus-shaped foundation which seems to emerge from the water. Wound around the base of the small island are two enormous serpents. During the dry season these artificial lakes are without water. The arrangement of this temple recalls one dedicated to Vishnu, which has a similar serpent wound around its base—a characteristic of the religious syncretism of the period. (Photograph by Claude Guioneaud.)

351. CAMBODIA, ANGKOR, NEAK PEAN ARTIFICIAL LAKE, NORTH PAVILION, *Bayon II Style.* The four pavilions enabled the water from the central lake to feed the smaller lakes. This was accomplished by means of outlets (here, in the form of an elephant's head) at the bases of the chapels of the four subsidiary lakes. Neak Pean water was famous for its miraculous power. It is easy to imagine the crowd of worshipers who came here during Angkor's great period to dip their bodies in the water of this Khmer "Lourdes." The pediment bas-reliefs show the ill and the lame plunging into the water and, once healed, coming to thank the bodhisattva Lokeshvara.

352. CAMBODIA, ANGKOR, NEAK PEAN TEMPLE, DECORATION OF THE NORTH FALSE WINDOW, *Bayon II*

Style. This temple boasts fine decorations, and was rebuilt in 1935 by M. Glaize, then Curator of Angkor. In this detail Lokeshvara is shown standing on a lotus and holding serpents. Celestial beings seem to be playing with serpent-garlands. Above this false window, a pediment bears dancing girls, and above them is a horseman (?) who is sheltered by a parasol. Although hieratic and somewhat heavy, this style is not lacking in quality. Sandstone.

353. CAMBODIA, ANGKOR THOM, SOUTH GATE, CAUSE-WAY BORDERED BY DEMONS AND DEVAS. Crossing the huge moats which separate the fields from the city walls of Angkor Thom, the causeways leading to the city gates (towers decorated with faces) are bordered by huge railings consisting of giants holding a naga on their knees. On one side are devas, on the other asuras (demons). The theme depicted is the Churning of the Sea of Milk, divided here into two parts, and the pivotal mountain is taken as being at the center of Jayavarman's city; his mountain-temple, the Bayon. Here a Brahmanic legend has been employed for Buddhist purposes— an artistic-religious synthesis that enabled the formula to triumph. Although conceived in a heavy, inexpressive style, these sandstone giants create a powerful effect, and their repetition lends a note of grandeur. Although they had previously collapsed, these statues have since been restored by the Ecole française d'Extrême-Orient and the Conservation Department of Angkor.

354. CAMBODIA, ANGKOR THOM, SOUTH VIEW OF THE BAYON. A Buddhist temple, the Bayon lies at the geometrical center of the city of Angkor Thom, and the latter's walls serve as the temple's outer enceinte. The monument is an unparalleled creation, not only for its architectural conception, but also for its strange towers. Square in plan and surrounded by galleries decorated with bas-reliefs as at Angkor Vat, the center of the structure was subsequently filled in by the addition of a high terrace which brought the floor of the third terrace up to the roof level of the second gallery. An oval tower was built in the center of the mass, transforming the sanctuary into a mountain-temple. This tower is the only one of its kind in Khmer art, and its base is hollowed out into 13 very deep chapels. The main cella is placed in the center of the tower, with its entrance facing east. It is undecorated and shelters an image of Buddha seated on the coils of the Naga king, Mucilinda. The chapels, as well as the corner prasats, the prasats of the axial chapels, and those of the gopuras, are all surmounted by towers, each of which are decorated by four enormous faces oriented to the cardinal points. Since this monument is still largely in ruins and no detailed study of it is possible, the actual number of these face-

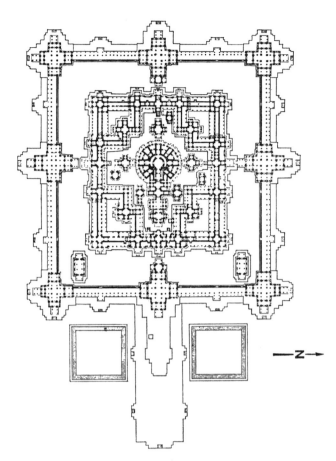

FIG. 35. PLAN OF THE BAYON AT ANGKOR THOM
(*After Glaize*) (1 inch = 164 feet)

towers has yet to be ascertained. However, the plan appears to be relatively uncomplicated (fig. 35). The first enceinte contains a gallery and is adorned with cruciform pavilions at each corner and on each axis. The pavilions open onto a paved terrace containing two libraries at both corners of its east end. The terrace contains another enceinte, galleried, adorned with five towers on each side, and courtyards placed within its corners. This ensemble delimits a cruciform space that is entirely filled in to roof height by a terrace. This final story or level is crowned by the central tower rising 150 feet above the ground and surrounded by subsidiary chapels. (Photograph by Claude Guioneaud.)

355. CAMBODIA, ANGKOR THOM, THE BAYON, SIDE VIEW FROM THE SOUTH. At first sight the temple appears a chaotic ruin. Wind, rain, and especially the astonishingly bad building methods have metamorphosed its original design into wreckage. Whereas at Angkor Vat the general view was carefully designed, the same does not apply here; but the successive piling up of galleries and towers really creates the image of a mountain. We still do not know whether the main tower was adorned with faces or treated merely as a prasat. On the left, we can see the bas-reliefs of the first gallery whose roof has collapsed, the main base adorned with lions and naga railings, and the towers—almost all of which have lost their upper parts, probably a lotus surmounted by a bronze motif (*trisula*) placed on top of a conical stone. The bases of the pillars are adorned with tevodas and dancing groups. Surrounded by the jungle and often bathed in an atmosphere heavy with mists, the temple looms like a ghostly skeleton. We must cross the main base, look at the bas-reliefs, and examine the towers in order to comprehend fully and appreciate the true beauty of this building—a masterpiece created by a king who, in a last supreme effort, revived Khmer grandeur. But this outstanding achievement exhausted the country, leaving it an easy prey to the armies of the Thai which threatened from the west.

356. CAMBODIA, ANGKOR THOM, THE BAYON, FACE-TOWER. The somewhat haughty smile that greets the visitor remains one of the most astonishing creations of Khmer artists who, with rare mastery, treated the colossal with the same ease that they expended on carving small, detailed decorations. Accent pieces and garudas decorate the corner towers between the masks rising above detailed pediments.

357. CAMBODIA, ANGKOR THOM, THE BAYON, FACE-TOWERS. By their number and size (from 5 feet 10 inches to 8 feet 4 inches high), the faces on these towers form a landscape repeated a thousand times, ever different, and sometimes hallucinatory, according to the angle from which they are seen. Although poorly set in place, the sandstone blocks are remarkably cut. Endlessly scanning the horizon, these smiling faces of Lokeshvara appear to be commanding that a golden age descend upon the world.

358. CAMBODIA, ANGKOR THOM, THE BAYON, PEDIMENT HIDDEN BY THE ADDED TERRACE. Many of the historiated pediments representing Lokeshvara were destroyed during the Shivaist reaction that followed the reign of Jayavarman VII. Hidden by the addition of the final terrace, a few of these have survived intact and were revealed during the work of excavation. Here we see the detail of one of them: apsaras or tevodas are sitting beneath parasols and are fanning a figure seated on a folding stool and pointing to Lokeshvara (at left, and not shown in the photograph). Stereotyped faces, rather clumsy poses, and sketchily treated legs are witness to the haste in which the Bayon was built.

359. CAMBODIA, ANGKOR THOM, THE BAYON, APSARAS. Almost all the pillars are adorned with apsaras, either singly or in groups of two or three, dancing on lotus flowers. Many of these bas-reliefs are merely sketched in with incised lines and left

uncompleted. Others, like this one, reveal a combination of bas-relief and incision. Art is absent here since there is really no creation but only a tiresome repetition of movements belonging to drawing rather than to sculpture.

360. CAMBODIA, ANGKOR THOM, THE BAYON, FIRST EAST GALLERY, NORTH WING, BAS-RELIEF, *Bayon III Style*. The bas-reliefs decorating the galleries of the Bayon are more animated and less rigid than those at Angkor Vat. Although certain parts executed at a later date are by mediocre artists, they nevertheless offer a wealth of information about events that took place during the reign of Jayavarman VII, and about the manners and customs of the period. Sculpture is everywhere animated by a concern for realism, not only in the correctly rendered and well-observed poses of the figures, but in the battle detail as well. Here we see a battle scene between Khmer warriors and Cham soldiers. Bareheaded, and wearing either heavy belts made of rope or short embroidered jackets, the Khmers are protecting themselves with small round shields held in their left hands. The Chams wear curious helmets shaped like reversed flowers, and protect themselves with long shields slipped through their arms. Behind the group is an elephant ridden by Chams; one of the warriors is about to be killed by an arrow aimed at his forehead, and the other is shielding himself from a volley of arrows. Fluttering in the wind are the standards of both armies. Details of weapons, clothing, elephant harness and trappings, and standards, are well defined. The treatment of bodies recalls Egyptian art—hips in profile and frontal torsos. All in all, this is a handsome piece of sculpture.

361. CAMBODIA, KOMPONG SVAY, PRA KHAN, PRESUMED HEAD OF JAYAVARMAN VII. One of the finest pieces of sculpture in all Khmer art, this head in the Bayon style is the work of a very talented artist. Although idealized, it probably represents King Jayavarman VII. G. Coedes, who has made a special study of this sovereign, says, "Physically he was rather corpulent, and his hair was swept to the top of the head into a small chignon." A portrait rather than a divine image, this typically Khmer head is no longer treated with an eye to the forceful lines in the face (those of the eyebrows, the nose, the angles of the jaw) but to volumes, so masterfully interpreted that light alone gives living form to this very coherent mass. No line is used to emphasize the delicate sweep of the eyebrows and mustache. Behind the thin, lowered eyelids we can sense the presence of the eyeballs. The lips with their delicately curved outlines seem to be flesh and blood. The powerful, clear forehead leads naturally into the hair, which the sculptor has purposely treated in fine, incised lines so that its mass does not interrupt the continuous flow of forms in the face, whose serenity, sweetness, and power combine in creating one of the finest expressions of human genius. Late twelfth century (?). Gray sandstone. Height: 16 inches. *National Museum, Phnom Penh.*

362. CAMBODIA, ANGKOR THOM, THE BAYON, EAST WING OF THE SOUTH GALLERY, DETAIL OF A BAS-RELIEF. According to the rules of Khmer perspective, the figures nearest the spectator are represented below and those farthest away, above. Their size does not depend upon their distance but upon their social importance. In the upper part of this detail a boat (only the keel is shown here) glides along a river filled with fish and crocodiles. On the near bank (and therefore at the bottom of the scene) scenes of everyday life follow one another without transition; these are similar to those which may be seen in present-day Cambodia. Sheltered by a light, porch-like structure, a woman is selling fish. In front of her a couple are seated with their arms tenderly entwined. They seem to be engaged in a transaction with a jewel merchant. At right, a group of men is excitedly watching a cock fight. Well-observed, correct poses, humorous details, naturalistic rendering of the fish, combine to give this cross section of Khmer life an authentically lifelike quality that reveals more about thirteenth-century Angkor than any long text could possibly give.

363. CAMBODIA, KOMPONG SVAY, PRA KHAN, CARYATID BUDDHA, *Late Style.* This sandstone statue of Buddha in an unusual position was probably used to decorate a foundation. It has the characteristics of the Bayon style, but the treatment is rather clumsy. However, the block is well-balanced, the pose strong, the masses solid. Although not a masterpiece, this sculpture clearly shows the tendencies of late Bayon art. A likely date is the close of the thirteenth century. Sandstone. Height: 3 feet 2¾ inches. *National Museum, Phnom Penh.*

364. CAMBODIA, ANGKOR THOM, THE TERRACE OF THE LEPER KING, BAS-RELIEF, *Bayon IV Style.* Cleared by the restoration work done on the terrace, these sculptures can now be seen in their original aspect. Aligned in several rows, devatas and demons seem to form a supramundane world around a horse with five heads, the zoomorphic manifestation of Avalokiteshvara. These bas-reliefs have been very carefully executed. The style of the faces is liberated from the conventional style of Bayon art and seems to return to such former characteristics as the dividing line between the eyebrows and the diadem. Sandstone.

365. CAMBODIA, BANTEAY CHMAR, EAST GATE, *Bayon IV Style.* This huge temple standing in the heart of the scrublands on the Thai-Khmer border, more than 37 miles north of Sisophon, was built during the last years of the reign of Jayavarman VII and was used as both a citadel and a royal city. Square in plan, surrounded by galleries containing huge bas-reliefs relating the king's life, the temple was hastily constructed and then abandoned to the forest. Badly cut sandstone, poor foundations, crude bas-reliefs—all indicate decadence. This was one of the last great Khmer temples.

366. CAMBODIA, ANGKOR THOM, VIEW OF THE TERRACES, *Bayon IV Style.* Built of sandstone and 26 feet high, the terraces of Angkor were probably erected to support light pavilions. Bordered by naga railings, they were situated west of a large square where parades took place. The sides are decorated with rather good bas-reliefs, and the corners have either garudas or elephants with three trunks. The Terrace of the Leper King (so called because of a statue which was thought to be that of Jayavarman VII, who had leprosy in his youth and was later miraculously healed) was modified by a filling which long hid all these bas-reliefs on the sides of the terrace. The Terrace of the Elephants was much longer (105 feet) and probably formed the foundation of a long large room "decorated with mirrors," according to the description by Chou Ta Kuan. Its sides are decorated with bas-reliefs of elephants. Here we can see the northern part of this terrace, decorated with bas-reliefs which seem to depict games (chariot races, horse races, boxing contests). At the far end of the square, among the trees, we see the outlines of 6 of the 12 laterite towers known as Prasat Suor Prat. They are partly unfinished and their purpose is unclear; they may have been used as temples dedicated to the planets.

367. CAMBODIA, ANGKOR, TEMPLE OF ANGKOR VAT, TORSO OF BUDDHA. This richly bedecked Buddha, found in the ruins of the temple of Angkor Vat that was occupied by Buddhist monks, has many affinities with Thai art—especially in the decoration. Frontality, stiffness of gesture, and ornamental excess indicate a late date, perhaps fifteenth century. Lacquered and gilded sandstone. Height: 2 feet ½ inch. *Conservation Storehouse, Siem Reap.*

368. CAMBODIA, ANGKOR, BEJEWELED WORSHIPER. This wonderful lacquered and polychromed wood sculpture (only the head is shown) happily combines Thai decorative elements (*mukuta*, or choker) with Khmer sculpture in the round. About the fifteenth century, when this sculpture was made, artists seem to have turned away from sandstone, then rare at Angkor, and were satisfied with the almost mechanical repetition of standard types. This work, therefore, is rather surprising for its litheness and sweet and humble attitude, recalling the splendor of Khmer art. Its perfect expression and idealization give intense inner life to this late work which is the final example of an art that now belongs to the past (fifteenth century?). Wood with traces of polychrome. Life-size. Height: 3 feet ¹/₂ inch. *National Museum, Phnom Penh.*

369. CAMBODIA, UDONG, STUPAS OF THE TOMBS OF THE LAST KHMER KINGS. After definitely abandoning Angkor after it had fallen into the hands of the Thai, the kings of Cambodia moved from capital to capital until they settled at Phnom Penh in the sixteenth century. By this time they were no longer the great builders they had been. Here at Udong, near one of their cities and on the hill where they were buried, are three Thai stupas, one of which bears a weak finial adorned with four faces, the sole reminder of the prodigious Khmer past. A time of troubles followed this period and Khmer art was forgotten.

292

293

294

295

301

302

305

304

307

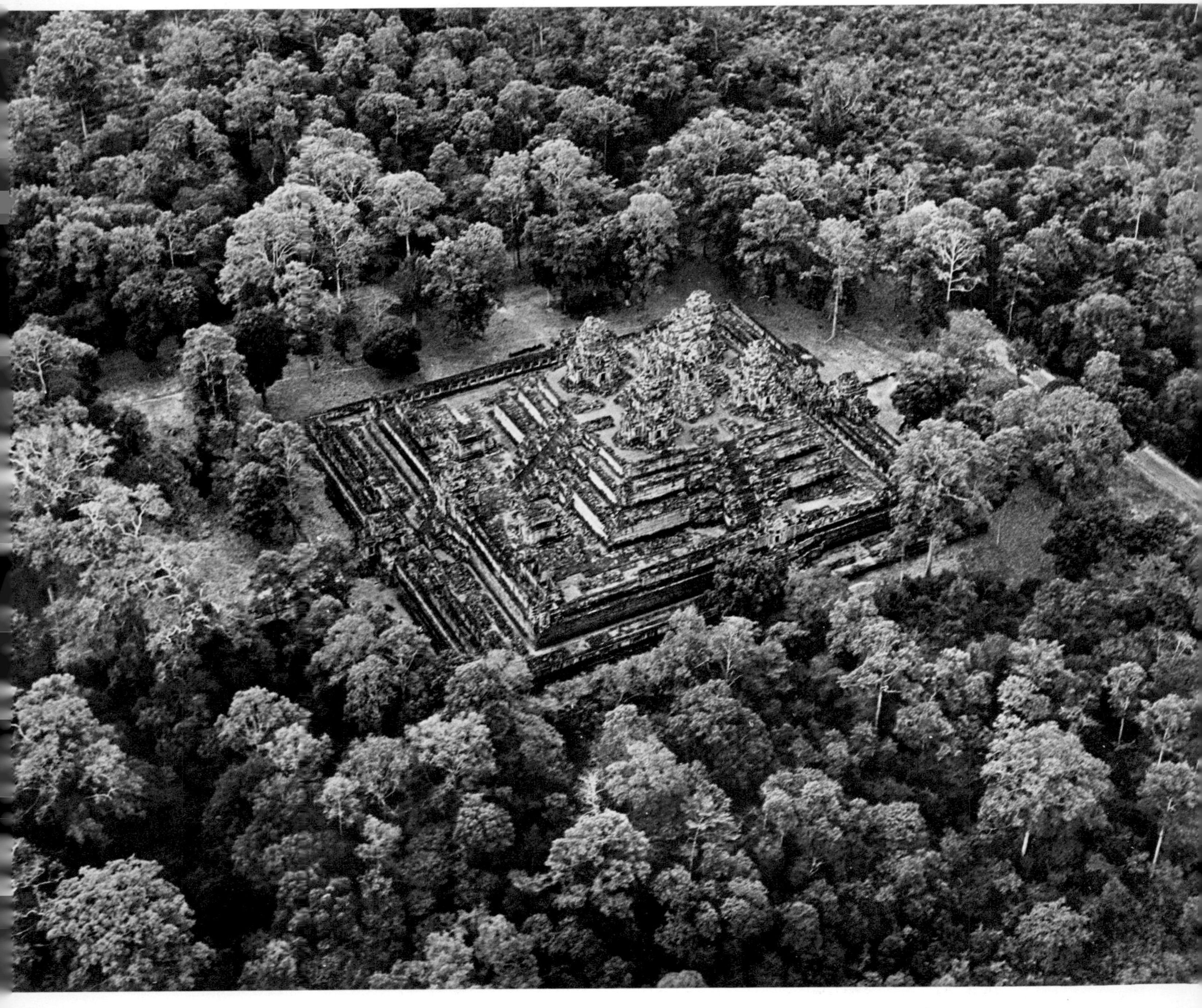

308

309

312   313

315   316

322   323

324

325

331

332

333

334

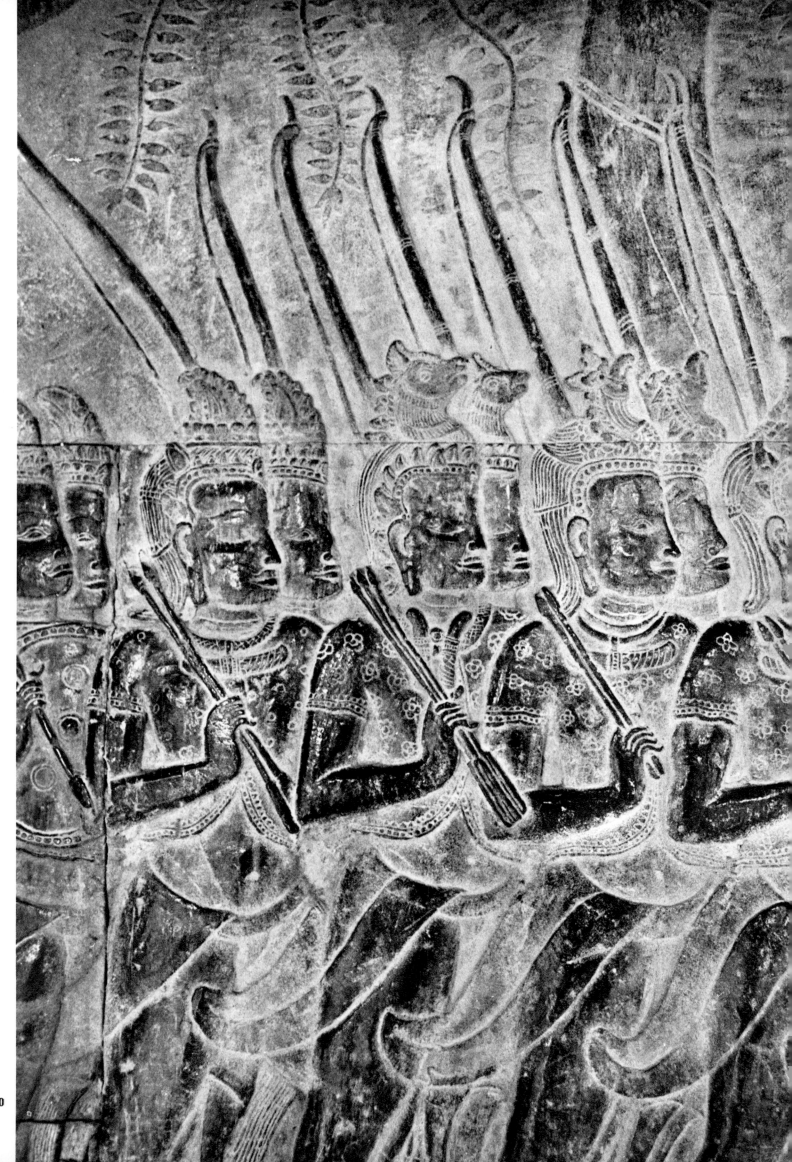

344   345

346   347

348   349

350

351

352

359

360

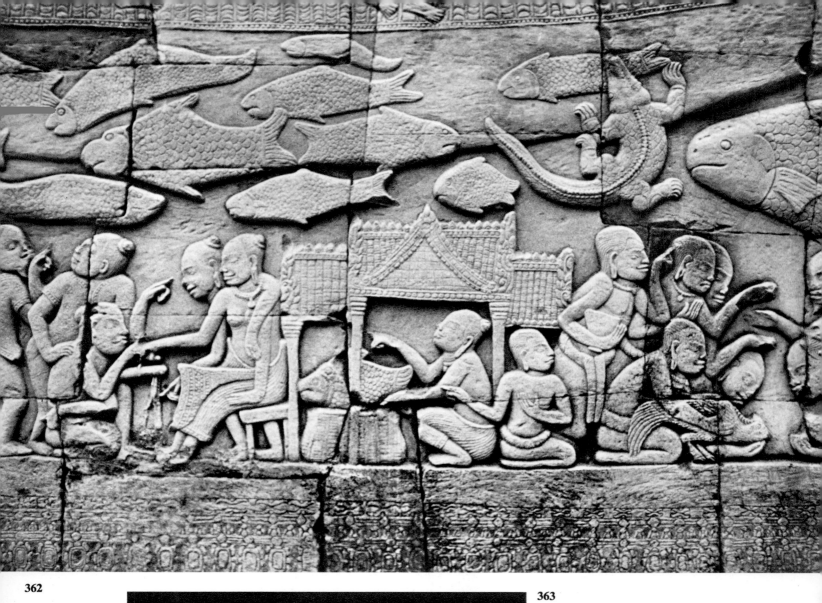

362

363

5. THE SOUTHERN CHAMS (Tenth–Fifteenth Century)

THE entire history of Champa is nothing more than a long struggle against the Vietnamese, who after several centuries forced the Chams to retreat south and to the mountains. This retreat resulted in Cham wars against the Khmers. Although Indravarman was audacious enough to set fire to Angkor in 1177 and, for a time, thought he was master of his destiny, the time was indeed a brief one. For, as we have related, the Khmers soon took a signal revenge and made Champa a vassal state until 1220. But the history of this unfortunate people does not end here. Five years after Cham sovereigns were rid of their Khmer suzerain, the Vietnamese made a new thrust toward the south. At the close of the thirteenth century, Kublai Khan's troops inflicted severe punishment on the Chams for daring to refuse allegiance. Finally, in 1313, Vietnamese troops imposed their power on the Vijaya sovereigns. Despite a sudden resurgence of action during the reign of Che Bong Nga (1360–90), who made raids as far as Hanoi, the cause was lost. The conquest of Vijaya by the Vietnamese in 1471 marked the disappearance of the Cham Kingdom. The few tribes who still resisted in the most southern part of the peninsula were gradually destroyed.

In the early twelfth century, the struggle against Angkor resulted in a decline of art. Architecture, now cubic, was deprived of even its decoration, and became austere. The most striking example of this transitional style is the small Po Nagar temple at Nha Trang. Shortly after, however, Khmer influence seems to have produced a brief architectural revival. Although decoration remained meager, forms became elongated and more graceful, and arches acquired their characteristic spearhead shape. Now reduced in size, the corner edifices on false stories of roofs became simple "piles of square dishes" (with "silver towers" at Binh Dinh). "Ivory towers" were imitations of ogival prangs of Angkor Vat and bore clumsily copied Khmer-type lintels.

Toward the close of the thirteenth century, "copper towers" and "gold towers" and the sanctuary of Thua Thien showed a definite decline of art. Excessive stylization of foliage and lotus buds led to the most unusual results. Reduced edifices were hypertrophied. This general decline of art did not spare sculpture which often attempted to copy certain Khmer details; only the mythical animals on the Thap-Mam sanctuary reveal a certain vigor and fine sense of movement. The monuments erected toward the close of the thirteenth century were, increasingly, simplified and schematized. Decoration disappeared almost completely, leaving only incoherent, heavy elements. Although the late-thirteenth-century Po Klaung Garai temple still reveals certain Khmer characteristics, the sixteenth-century (?) towers of the Yang Prong and Po Rome temples are no longer related to the Cham spirit. Sculpture alone seems to have retained some vitality, but legs tend to disappear more and more into the stone block, and at the close of this backward development only a vague outline of the face is indicated.

Once the Chams had disappeared and had integrated themselves with mountain tribes, their art returned to primitive stone, and thus the last bulwark of Brahmanism vanished from the locality. Triumphant, Theravada Buddhism was to encounter no obstacle until the realist philosophy of Confucius. The period of great achievement had come to an end and the peoples of the Indochinese Peninsula turned to a doctrine of renunciation. To our great regret, circumstances made it impossible for us to go to Mi-Son. Since its monuments were not accessible, only sculptures are shown in this book.

SUMMARY OF CHAM STYLES

Unknown Beginnings: Born of Indian influence—Wooden architecture perhaps related to that of Funan.

Early Style: Already well defined, typically Cham, but treatment still Indian. First centered at: Mi-Son E1—Light architecture on brick base. Seventh–eighth century.

Second Style: Centered at Hoa Lai: Architecture with pilasters and strong arches. Eighth–ninth century. Po-Dam—Mi-Son F3—A2—C1.

Third Style: Centered at Dong-Duong: Free of Indian influence. Excessive décor. Ninth–tenth century. Mi-Son A3—A13—B4.

Transition: Mi-Son A10: Javanese and Khmer influences.

Fourth Style: Mi-Son A1 (tower-sanctuary-top). Tenth–eleventh century. Mi-Son B5.

Transition: Mi-Son E4—B6.

Fifth Style: Po Nagar: Cubic style, decadence (early twelfth century).

Sixth Style: Binh Dinh:
  Silver towers
  Gold towers
  Mi-Son G1 (?)
  Ivory towers (Khmer imitation)
  Thua Thien
  Copper towers (late thirteenth century)

Seventh Style: Late works in decadent style
  Po Rome (sixteenth century?)
  Po Klaung Garai (late thirteenth and beginning of the fourteenth century)
  Yang Prong

370. VIETNAM, BUST OF A WOMAN. Probably of Durga, since the ascetic-type chignon—a Shivaist symbol—is topped by a stylized buffalo head. This head is outstanding for its realism and conception, which appear to have been influenced by Javanese art. The expression of femininity is in contrast to other works of the same period. The eyes were probably inset with metal or porcelain. Sandstone. Height: 12 inches. *National Museum, Saigon.*

371. VIETNAM, BINH DINH, UMA. This very conventional pediment is rather striking for its perfect symmetry. It probably represents Uma, one of the forms of Shiva's shakti; it appears to have all the attributes. Note the curious headdress consisting of a tiara and diadem, one above the other. The face seems to have been inspired by Khmer art. Sandstone. Height: 3 feet 4 inches. Thap Mam style. *National Museum, Saigon.*

372. VIETNAM, BINH DINH, RAMPANT SINGHA. This late piece (to be compared with the dancing singha of the northern Chams shown in plate 287) with its profuse detail is in contrast to the architecture of the period when all decoration seems to have been suppressed. A corner piece treated as a caryatid, this lion crushing a serpent has nothing demonic about it. Treated in a baroque manner without the slightest attempt at anatomical accuracy, it shows the decline of the style Thirteenth–fourteenth century. Sandstone. Height: 3 feet 4 inches. *National Museum, Bangkok.*

373. VIETNAM, YANG NUM JARAI, TORSO OF A DVARAPALA. It is very likely that the Vietnamese introduced the ceramic technique to the Chams, as the Chinese had to the Thai. This unfortunately mutilated but beautiful piece seems to represent a dvarapala, an assumption suggested by the serpent wound like a rope around its chest. The well-depicted loincloth shows what the Chams wore in the fourteenth century; the rosette on the right thigh may be a tattoo, for this custom was quite common among the peoples of Southeast Asia; the choker has a typically Khmer decoration. Thirteenth–fourteenth century. Light-brown glazed terra cotta. Height: 3 feet 4 inches. *National Museum, Saigon.*

370

372

VII. THE THAI KINGDOMS

About the close of the eleventh century, Yunnan tribes (who for centuries had been driven back by the Chinese and who had assimilated themselves into the Nan Ch'iao tribes), taking advantage of Khmer weakness and the easy prey offered by the Dvaravati Empire, advanced into Laos and into the present territory of Thailand along the upper valleys of the Mekong and the Chao Phraya. Before this, however, these Thai tribes had been infiltrating peacefully for a long time into the ancient Mon country. But they had not yet formed groups sufficiently strong to impose and create a Thai state. Employed by the Khmers as scouts and shock troops, these "Syam" became civilized after contact with their masters. Soon converted to Theravada Buddhism by the Mon peoples of the ancient Dvaravati Empire, they became the champions of this religion. But far from remaining an isolated ethnic group, they intermarried with the Mon population and adopted their customs and way of life. They had no writing, but they nevertheless retained their language, which they finally imposed on the entire country. Some of them (the Chams) settled in Burma and, coming against the Burmese, sought refuge in the upper parts of the territory. Others settled in north Laos and in the northern part of the Chao Phraya basin. Taking advantage of Khmer weakness, they descended into the plains and replaced them at the close of the thirteenth century. But during the period of Khmer occupation, they had already formed themselves into local districts, in the Haripunjaya (Lampun) region, the northern bulwark of the Mon-Dvaravati. About 1220 they formed small kingdoms at Luangprabang, Bhamo, Xieng Sen, Xieng Mai, and elsewhere. Fifty years later the leaders united and formed the first Thai Kingdom, that of Sukhothai. The scholarly king, Rama Kamheng (close of the thirteenth century), gave laws to the Thai, adopted the Khmer alphabet into the Thai language, and extended his conquests as far as the city of Lopburi (Lavo). During this time, the northern part of the country united into the Nan La Kingdom with Xieng Mai as its capital (1296). In the south, the Thai and Mons formed a unified state whose economy was based on agriculture, but was not yet politically defined.

Henceforth, the entire history of the Thai centered about southernward expansion, the constant struggle against the Khmers in the east, and a desperate defense against Burmese attacks.

A NOTE ON THAI CERAMICS

Coming from Nan Ch'iao, the Thai brought with them the refined techniques of Chinese ceramic making, especially the secret of celadon ware which made the Sung dynasties famous. Many kilns were established at Sawankalok (Thuriang Ko Noi), a few miles north of the Luang River rapids, and then at Sukhothai (Thuriang), several hundred yards north of the city. There were 12 kilns at the latter, each divided into three vaulted sections: hearth, firing room, and chimney. The pieces to be fired were piled in and separated from one another by resting on either tubes or tripods made of fireproof clay. According to the place where the work was made, there are at least five kinds of pottery in Thailand, generally designated as a group by the term *Sangkalok*.

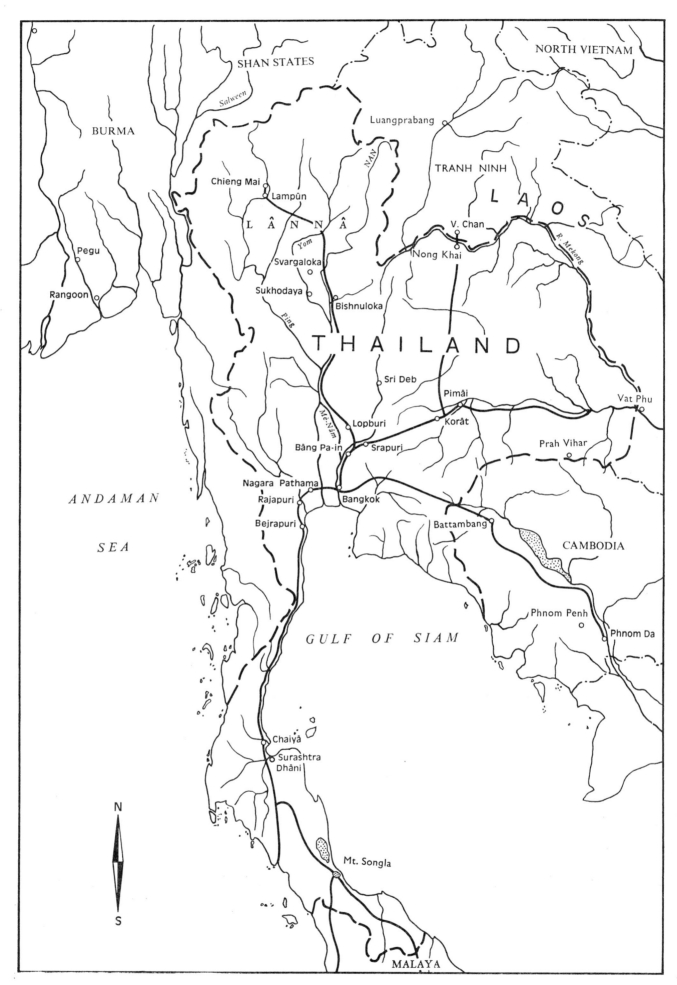

FIG. 36. ARCHAEOLOGICAL SITES IN THAILAND AND LAOS

XALIENG

These ceramics come from the Sri Satchanali (Sawankalok) kilns installed near the Yom River. They appear to be the most ancient and have a dark-brown glaze applied on a rather crude clay; their style often denotes a Khmer influence. However, they are the logical development of Thai nonglazed pottery. This type was made at the same time as the following examples.

SAWANKALOK

Certainly the most beautiful productions of Thai ceramic ware, this type of pottery was made especially for export and in large numbers during the Sukhothai period (thirteenth–fourteenth century) in the Sawankalok kilns. Ware of this type has been found as far away as the Philippines and Borneo, as well as in the Near East and India. The clay is of excellent quality and the celadon glazes range from very light greenish-gray to deep yellow-green. The forms show great variety—not only vessels (bowls, jars, bottles, various vases), but decorative objects as well (elephants, tiles, acroteria). Certain vases are supported by animals, others by figurines. Of special interest are maternity figurines that represent a kneeling woman nursing a child. These statuettes (all decapitated in order to ward off evil spirits—a kind of sham sacrifice) were offered to the god by women who wanted children. Such celadons had much in common with the Luang Ch'uan ceramics of China.

FIG. 37. *Left:* SUKHOTHAI CELADON WARE WITH BROWN DECORATION (Height: 9½ inches); *Center:* SAWANKALOK CELADON WARE WATER JUG (Height: 8 inches); *Right:* XALIENG CERAMIC JUG (Height: 6½ inches)

SUKHOTHAI

The products of the Thuriang kilns resembled the Chinese T'zu-Chou style. Tradition says that about the close of the thirteenth century, ceramists were brought from T'zu-Chou to Sukhothai by order of King Rama Kamheng. However, the works produced at Sukhothai had typically Thai forms. Generally they were made with great care, and were in a light gray-green celadon. As a rule, fish motifs and floral decorations predominated. This pottery was found throughout Southeast Asia.

KHMER OR LOPBURI POTTERY

Produced between the eleventh and fourteenth century, this pottery, with mainly Khmer motifs, was hardly decorated. Modeled in low relief, it has a gray-green glaze but lacks the fine effect that made north Thai pottery famous. These kilns are found in Cambodia (Koulen Plateau) and near the city of Lopburi in Thailand.

About the middle of the fifteenth century, kilns were built on the outskirts of Xieng Mai by prisoners of war who had been brought from Sawankalok. The clay is inferior, but the quality of the ceramic ware is still fine. Decoration is generally the same as that of Sawankalok. Until the middle of the sixteenth century these kilns were still in use.

Thai ceramic production followed the same formula until the eighteenth century, keeping to gray-greens and browns, but the quality never equaled works produced at Sawankalok (see fig. 37).

FIG. 38. DESIGN IN THE CENTER OF A SAN KAMPAENG STYLE PLATE

1. THE SUKHOTHAI STYLE (Thirteenth–Fourteenth Century)

Thai architecture of Sukhothai, though still poorly defined, utilized several influences and styles. Here again we find the Khmer prang, although greatly modified, its corners so flattened that the tower section becomes almost round, and its upper part so attenuated that with its antefixes and geometricized forms it almost becomes a stupa. Ceylonese influence also can be seen in the slender stupa (probably copied from imported reliquary caskets) terminating in a slender spire, and in the arrangement of the monuments which, adapted to Buddhist requirements, had to include not only the stupa (chedi), but also a vihara (*viharn*) to house the faithful, as well as an ordination hall (*uposatha, bot*) reserved for monks, libraries for sacred writings, a mandapa (*mondop*) to contain an image of Buddha or his footprints, and, finally, various buildings for monks in the monastery enceinte (*vat*). These buildings are the result of different styles. The viharns or bots probably developed from a type of Chinese construction with incurved roofs having decorative elements rising on the corners. The mondops and their roofs are generally square and strangely resemble Mon buildings—simple cells covered by many roofs superposed like stories (like the roofs of Pithakat Taik at Pagan). Certain details are still copied from the Khmers, but building methods are quite different. Brick and wood are common. This explains why a large number of edifices has perished, especially those in which the naves were separated by colonnades supporting the principal roof beams. Laterite was preferred for foundations. Decoration consisted of stucco-coated brick.

Stupas show great variety and in general are quite slender; they range from the late Dvaravati square or octagonal towers with many stories adorned with Buddhas (for instance, Vat Kukut at Lampun, which may have influenced the Sat-Mahal-Prasada of Polonnaruva in Ceylon) to the slender spires. In the intermediary phase were many generally composite architectural forms—

square base, bulbous dome, recessed drum-dome—which formed a large cross section of different styles or attempts at novelty, which are commemorative monuments as well. The sculpture of Sukhothai shows more homogeneity. The statues of Buddha are a unique type, probably influenced by south Chinese Buddhist art, but also by Burmese and Ceylonese works. Treated in a very lithe manner (displaying an ignorance of anatomy), the sculptures of this period (seated or walking Buddhas) are characterized by very elongated arms and soft, fine hands, which become conventionalized through the repetition of the forms. The beautiful oval faces have fine, regular features: a long, slightly hooked nose with a drooping tip and thin bridge, greatly curved eyebrows, and heavy eyelids above large, staring eyes. The hair is treated in tight curls, and falls to a rounded point on the forehead and has a thick ushnisha on the top, often surmounted by a kind of flame symbolizing the spiritual fire. In the early period this art is characterized by certain innovations: the type of face that later was to have a strong influence on the faces of Thai Buddhas, and the type of walking Buddha represented for the first time sculpted in the round,

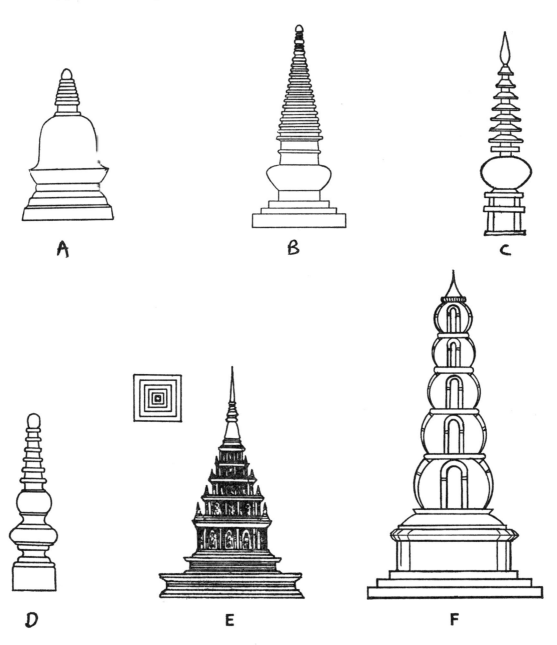

FIG. 39. DVARAVATI-STYLE STUPAS. A, B, C, D. TYPES TAKEN FROM BAS-RELIEFS; E. LATE-STYLE STUPA OF VAT KUKUT AT LAMPUN; F. LATE-STYLE STUPA OF GU THAO AT XIENG MAI

357

perhaps inspired by certain figures in the Ananta Pannya at Pagan. As in all Mahayana Buddhist art, Buddha's positions are one of four: standing, walking, seated, or reclining (on the right side). The sole exception to this last position is the reclining Buddha sculpted on the summit of a rock on the Phnom Koulen in Cambodia, in a style strongly influenced by that of Dvaravati, represented (in contradiction to the texts) reclining on his left side.

WALKING BUDDHAS

When executed in the round, these bronze sculptures are medium-sized, often lacquered and gilded. The forms generally correspond to the description of the Sage given in the Pali canon (or rather to the interpretations thereof), and we have good reason to believe that King Rama Kamheng had personal ideas about this. The feet are treated flatly with predominant heels, the legs have strong thighs with summarily modeled fine calves, the shoulders are unusually wide, the hands very delicate and lithe, "like lotus flowers which have just blossomed." The chin is cleft by an incised line, the lips are well designed beneath a hooked nose "like that of a parrot." The ears have very pendulous lobes, the lower part curving slightly outward. The clothing has almost no folds, and lies flat against the body, with the right shoulder exposed. The end of the robe is draped beneath the right arm, carried around the back in toga fashion, and thrown over the left shoulder, its supple, finely pleated folds falling to the navel. The bottom edge of the robe flares out and upward, creating a hook-shaped contour. The belt is often emphasized by one or two wavy pleats. Several of these walking Buddhas are treated the "wrong" way, that is to say, with the right hand raised. However, in most cases it is lowered to the side, while the raised left hand has the palm extended in a gesture of appeasement. The treatment of the hip movement may be related to certain Gupta-style sculptures. Some of these walking Buddhas of brick and stucco (still *in situ* at Sukhothai) are gigantic and are set against a wall. But in treatment and style they are quite similar to those of bronze images.

As the style came to an end, movement was more rapid, the thighs less round, the robe less flat against the body.

STANDING BUDDHAS

These images are scarcer and generally have the same typical characteristics as the walking Buddhas. But the entire attitude is stiffer. Both hands are raised in the attitude of Buddha descending from Trayastrimsa, or else the statue has only one hand raised in a protective gesture.

SEATED BUDDHAS

By far the most numerous representations both in bronze and stucco, these Buddhas have the characteristics of the style just discussed, but the legs are in the hero position—that is, folded; sometimes (but only rarely) they are in the lotus position, which seems later in date.

RECLINING BUDDHAS

These are the scarcest images of Buddhist art. Except for a very few examples in bronze, they are generally of brick and stucco and often reach gigantic proportions.

FOOTPRINTS OF BUDDHA

Generally sculpted on a round base in the form of a lotus, they include the 800 distinct marks arranged around the Wheel of the Law indicated on the entire surface of the footprint. These footprints are often incised on sheets of metal as much as 6 feet 8 inches long. Occasionally the enclosed section is adorned with figurines. These marks are both pedomantic (divination by reading the soles of the feet) and an image of the Buddhist universe representing the worlds, the planets, and the stars arranged around mythical Mount Meru, pivot of the world.

358

Decoration consists almost exclusively of applying stucco to brick and terra cotta, which is often glazed. Chinese potters had established many kilns at Sawankalok (Sri Satchanali) where they turned out pottery and figurines having the same light gray-green glaze as the famous Chinese celadon; these pieces were highly prized in Java. In imitation, the Khmers also produced a glazed pottery, but of very inferior quality. Decoration during the Sukhothai period consisted of glazed tiles representing mythical animals: nagas, or makaras, and often *tepanoms* (celestial figures). Walls and pediments were sometimes decorated with finely incised stucco floral motifs. The bases and tops of walls were decorated with friezes and demons' heads. Inspiration was Dvaravati derived but appears to have been primarily influenced by Chinese art.

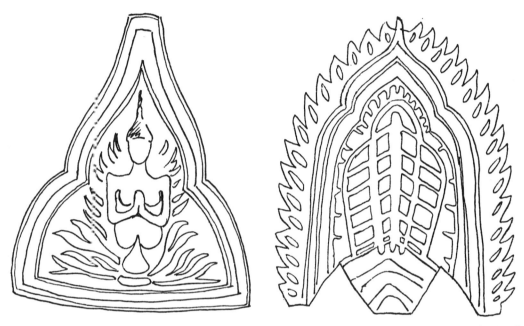

FIG. 40. *Left:* UNGLAZED ROOF-TILE FINIAL, SUKHOTHAI STYLE (Height: 7¼ inches)
Right: GLAZED ROOF-TILE FINIAL, KOULEN STYLE (Height: 5½ inches)

BRAHMANIC IMAGES

Buddhist tolerance allowed inclusion of gods foreign to Buddha's Law. It is therefore not unusual to find the ruins of some Brahmanic temple among the many Buddhist monasteries, together with representations of gods of the Hindu pantheon. Generally bronze, these images are in a more hieratic style than the Buddhas, but their proportions and facial treatment are distinctively Sukhothai in style.

The Sukhothai style continued very late, long after the center of Thai culture was moved toward the south. Until the close of the fifteenth century many pieces still show the imprint of the Rama Kamheng style. This style is generally classified according to three periods: pre-classic (thirteenth century), classic (fourteenth century), and post-classic or late (fifteenth and even sixteenth century). However, as these periods overlapped greatly, their limits cannot be ascertained with exactitude.

Some kings and bonzes continued to remodel their monasteries and monuments, and it is often extremely difficult (since documents are lacking) to assign an exact date to an edifice. Because of this, we are going to present monuments originating from the middle of the fourteenth according to geographical order—Sukhothai, Phitsanulok, Sawankalok—and end with the sculpture.

374. THAILAND, SUKHOTHAI, VAT MAHA THAT, EAST VIEW. Surrounded by a brick enceinte 623 by 646 feet, pierced by four gates, this huge sanctuary (no monks lived here) was part of the royal palace. It consists mainly of a very high chedi, the front of which is embellished with a niche surmounted by a Khmer-inspired pediment. Along the base is a frieze representing disciples in pradakshina (rite of circumambulation). An enormous bronze seated Buddha was placed in front of this sanctuary at the far end of the viharn, the laterite pillars of which are visible on either side of the photograph. The statue was brought from Bangkok by King Rama I and was supplemented by several smaller copies. The floor of the viharn is paved with brick. A combination of a stupa and a Khmer prasat, the 55-foot-high chedi is stucco-coated brick. Many small chedis (149 in all) are arranged around this elegant structure. Sometimes called Vat Yai, it was built by the kings of the Phra Ruang Dynasty (1257-1376).

375. THAILAND, SUKHOTHAI, VIEW OF THE SITE. The old city of Sukhothai lies some 7 miles west of the new city, on the edge of a plain surrounded by hills. It was the Thai capital from the middle of the thirteenth century until 1365, and was governed by eight kings of the Phra Ruang Dynasty. During that time it was a very rich city and was walled in by triple earthen ramparts pierced with gates at each cardinal point; the ramparts measured 5620 feet east-west and 4080 feet north-south.

The buildings of this period include:

1. A pagoda or chedi generally fronted by a hall or viharn.
2. A mondop (a square room) also fronted by a viharn.
3. A prang or sanctuary-tower (Khmer influence) with a viharn.
4. A viharn; a kind of combination of a hall and several small chedis and prangs used for gatherings of the faithful.
5. Finally, a bot or uposatha, a kind of small covered hall where monks were ordained. This building is always surrounded by eight standing stones known as *sima*, with a ninth one lying buried beneath the altar. When the monastery is a royal foundation, these sima are doubled.

Each of these complexes, or monasteries (vats), was generally surrounded by earthen ramparts and moats. The buildings were built of laterite, stucco-coated brick, and wood, and roofed with tiles which were often glazed. This chedi on the shores of Lake Traphang Takuan is the Vat Sra Sri.

376. THAILAND, SUKHOTHAI, VAT MAHA THAT, FRIEZE OF THE DISCIPLES. Forty disciples (10 per

side), hands joined, are represented walking around a chedi, sheltered by an overhanging cornice. Made of brick and stucco, and well preserved, they are all alike. About 3 feet 4 inches high.

377. THAILAND, SUKHOTHAI, VAT MAHA THAT, SQUARE CHEDI. The laterite and brick base of this chedi—the facing and stucco decoration of which have perished—is adorned with small niches containing lions and demons acting as caryatids, as well as celestial beings (tepanoms). Three of them may be seen at the extreme left of the photograph. In front of the chedi is a large restored Buddha in the Sukhothai style seated in a projecting niche which has collapsed.

378. THAILAND, SUKHOTHAI, WALKING BUDDHA. A gilt-bronze statuette representing Buddha either walking or pressing his footprints into the ground. The lines are sinuous and the robe clings to the body. The errors in proportion are intentional, giving a fragile elegance to this type which is characteristic of Sukhothai Buddhas. The base is of a later date. Height: 20 inches. *Collection H.R.H. Princess Chumbhot, Bangkok.*

379. THAILAND, SUKHOTHAI, VAT SRI SAWAI. Instead of a chedi, this vat has three Thai prangs decorated with motifs in the Lopburi style (showing Khmer influence), with a central tower 65 feet high. Fronted by a viharn on the east, this sanctuary was probably dedicated to Shiva by the Khmers before being adapted for Buddhist worship. The foundation of this sanctuary, therefore, probably dated from the time of first Khmer settlement in this region. The structure is surrounded by laterite walls pierced by a single gate on the south side. The prangs are built of brick and mortar and the columns are made of laterite blocks.

380. THAILAND, SUKHOTHAI, VAT BENCHAMABOPIT, HAND OF A WALKING BUDDHA. This hand of refined, almost feminine elegance is a detail of a walking Buddha made of lacquered and gilded bronze. Height: 4 feet 6 inches. *National Museum, Bangkok.*

381. THAILAND, SUKHOTHAI, HEAD OF BUDDHA. This is a perfect example of the somewhat effeminate characteristics of the style: a perfectly oval face with a heavy jaw; a chin emphasized by an incised line; well-designed lips bordered by an incised line; a fine slightly hooked nose; slightly bulging eyes; eyebrows in relief, joined in the center to form the nasal ridge; and hair made up of small, spiral curls. The flame usually surmounting the ushnisha is missing. Pure in design, this head is a perfect example of Sukhothai art. The bronzes of this period are distinguished by the extreme thinness of the metal, which is a testament to the wonderful technical skill of the artists of the period, whose art was certainly greatly influenced by that of Chinese bronze workers. Bronze. Height: 12 inches. *Sukhothai Museum.*

382. THAILAND, PHITSANULOK, VAT SULAMANI, KINNARI. A beautiful terra-cotta dancing kinnari which was probably part of the pediment of a viharn or of an uposatha. It belongs to the monks of Vat Sulamani, who guard it zealously. Height: 18 inches.

383. THAILAND, SAWANKALOK, CHEDI OF VAT CHANG LOM. This classic Sinhalese chedi stands on three 45-foot square terraces bordered by columned balustrades. The pedestal of the chedi is surrounded by stucco-coated laterite elephants. Decorated with a balustrade, the upper terrace consists of niches holding seated brick and stucco Buddhas. This structure was probably built by King Rama Kamheng to contain the relics of Buddha (an inscription relates that in 1286 a chedi was erected in the center of the city of Sri Satchanali which took 6 years to build). In front of this chedi stood a viharn measuring 38 by 98 feet.

384. THAILAND, SUKHOTHAI, VAT CHANG LOM, ELEPHANTS. The base of this chedi is decorated with elephant heads in imitation of those which probably existed at the Mahatupa Stupa at Anuradhapura in Ceylon. The elephants are unfortunately in a very bad state of decay. Height: about 5 feet.

385. THAILAND, SUKHOTHAI, VAT SRA SRI. Standing on the shores of Lake Traphang Takuan, this vat is composed of a round Sinhalese-type chedi resting on a 59-foot-square base, and a viharn resting on a very high platform. The latter houses a large brick-and-stucco Buddha. At one time this chedi was surrounded by nine other small structures. The uposatha stood on a not-distant small island lying to the east.

386. THAILAND, SUKHOTHAI, VAT CHETUPHON. Situated south of the city, about a mile beyond the ramparts, this monastery is surrounded by moats and brick walls. At its center rises a mondop with only its far wall standing. Against this stands a large, handsome walking Buddha. The head has disappeared and most of the stucco is gone. On the outer sides of this I-shaped wall are sculpted standing Buddhas. A 1412 inscription seems to indicate that this vat was built at an uncertain earlier date. The lateral walls of the vinarn have disappeared, but "windows" have remained, sculpted in the stone in imitation of wooden pieces. The columns of the viharn are laterite and the foundation is brick.

387. THAILAND, SUKHOTHAI, VAT CHEDI SI HUONG, STUCCO HEAD. This comes from one of the bas-reliefs of a chedi with a 26-foot base not far from Vat Chetuphon. The relief represents lions and celestial beings with two or four arms holding vases of flowers. This wonderful stucco head shows how Sukhothai artists enlarged their works by coating them, and is a Thai example of the method commonly used by Burmese in the poromu at Pagan. It is likely that many Burmese artists had settled at Sukhothai after the fall of Pagan in 1287. Stucco and mortar. Height: 7 1/4 inches. *Sukhothai Museum.*

388. THAILAND, SUKHOTHAI, VAT SRI CHUM. This now-roofless mondop is fronted by a large viharn whose roof was supported by brick columns. Square in plan, the mondop is about 50 feet high and 54 feet wide. Its 9-foot-thick walls rise in the center of a raised 105-foot-square platform. The interior houses a colossal brick and stucco seated Buddha in the earth-touching pose, which can be seen through the curious curtain door (the flame above the statue's ushnisha is modern). The top of this unusual structure can be reached by a flight of steps built into the thickness of the left wall. The ceiling of this passage consists of slabs of reused stone decorated with wonderfully incised scenes from the Jatakas and imprints of Buddha's foot. It is an unparalleled example of its kind, though greatly ruined. The mondop was partially restored in 1956.

389. THAILAND, SUKHOTHAI, VAT SRI CHUM, HAND OF BUDDHA. This gigantic hand in the lithe Sukhothai style is more than 5 feet long. As signs of homage, pilgrims have pasted it with pieces of gold leaf which glisten in the sunlight. This statue of Buddha measures more than 37 feet from one knee to the other. An inscription by King Rama Kamheng names it "Phra Achana."

390. THAILAND, SUKHOTHAI, VAT MAHA THAT, HEAD OF KALA. The art of stuccowork achieved a high degree of competence during the Sukhothai period. This head of kala (or of Rahu, the demon of eclipses), probably formed the center part of garlanding. Stucco. Height: 2 feet 4 inches. *Sukhothai Museum.*

391. THAILAND, SAWANKALOK, VAT CHEDI CHET THAO, BUDDHA. Adorning a niche of a great vat-chedi, this handsome Buddha (sheltered by the Naga king, Mucilinda, a theme dear to the Khmers) was certainly Khmer-inspired. But here the treatment of the serpent's heads is different; the central head (missing) was probably that of a demon. The contrast between the calm meditative attitude of Buddha and the ferocity of the nagas is very striking. Brick and stucco. Height: about 6 feet 8 inches.

392. THAILAND, SAWANKALOK, VAT NANG PAYA, WALL DECORATION. The uposatha of this greatly ruined vat, still surrounded by its laterite walls, is pierced by narrow windows in the form of loopholes, whose intervening spaces are adorned with delicate stucco decorations reminiscent of Chinese rugs. Height: about 3 feet 4 inches.

393. THAILAND, SUKHOTAI, KOMPONG PHET, VAT SADET, SOLE OF BUDDHA'S FOOT. A large sheet of bronze embossed and incised with lines, this footprint of Buddha's displays animals, monks, and a ship, and represents the styles of light architecture of the period. This imprint is more than 3 feet 4 inches long. The ship alone measures 3¼ inches. It may be seen on the periphery of the chakra decorating the central part of the sole of the foot. (Fourteenth century.) *National Museum, Bangkok.*

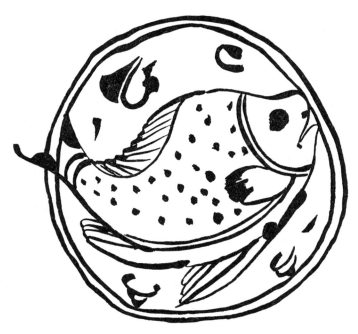

FIG. 41. DESIGN IN THE CENTER OF A SUKOTHAI DISH IN THE SANGKALOK STYLE

376

375

379

378

380   381

383

384

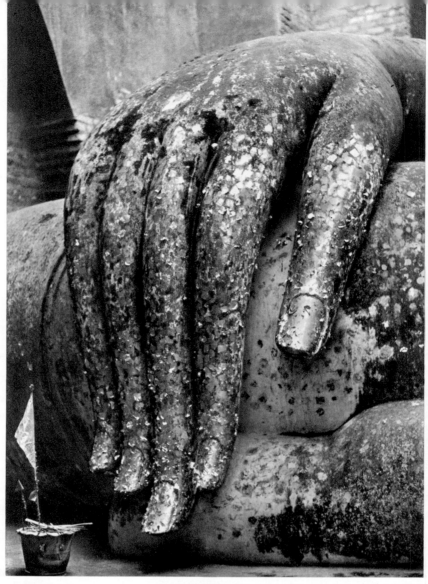

389

390

391

392

393

2. THE NORTHERN THAI STYLES (Fourteenth–Sixteenth Century)

During the period when the Sukhothai style flourished, northern Siam formed an independent state known as Lan Na, whose capital was Xieng Sen (later called Xieng Mai), a city situated not far from the old Mon city of Haripunjaya in Lampun. About the middle of the sixteenth century the kingdom was conquered by the Burmese, whose art greatly influenced the so-called late Xieng Sen style. It was not until the nineteenth century that this territory was restored to Thailand. Early Lan Na monuments are rare: one of the most important of these is the Chedi Si Liem, built about 1300. It still shows certain characteristics of the pre-existing Mon architecture of Haripunjaya. Certainly the most curious monument is the Vat Chet Yot, built during the reign of the reformer Tiloka in the middle of the fifteenth century to celebrate the 2000th anniversary of the death of Buddha (1457). It partially copied the famous Mahabodhi temple at Bodh-Gaya in India. But the very elegant stucco decoration of its walls, representing the gods of the Mahayana pantheon, is typically Thai and retains certain elements of the Sukhothai style. Surviving Xieng Sen style sculpture consists mainly of bronze images of Buddha. They are shown seated in the lotus or diamond position, the right hand in the earth-touching pose (bhumisparsa), already typical of Sukhothai Buddhas, the left hand resting, palm open, in the lap. Yet here,

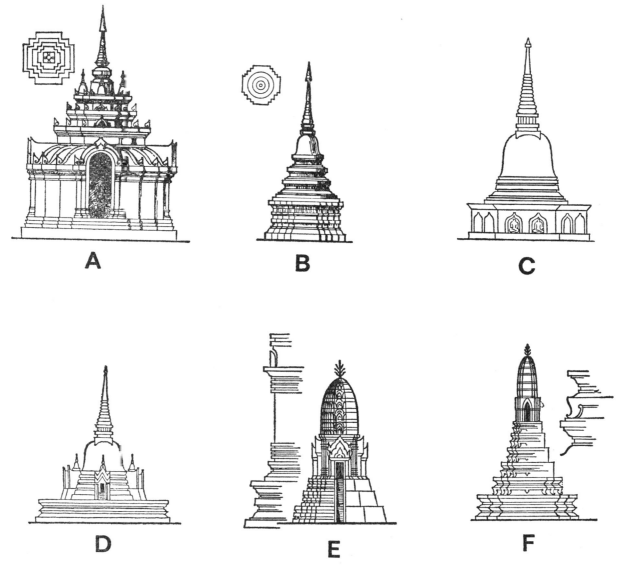

FIG. 42. TYPES OF CHEDIS. A AND B. NORTHERN THAILAND CHEDIS; C. CLASSIC SUKHOTHAI CHEDI; D. COMPOSITE AUYTHIA CHEDI; E. PRANG STYLE PRIOR TO THE SIXTEENTH CENTURY; F. PRANG STYLE AFTER THE SIXTEENTH CENTURY

375

395   396

397   398

400

401

403   404

3. THE U'THONG AND AYUTHIA STYLES (Fourteenth–Eighteenth Century)

The true Thai style was inaugurated about 1350, when a prince of the city of U'Thong founded a new capital a short distance north of the present city of Bangkok, on the Chao Phraya River. The city of Sukhothai was included in the new Thai Empire and rapidly developed to become one of the principal capitals of Southeast Asia. The successful wars fought by the Thais of Ayuthia against the Khmers, and the treasures brought back from Cambodia, increased the wealth of the kingdom. Many religious establishments were founded, and a large number of images of Buddha were cast not only in precious metals, but in bronze as well. Monasteries were built almost everywhere, and all the earlier styles were imitated, with the result that toward the close of the period they became stereotyped, dull, and affected. In 1767 this luxurious city was stormed and captured by the Burmese who did not withdraw until it was only a heap of ashes and pillaged of all its fabulous treasures.

The chief characteristics of Ayuthia art (in the beginning at least) were the adaptation of certain Khmer forms to architecture and sculpture. The Khmer prasat was taken as a model. Slightly modified in the beginning, about the close of the seventeenth century the upper part became somewhat slender, and in the following style, known as "national," it became a fluted spire (prang). Stupas also followed this tradition and became increasingly attenuated and needle-like. Bases were generally adorned with lions and niches modeled in stucco. By the diminishing arrangement of its piled-plate tiers, the terminal spire of the stupas was reminiscent of the chattras or parasols of Indian and Ceylonese examples. These stupas are surmounted by a prang, like certain pavilions and wooden palaces. The latter, however, have disappeared. The form of these stupas (almost identical to those of light Sukhothai monuments) is found only in relatively modern constructions. The telescoped roofs of these buildings are typical of this style and remain the glory of the national Thai architecture.

Sculpture is divided into several periods according to the types of Buddhas:

1. That known as U'Thong, or early Ayuthia, style which combines the characteristics of the Dvaravati and Lopburi (Khmer) styles. They are divided into four groups:
   Group A: Thirteenth-and fourteenth-century Buddhas in a style very similar to that of Dvaravati (round face, short flame on ushnisha).
   Group B: Buddhas from about 1350 to 1425 in a style greatly influenced by the Khmer type (square face, high flame, large ear lobes).
   Group C: Buddhas from 1400 to the close of the fifteenth century (oval face, refined features, thinner body, fingers of equal length).
   (All Buddhas of Groups A, B, and C bear wig-like headdresses, separated from the forehead by a light, flat band.)
   Group D: Fifteenth-century Buddhas (Long and ascetic figures, softer features, a narrow smile, and a very prominent chin).

2. The so-called national Ayuthia style follows the U'Thong style, groups C and D serving as transition. This style began even before the close of the U'Thong style and lasted until the fall of the city. During this period various interpretations of the Buddha figure were elaborated, many often following the inspiration of families of bronze workers. Production of images during this period was enormous; they were cast by the thousand, and Buddhas crowned with the mukuta (a motif perhaps borrowed from Khmer art) enjoyed great popularity. However, the overabundance of these works and their hasty execution mitigated against high quality, and a definite decline set in, not only in casting techniques, but also in art in general. Bearing geometrical features, stiff and conventional attitudes, overloaded with ornament, and bordering on the baroque, these final works are of little interest.

387

Decorations of monuments paralleled the variations of styles in statuary. However, since they were executed in stucco, they were unfortunately greatly damaged when the Burmese sacked the city. Tile was generally glazed and adorned with delightful tepanom motifs. Regrettably, wall paintings have survived only in sections, and these greatly ruined. An exception, though, may be found at Vat Rajpurana (1424), whose murals were miraculously preserved in a hermetically sealed crypt.

FIG. 43. TYPES OF THAILAND BUDDHAS. A. EARLY NORTHERN STYLE; B. LATE NORTHERN STYLE; C. SUKHOTHAI STYLE; D. U'THONG STYLE

406. THAILAND, AYUTHIA, VAT CHEDI CHAO PHYA THAI. This is at a monastery also known as Vat Chai-Mongkol, erected in 1357 or 1363 (depending on the chronicles) by the king of U'Thong at the time of the founding of the city of Ayuthia. King Naresuen the Great built this very high chedi about 1592. It follows the classic style, and is constructed of brick and mortar, with a pagodon at each corner of its square base.

407. THAILAND, AYUTHIA, VAT PHRA CHAO PHANANG CHOENG. Built in 1324, before the founding of the city of Ayuthia, this is the most ancient vat of the south Thailand style to have survived. It is uncer-

tain whether the present structure exactly reproduces the original, since it was first repaired by King Naresuen the Great, then by kings of the Chakri dynasty, by King Mongkut in 1854, and finally by King Chulalongkorn in 1901. This vat contains an enormous 62-foot-high seated Buddha.

408. THAILAND, SUKHOTHAI, VAT MAHA THAT, HEAD OF BUDDHA, A fine example of the U'Thong style which found its way to the north, this stucco head at Vat Maha That displays certain characteristics of portraiture from about the close of the fourteenth century. Stucco. Height: 12 inches. *Sukhothai Museum.*

388

409. THAILAND, SAWANKALOK, VAT PHRA SRI RATANA MAHA THAT. Also known as Vat Phra Prang, this complex features a very high prang imitating Khmer prasats and is built of laterite, brick, and mortar. The tower stands on a 72-foot-square pedestal adorned with a projecting chapel that is reached by a very steep flight of steps. A reliquary is installed in the center of the chapel which is surrounded by two galleries. Near this prang are ruins of a viharn which (though probably founded by the Khmers) was rebuilt by the Thais about 1490 in the style then current at Ayuthia. The summit of the prang is crowned by a bronze ornament of Khmer origin symbolizing a triple trisula, or Buddhist trident.

410. THAILAND, LOPBURI, VAT PHRA SI RATANA MAHA THAT, VIHARN LUANG. Founded by the Khmers in the twelfth century, this vat was rebuilt during the reign of King Narai and, like many Thai vats, was restored several times thereafter. It is in the Ayuthia style, but it is practically impossible to assign it an exact date, a case with most Thai monuments. Here, only the motif above the main entrance of the viharn is of real interest; this represents a mondrop with superimposed roofs. This type of ornament, which later was very popular in Thai art, is represented in its most primitive, if not initial, form. Brick and stucco.

411. THAILAND, AYUTHIA, VAT PHRA MAHA THAT, OCTAGONAL CHEDI. Situated in the midst of an enormous complex of temples and prangs, this curious octagonal construction east of the royal palace undoubtedly has its origins in northern-style chedis. It was erected in the early fifteenth century—possibly as early as 1384—by King Naresuen the Great upon his victorious return from Xieng Mai. It was originally seven stories high, and its niches must have held terra-cotta bas-reliefs, which, together with the upper stories, have now disappeared. It is possible that this monument was topped by a Khmer prang.

412. THAILAND, LOPBURI, HEAD OF BUDDHA. In this wonderful U'Thong bronze we can see the influences of both the Khmer and the Dvaravati styles. The square face, the connecting eyebrows, the band between the hair and forehead, and the cleft chin are characteristic of late-fourteenth-century art. Bronze. Total height of the statue: 2 feet 10 inches. *Lopburi Museum.*

413. THAILAND, AYUTHIA, VAT PHRA SRI SAMPET, HEAD OF BUDDHA. About the close of the fifteenth century, the Ayuthia style, greatly influenced by northern styles, freed itself of Khmer and Dvaravati influences and a new type of Buddha was the result. The curls of the hair became very small, the face rounder, with the features tending to be more conventionalized. A flame-like *urna* (whorl of hair) adorns the forehead of this Buddha. Its eyes were probably inlaid with enamel, mother-of-pearl, or precious metal. Gilt bronze. Width of the mouth: 18³/₄ inches. *National Museum, Bangkok.*

414. THAILAND, PHITSANULOK, VAT NANG PHRA YA. This uposatha (bot) where monks were ordained is built in the ancient style and probably dates from the fifteenth century. It may, however, have been rebuilt several times since then. Low walls and superimposed saddle roofs relate the style of this bot to the viharn of Vat Phra Chao Phanang Choeng at Ayuthia (plate 407). The chedi seen at the far left also probably dates from the fifteenth century and seems to have been erected on the ruins of a more ancient structure.

415. THAILAND, AYUTHIA, VAT SRI SAMPET. Built by King Boroma-Trailokanat on the site of the first royal palace, this sanctuary was the largest in the capital. It consists of a viharn built in 1499 and three aligned chedis. The first two chedis were erected by Boroma-Trailokanat's son, King Rama-dibodhi II, to contain the ashes of his father and of his brother, Boroma-Raja III, while the third was built 40 years later by King Boroma-Rajanah Buddhang Kun in memory of Ramadibodhi II. Many small chedis meant to contain the ashes of royal princesses were added to the original edifices. This temple was repaired twice, in 1631 during the reign of King Prasat Thong, then in 1742 by King Boroma-Kot. It was mostly destroyed during the Burmese invasion of 1767 which reduced the city to ashes. The three large chedis stand on a common terrace and consist of bell-shaped anda surmounted by a cubic harmika topped by a columned drum supporting the high terminal spire. This is a classic type of stupa in the Ayuthia style. In the foreground are the pillars of the ruined viharn, with capitals formed like lotus blossoms.

416. THAILAND, AYUTHIA, LUANG SOP SAWAN, VAT SUAN, SURIYOTHAI CHEDI. This monument was erected in memory of the wife of King Maha Chakraphat, Queen Suriyothai, who died in combat fighting on the back of an elephant alongside her husband in a war against the Burmese (1548). An unusual type, this structure introduced a new stage in the construction of chedis, completely freed of the stupa form and combining both the prang and the chedi into a successful architectural unit.

417. THAILAND, PECCHABURI, VAT YAI SUVANNARAM. Dating from the sixteenth century, this vat consists of extensively remodeled structures. However, it offers a general idea of what religious buildings of the period were like. The roofs were restored during the reign of King Mongkut (1851–68))

418. THAILAND, SARABURI, VAT PHRA BUDDHA BAT. Built in the reign of King Narai, this mondop was designed to contain a miraculous imprint of Buddha's feet; it stands on the side of a hill overlooking the Chao Phraya River. Columns surround a cubic structure bearing a roof that combines the characteristics of a chedi and the usual terraced roofs of mondops. This sanctuary stands on several superimposed square terraces bordered by balustrades. The vat enclosing this mondop is the object of a famous annual pilgrimage which attracts millions of the faithful.

419. THAILAND, LOPBURI, NARAI RAJA NIWET PALACE, GATE. Erected by King Narai (1656–88), the palace (now a museum) was surrounded by high walls with gates in a style evidently inspired by that of Indian Mogul forts. The roofs of these gates are reminiscent, however, of those on Khmer gopuras.

420. THAILAND, LOPBURI, VAT SAO TONG THONG. This ensemble was restored by King Narai at the close of the seventeenth century and has remained in that state ever since. Only the chedi seems to have been rebuilt during a more recent period. Standing on a platform, the viharn has all the characteristics of the late Ayuthia style: raised walls, slot openings, pilasters terminating in long leaves, telescoped roofs, and an entrance surmounted by a roof with a narrow pediment. Brick and mortar.

421. THAILAND, AYUTHIA, VAT SUAN DHARARAM, THE BOT. Typical of eighteenth-century constructions, this bot is clearly different from earlier edifices because of its windows, richer ornamentation, and, in the center of each pilaster, consoles which support the roof. This method was used in the construction of almost all the viharns and uposathas in the eighteenth and nineteenth centuries. The stucco decoration is painted. In the foreground we can see one of the double simas, indicating that this is a bot of royal foundation.

422. THAILAND, AYUTHIA, MODEL OF A VIHARN. A mid-eighteenth-century terra-cotta model inlaid with varicolored stones. The roofing imitates round tiles. Height: 2 feet 8 inches. *Ayuthia Museum.*

423. THAILAND, AYUTHIA, VAT MAI NANG PHIEM, PEDIMENT. A fine piece, probably dating from the eighteenth century, this once adorned a viharn or a bot. The relief depicts demons assisting a demon king who is holding a prince. Gilded wood. Height: about 16 feet 8 inches. *Ayuthia Museum.*

424. THAILAND, PECCHABURI, VAT PAI LOM, STUCCO DECORATION. It is unusual to find stucco bas-reliefs of typically foreign inspiration in the interior of a viharn—and a greatly ruined one at that. The many-storied chedi has been transformed into a Chinese pagoda and is surrounded by a halo of flames. The surrounding vegetation, houses, and figures are treated in a realistic and meticulous manner reminiscent of wall paintings of the period. Late eighteenth century.

425. THAILAND, AYUTHIA, LOKHAYA SUDHA, RECLINING BUDDHA. This figure is known as Phra Buddha Sai-Yat and is 91 feet long. Built of brick and mortar, it probably dates from the middle of the eighteenth century. Rigidity of form, verticality of the arms supporting the head, summary treatment of the clothing, and distorted proportions mark this huge sculpture as a typical work of the late Ayuthia style.

426. THAILAND, AYUTHIA, HEAD OF BUDDHA. After the U'Thong styles (still close to Khmer art) and those inspired by Lan Na or Sukhothai, the Ayuthia style asserted itself, and a new style of Buddhas developed. The heads became longer and were often related to the type of adorned Buddha: with earrings and crowned by a royal diadem or incised mukuta with precious stones. This beautiful, rather ascetic head belongs to the close of the third Ayuthia period (sixteenth century). Bronze. Height: 10 inches. *Ayuthia Museum.*

427. THAILAND, AYUTHIA, HEAD OF BUDDHA. Belonging to the last Ayuthia style, this attractive head combines all the characteristics of the style developed in the capital—a truly Thai style which inspired all subsequent Buddha images. The face is oval and tends toward a certain naturalism; it is also somewhat feminine. The very slit eyes recall Burmese Buddhas. The mukuta is geometrical. Late seventeenth century. Gilded bronze. Height: 10 inches. *Collecion H.R.H. Princess Chumbhot, Bangkok.*

409

410

411

412   413

414

415

419

420

426   427

4. THE LAOTIAN STYLES (Fifteenth–Twentieth Century)

Laos has little in common with Siam. Its population (a combination of Thai and Mon-Khmer elements known as Khas) was scarcely affected by the Khmer occupation. The Khmers were content to exercise their influence over lands bordering the middle course of the Mekong, in the surroundings of the sanctuary of Vat Phu. The real beginnings of Laotian art are little known, and the war which has raged there for several years now has resulted in the destruction of a large number of monuments. In addition, in an effort to keep up their monasteries, the monks have torn down many structures and rebuilt many others, evidently with no concern for style. Since there is no law to protect works of art, they have also been pillaged of many treasures which are now scattered and difficult to identify or date. However, it seems that in the Lan Xang Kingdom (capital: Luangprabang), founded in the middle of the fourteenth century, there was a strong northern influence, and we can almost say that the Laotian Lan Xang style is nothing more

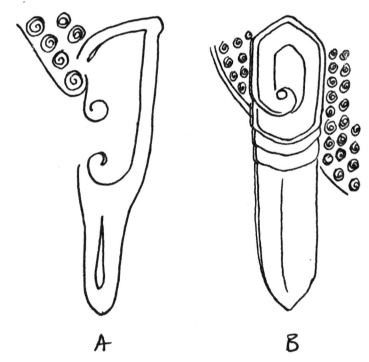

FIG. 44. A. EAR OF A SIAMESE-TYPE BUDDHA; B. EAR OF A LAOTIAN-TYPE BUDDHA

than a local variant of that of Xieng Sen. After conquering north Siam, the Burmese introduced their own style which could still be discerned at a very late date in the roofs of certain edifices, such as the library of Vat Sisaket at Vientiane.

Relatively isolated by their mountainous country, the Laotians probably did not develop their own art until much later. Their stone or bronze statues have survived in small quantity, while pre-eighteenth-century works in wood have practically disappeared, destroyed either by dampness or termites.

The Sukhothai style also reached Luangprabang when a Sukhothai sovereign sought refuge in the city. Two examples of walking Buddhas have been found; the treatment is Sukhothai, but the execution seems later in date (seventeenth–eighteenth century). However, they are all rather clumsy copies (Vat Ho Phra Kheo). About the seventeenth century, a typically Laotian style began, characterized by standing or seated bronze Buddhas with full faces, subtle smiles, sharp and heavy noses, and globular eyes surmounted by distinctively incised arched eyebrows. The ears are stylized in snail shapes, a characteristic of all the later Laotian Buddhas. The slightly

403

hooked noses seem to continue the line of the foreheads. Treated as small conical curls, the hairline is bordered by a flat band. Their rather heavy bodies wear clinging robes, beginning flush with the neck in several folds, and gathered in at the waist by a belt having a round buckle which acts as navel. From this belt the lower part of the robe falls in straight folds to the base. The thighs are large and the legs are distinctively neglected.

At a somewhat later date, the type becomes geometrical with emphasized features which seem to have been cut out with an axe; arms and legs are stiff, with no concern for anatomy, and the body is covered with ornament. In the last period of this style (nineteenth century), the face and ear lobes become longer, the eyes blend with the round cheekbones and are merely incised, eyebrows are prominent, and the ridge of the nose continues upward into the hairline, and the flame of the ushnisha terminates in a point. Quite often the Buddhas are seated on a high, molded base which extends and continues the triangular form of the figure. The standing Buddhas are stiff and their garments seem to hem them in tightly. Their excessively long arms descend as low as the knees. Clumsy treatment of these Buddhas often denotes the lack of models. We can easily say that Laotian sculpture is more the work of regional artisans than a national art.

The same is not true of architecture, however. Although the roofing of certain buildings retains Burmese characteristics, a completely Thai art imposes its style on the many structures which compose the pagoda complexes. The telescoped roofs with their concave lines descend quite low and are supported either by low walls or massive columns of wood or stucco-coated brick, their tops decorated with foliage in imitation of a capital, just as in the Thai art of Siam. The most typical monuments are the pagodas of Tran Ninh and Luangprabang. Certain vats are fronted by a columned porch with a roof that is often perpendicular to the axis of the building. The generally square columns support a richly decorated gable to which is attached a hanging motif.

These arches are often multilobulate; in the case of small pagodas the arch is simple and thus a pendentive is not needed. The roofs are decorated with long, bent thorns at the corners and with an open crest motif on the peak. Windows are few and interiors dim. Pillars (round at Luangprabang, square at Vientiane) lean inward and are generally wider at the base.

One of the most fascinating characteristics of the monuments of the Laotian vats are their chapels. Small, entirely built of brick (including roofs), they are decorated with stucco motifs. Seen from the front, these chapels are shaped rather like a thick-handled pike. The roof is massive and the interior is lit only by means of a door, which is usually richly decorated. The origin of this curious elephant-seat-shaped door is hard to explain.

Another element of pagoda design to which Laotians have given many forms is the *that* (the Laotian word for stupa). They exist in every form imaginable—from the enormous, low, seemingly squashed structure surrounded by pinnacles of That Luongat Vientiane; to the almost pyramidal-storied Vat Vixum at Luangprabang; to the slender point-like (a real needle rising toward the sky) That Phong Peng at Ban Na Sri in Tranh Ninh; including (in the intermediary phase) many *thats* in the form of decanter stoppers.

Like certain doors (Vat Aram at Luangprabang), other parts of buildings show combined Khmer and Burmese elements with a barrel vault made of rows of successive corbeled bricks.

Almost always consisting of stucco, decoration tends to emphasize the corners of the raised, horn-shaped moldings, giving the buildings a distinctive appearance. Stucco decoration on vat walls, chapel façades, or altar bases (most often floral) is treated in a lace-like manner. There is an unpleasant modern tendency to replace this with colored glass imbrication which, of course, creates a certain luster, but the result is in rather dubious taste.

A type of decoration special to Laotian art (although employed at different periods in Thailand) is that adorning vat pediments. Generally in the form of an equilateral triangle, it is decorated with very skillful wood carvings whose design is strictly adapted to the shape of the pediment. It is entirely floral, with the possible addition of one or two figures. Traditional motifs are employed even today to decorate household furnishings, ceremonial barges, and catafalques.

404

Traditionally extreme in all artistic manifestations, the Laotians adapt cherished designs to modern materials: cement replaces stucco and wood, while oil painting is substituted for other decorative media. Here again, unfortunately, since the new seemed more appropriate and more valued, the old magnificent decorative panels, now considered old-fashioned, were destroyed to make way for new ones.

428. LAOS, VIENTIANE, VAT HO PHRA KHEO, BUDDHA. Laotian Buddhas exist in many varieties, some as yet uncatalogued; most types have scarcely been studied and are still rather poorly described. This fine bronze head combines Xieng Sen and Sukhothai styles with Burmese art, while still retaining purely Laotian characteristics. The result is a kind of geometrical stylization of forms. The ears, pointed nose, and the folds of the neck appear at first glance to be clumsy copies of Siamese models. This is not the case, however, as the style is typically Laotian. The eyes are inlaid with precious metals. Bronze. Total height of the statue: approximately 3 feet 4 inches.

429. LAOS, LUANGPRABANG, VAT NANG, DOOR. In Laos more often than in Thailand, the door and window panels of viharns and uposathas are generally decorated with carvings of a figure, sometimes European, standing on an animal (in this instance the four lions of early Buddhism, similar to those on the capital of the Ashoka lat at Sarnath in India) amid an exuberant vegetal decoration. Gilded and often inlaid with mother-of-pearl, these panels are generally quite handsome. Except in certain isolated cases, an exact date cannot be assigned to these works.

430. LAOS, LUANGPRABANG, VAT XIENG THONG. The royal building where Laotian kings were invested and crowned is the perfect example of a Laotian vat. It is situated on the banks of the Mekong, almost at the junction of the Nam-Khan River. The greatly curved telescoped roofs and projecting porch adorned with columns show it to be directly inspired by northern Siamese vats. Founded in 1561, it is one of the most ancient in the city (after Vat Vixum whose stupa or *that* was built in 1503). Its decoration, also Siamese in derivation, consists of an attractive triangular motif formed of miniature *thats* on the roof ridge, surmounted by a Burmese hti.

It is often difficult to know where northern Thai art begins and Laotian art ends; both of them are closely related Thai arts which developed independently of one another in the sixteenth century. In general, the art of Laos (which was more isolated than its neighbor) has remained almost unchanged to this day. As the buildings were built almost entirely of wood, they were often rebuilt and

remodeled, but the basic design has remained the same. The chapel shown in the foreground, whose curved roof is typical of the Laotian style, is entirely built of brick and mortar, and its stucco decoration is similar to the vat's. The columns of the latter, together with the roofs and ornaments, are painted in lively colors—red, gold, and black. A recent decorative addition of plaques of colored glass is in the worst taste imaginable.

431. LAOS, PAK OU, VILLAGE VAT. This is a very simple type of viharn built on an ancient system of construction. The porch is built into the building and does not project; longitudinal wings have been added on each side, and their roofs are supported by masonry pillars. High wooden columns support the main roof. The four front columns are topped by pierced wooden arches and a carved pediment.

432. LAOS, LUANGPRABANG, VAT ONG THU. The Laotian vat style can be divided into two types of buildings. At Luangprabang, as at Tran Ninh, the walls are low and less important than the saddle roof, the columns are round and larger at the base than at the top. At Vientiane (or Vieng Chan) the roofs rest on high walls and the columns are square and recessed. Here we see a somewhat intermediary type, which nevertheless retains certain characteristics of the northern style. The railings are decorated with Burmese-type serpents and the ridge of the roof is adorned with a small stupa of a similar type. The carved consoles contrast to the simplicity of the walls and window embrasures.

433. LAOS, LUANGPRABANG, VAT MAI SUVANNABU-NARAM. This vat has a very high main roof topped by a secondary saddle roof. It is fronted by a columned porch with a double sloping roof in a direction perpendicular to that of the roofs of the main structure. This greatly ornamented porch (the columns and ceiling are painted with designs in red, gold, and black) is probably a late addition. A likely date for the structure is 1796.

434. LAOS, VIENTIANE, THAT LUONG. This structure is a unique example; walled in by a kind of cloister-gallery, it is topped by a decanter-cork type of bulb whose square base is decorated with lotus leaves. This, in turn, stands on a flattened, truncated pyramid surrounded by 30 spires fenced in by a promenade-gallery, the wall of which is adorned with merlons decorated with small standing Buddhas. The entrance is through a porch at the top of a flight of steps. The needle of this *that* is entirely gilded. Probably erected in 1586, it has been transformed on several occasions since then. It is related to a large monastery in the center of a village which is no longer standing, since it was completely destroyed during the Siamese invasion of 1827.

435. LAOS, VIENTIANE, THAT DAM. This is a typical octagonal decanter-stopper *that* mounted on a high, molded base. The summit is modern and replaces the one seen on the ground, to the right. It is a completely solid brick-and-mortar structure.

436. LAOS, VIENTIANE, BUDDHA OF PHYA VAT. This gigantic 45-foot-high brick-and-mortar Buddha decorated the far end of the three-aisled hall of Phya Vat. It is seated on a pedestal sculpted with friezes depicting mythical animals. Since the building has completely disappeared, a modern wall—an unfortunately abandoned attempt to rebuild the vat—has been built to support the statue, which is in deplorable condition.

437. LAOS, VIENTIANE, VAT THAT KHEO, THE BOT. This is a building in the Vientiane (Vieng Chan) style, probably rather recent in date but constructed in the traditional manner. The masonry porch has a carved gable pediment; the massive brick columns have a square recessed section and false capitals of long leaves; and the ridge of the roof is decorated with a serpent. The courtyard of this vat is cluttered with many small *thats*.

438. LAOS, VIENTIANE, VAT HO PHRA KHEO. This royal vat (larger in size than many other Laotian ones) hardly resembles its original design, for it was extensively destroyed and subsequently rebuilt. Erected on a high foundation, it is surrounded by a veranda with square columns. Originally, the roofs were probably less complex and higher. The overall design shows a decided Siamese influence.

439. LAOS, VIENTIANE, VAT SISAKET, LIBRARY. A typically Burmese structure erected about 1820. It is square in design, with a roof supported by square columns, built on a masonry platform, and having ogival bays. It was entirely rebuilt in 1931 by the Ecole française d'Extrême-Orient. The roof terminates in a small, square *that*.

440. LAOS, VIENTIANE, VAT HO PHRA KHEO, BUDDHA. Represented in a very rare pose (hands crossed), this Buddha is a typical example of Laotian art. Rigid arms and legs; simplification of volume; turned-up lower part of the robe (Sukhothai influence); nails and toes of equal length; beak-like nose; and stylized ears—all characteristic of Laotian Buddhas. Behind the statue is the wall of Vat Ho Phra Kheo bearing modern stucco decorations. Bronze. Height: 4 feet 4 inches. *Vat Ho Phra Kheo Gallery, Vientiane.*

441. LAOS, LUANGPRABANG, THAT OF VAT ARAM. This is a composite structure stemming from the decanter-stopper type of prang and *that*. Several of these monuments are quite high and (especially in south Laos) terminate in a true needle shape. This one is relatively recent.

442. LAOS, PAK OU, LOWER CAVES. At Pak Ou, on the Mekong, facing the mouth of the Nam Ou River, are two caves hewn from the side of the rock, the entrances adorned with wooden porches. For generations peasants of the surrounding area have placed statues of Buddhas here. There are now thousands of them, the majority in gilt wood, representing all the Laotian types—from those commissioned by kings to the humblest peasant's wood carving.

430

429

431

432

433

435   436

437

438

439

440   441

442

5. THE BANGKOK STYLE (Late Eighteenth–Twentieth Century)

After the destruction of Ayuthia, the Siamese established a new capital at Tonburi, on the right bank of the Chao Phraya; several years later, in 1782, they transferred their capital to Khrung Thep, on the opposite bank. This was to be known as the "City of Angels"—the name given by Europeans to one of its villages: Bangkok. The kings of the new city promoted a style which (logically derived from Ayuthian art) was really nothing more than a baroque continuation of the Ayuthia style. Many of the more important monuments were erected by Kings Rama I and II (1786–1851), Mongkut (1851–68), and Chulalongkorn (1868–1910). European influence (structures) and also Chinese (gardens, ornamental sculptures) are also quite evident. All the traditions of Ayuthian art are here developed, enlarged, and overdecorated to the point of paroxysm. The prang is developed to such a degree that it replaces the stupa as a monstrous needle, and is built of reinforced concrete adorned with inset fragments of Chinese porcelain (Vat Arun). The example started in Bangkok was followed throughout the province. At Nagara Sri Dhammaraja, the Sinhalese-type stupa is surmounted by a needle formed of piled plates similar to those which existed at Ayuthia. At Saraburi, the roof of the mondop (mandapa) containing the famous imprint of Buddha's feet, combines the prang styles, the Burmese roof, and the stupa needle. Finally, the telescoped roofs of the palaces are developed on a Greek cross plan, and their ridge crossing was embellished with a mondop roof or a reduced prang.

It is only fair to add that Thailand, like Cambodia, is one of the rare countries which has attempted to adapt its traditional architecture to the requirements of modern techniques. Many official buildings retain a definite charm, and represent a valid attempt to harmonize tradition and progress. It is interesting to note that the present-day architects of Thailand have been quite successful in this venture.

Wall painting developed: the inner walls of the vats were decorated with scenes combining Buddhist religious themes and great princely feats with architectural representation, often with pleasant effect. Sculpture is affected and mannered, lacking in genius, and excessively ornamented with wings, flames, and lace-like motifs of great complexity. Gold predominates. Wooden or bronze Buddhas have the same stiffness, the same insipidity. The wealth of costume, the head-dress topped by a high point, takes precedence over the body and the sense of plastic form. This is a traditional, baroque period.

443. THAILAND, BANGKOK, VAT PHRA KHEO. Also known as the Vat of the Emerald Buddha (or royal temple), this impressive complex of buildings lies within the enceinte of the great royal palace. Built in 1785 and continually repaired and enlarged, it is adorned with chedis of every style, with viharns, bots, mondops, and gigantic cement statues of demons painted in brilliant colors and decorated with glass mosaics. It is all pleasant to see, but overly baroque in taste.

444. THAILAND, BANGKOK, VAT PHRA KHEO, UPOSATHA.

445. THAILAND, BANGKOK, VAT PHRA KHEO, WALL PAINTING. This late-nineteenth-century work represents the royal palace; the lantern-form tower is adorned with Khmer-influenced figures. The Thai never used fresco technique; they painted directly on a previously whitewashed wall surface, which

explains why ancient paintings have not survived: they soon flaked off.

446. THAILAND, BANGKOK, VAT PHRA KHEO, WALL PAINTING. This scene illustrates an episode from *The Ramayana* and shows Rama on his chariot. Late nineteenth century.

447. THAILAND, BANGKOK, VAT MAHA THAT, ROOFS. Late nineteenth century.

448. THAILAND, BANGKOK, VAT BENCHAMABOPIT, VIHARN. Also known as the Temple of Marble, this edifice was erected by King Chulalongkorn (Rama V), on the site of the destroyed Vat Sai Thong. This viharn with its many telescoped roofs, is richly adorned with gold and red, and is one of the most characteristic vats of the Bangkok style. It has many galleries containing numerous types of Buddhas. Late nineteenth century.

415

449. THAILAND, BANGKOK, VAT PO, GARUDA FRIEZE. Built by King Rama I and enlarged by Rama II in 1793, this vat is richly decorated in a very ornate style. The chedi's base shows garudas (which act as false caryatids) crushing nagas. Gilded stucco.

450. THAILAND, NAKHON PATHOM, PHRA PATHOM, CHEDI. Founded in the fifth century by the Dvaravati Mons, it was converted to Brahmanic use by the Khmers, who added a prang. This 393-foot-high chedi was then completely rebuilt in 1860 by King Mongkut and finished by King Chulalongkorn who faced it with beautiful gilt-brown Chinese ceramic tiles.

451. THAILAND, BANGKOK, VAT ARUN RAJVARARAM. This huge brick and cement prang is located at Tonburi, the first site of the capital, on the right bank of the Chao Phraya River. Begun by Rama II in 1792, it was finished in the reign of Rama III. Also known as the Tower of Dawn, the Porcelain Tower, or Vat Cheng, this tower is 269 feet high and towers over the city of Bangkok. The profusion of its ornamentation, composed of fragments of millions of Chinese ceramic vessels and bowls, is disconcerting. It is the most spectacular and baroque work in all Thai art and is a perfect stylistic example of the Bangkok period, a style notable for its excess of detail, which is so overdone that it tends to cancel out any individual features. A new Thai period was about to develop, combining contemporary techniques and a traditional style, resulting in a style adapted to twentieth-century needs while still remaining original.

452. THAILAND, BANGKOK, SUAN PAKKAD GARDENS, HO TRAI LIBRARY. The structure now known as the Lacquer Pavilion stands in the Suan Pakkad Gardens. It was originally located at the Ban Khling Monastery, not far from Ayuthia, where it served as a library which some think was part of the royal palace of Ayuthia. Like all Thai libraries, it is built on piles. In danger of collapse, it was restored by Princess Pantip Chumbhot at her Bangkok residence. Extensive restoration work has re-created the wonderful gold paintings on black lacquer decorating the wooden walls of this pavilion. According to researches carried out by Somask, these paintings date from the early Bangkok period (late eighteenth century).

453. THAILAND, BANGKOK, SUAN PAKKAD GARDENS, HO TRAI LIBRARY, PAINTING. The scene represents rain-drenched fire-worshipers on a ship watching Buddha (below left) floating miraculously in mid-air. With its steady and incisive treatment, this panel reveals a wealth of detail relating to ships and costumes of the period. The rain is treated in broad, sweeping bands, as is the sea, and is curiously stylized. Panel number 2, on the upper row. Gold paint on black lacquer. (*Photographed by the kind permission of H.R.H. Princess Chumbhot*).

454. THAILAND, BANGKOK, SUAN PAKKAD, GARDENS, DECORATED DOOR PANEL. This is the central part of a door entirely decorated with inlaid mother-of-pearl on black lacquer. Height of the figure: about 8 inches. Late nineteenth century. *Collection H.R.H. Princess Chumbhot, Bangkok.*

446

447

453 452

SELECTED BIBLIOGRAPHY

General

AUBOYER, J.	*Arts et styles de l'Inde*, Paris, 1951
————.	*De l'Inde au Cambodge et à Java*, Monaco, 1950
BAREAU, A.	*Les sectes bouddhiques du petit véhicule*, Paris, 1955
BASHAM, A. L.	*The Wonder That Was India*, London, 1954
COEDES, G.	*Les États Hindouisés d'Indochine et d'Indonésie*, Paris, 1948
FOUCHER, A.	*La vie du Bouddha*, Paris, 1949
————.	*Les vies antérieures du Bouddha*, Paris, 1955
FRANCE-ASIE.	*Présence du Bouddhisme*, Tokyo, 1959
FRÉDÉRIC, L.	*The Art of India: Temples and Sculpture*, New York, 1959
GROSLIER, B. P.	*Indochine, carrefour des arts*, Paris, 1960
GROUSSET, R.	*Histoire de l'Asie*, Paris, 1950
LE MAY, R.	*The Culture of South East Asia*, London, 1954
LE THANH KHOI.	*Histoire de l'Asie du Sud-Est*, Paris, n.d.
MARCHAL, H.	*Architecture comparée de l'Inde et de l'Extrême-Orient*, Paris, 1944
PARMENTIER, H.	*L'art architectural hindou dans l'Inde et en Extrême-Orient*, Paris, 1948
RENOU, L. and FILLIOZAT, J.	*L'Inde classique*, Vol. 1, Paris, 1947; Vol. 2, Paris, 1953
SPINKS, C. N.	*Prehistory and Protohistory of Eastern Asia*, n.d.
STERN, P. and BENISTI, M.	*Évolution du style indien d'Amaravati*, Paris, 1955
WALES, H. G. Q.	*The Making of Greater India*, London, 1951
ZIMMER, H.	*The Art of Indian Asia*, New York, 1955

Ceylon

DEVENDRA, D. T.	*Classical Sinhalese Sculpture*, London, 1958
MITTON, G. E.	*The Lost Cities of Ceylon*, London, 1928
MODE, H. A.	*Die Skulptur Ceylons*, Basel, 1942
ROWLAND, B.	*The Art and Architecture of India: Buddhist, Hindu, Jain*, London, Baltimore, 1953
VOGEL, J. P.	*Buddhist Art in India, Ceylon and Java*, Oxford, 1936

The Indianized Kingdoms of the West and the Burmese Kingdoms

DUPONT, P.	*Archéologie Mône de Dvâravatî*, Paris, 1959
HARVEY, G. E.	*History of Burma*, London, 1925
KRAMRISCH, S.	*Pala and Sena Sculpture*, Calcutta, 1929

PHAYRE, A.   *Ancient Monuments in Burma*, Rangoon, 1921
———.   *History of Burma*, London, 1883
SHIN, U, BA.   *Lokahteikpan*, Rangoon, 1962

The Island Kingdoms

BERNET-KEMPERS, A. J.   *Ancient Indonesian Art*, Amsterdam, 1959
COVARRUBIAS, M.   *The Island of Bali*, New York, 1937
DAMAIS, L. C.   *Études balinaises*, Paris, 1960
GALESTIN, T. P.   *Houtbouw op Oost-Javaansche tempelreliëfs*, The Hague, 1936
GROENEVELD, W. P.   *Historical Notes on Indonesia and Malaya Compiled from Chinese Sources*, Djakarta, 1960
IVANOFF, P.   *Indonésie, archipel des dieux*, Paris, 1962
KROM, N. J.   *Inleiding tot de Hindoe-Javaansche kunst*, The Hague, 1920
LOEB, E. M.   *Sumatra: Its History and Peoples*, Vienna, 1935
MUS, P.   *Baraboudour*, Hanoi, Paris, 1935
PLEYTE, C. M.   *Die Buddha-Legende in den Skulpturen des Tempels von Borobudur*, Amsterdam, 1901
SCHNITZER, F. M.   *The Archaeology of Hindu Sumatra*, Leiden, 1937
SHELTEMA, J. F.   *Monumental Java*, London, 1912
SIVARAMURTI, C.   *Le Stoupa du Baraboudour*, Paris, 1961
SOEDARSONO, A.   *Menudju Borobudur*, Jogjakarta, 1953
STUTTERHEIM, W. F.   *Studies in Indonesian Archaeology*, The Hague, 1956
VERNEUIL, M. P.   *L'Art à Java, temples de la période classique*, Paris, 1927
WAGNER, F. A.   *Indonésie, art d'un archipel*, Paris, 1961

The Oriental Kingdoms

THE KHMERS

BOISSELLIER, J.   *La statuaire khmèr et son évolution*, Saigon, 1955
———.   *Tendences de l'art khmèr*, Paris, 1956
BRIGGS, L. P.   *The Ancient Khmer Empire*, Philadelphia, 1951
COEDES, G.   *Pour mieux comprendre Angkor*, Paris, 1947
CORAL-REMUSAT, G. DE.   *L'art khmèr, grandes étapes de son évolution*, Paris, 1939
DUPONT, P.   *La statuaire pré-angkorienne*, Ascona, 1955
FRANCE-ASIE.   *Présence du Cambodge*, Saigon, 1955
GITEAU, M.   *Histoire du Cambodge*, Paris, 1962
GLAIZE, M.   *Les monuments du groupe d'Angkor*, Saigon, 1944
GROSLIER, B. P.   *Angkor, hommes et pierres*, Paris, 1956
LEVY, P.   *Recherches préhistoriques dans la région de Mlu Prei*, Hanoi, 1943
MAJUMDAR, R. C.   *Kambuja desa*, Madras, 1944
MARCHAL, H.   *Angkor*, Paris, 1955
PARMENTIER, H.   *L'art khmèr classique*, Paris, 1939
———.   *L'art khmèr primitif*, Paris, 1927

CHAMPA

CLAEYS, J. Y.   *Introduction à l'étude de l'Annam et du Champa*, Hanoi, 1934
PARMENTIER, H.   *Inventaire descriptif des monuments chams de l'Annam*, Paris, 1909
STERN, P.   *L'art du Champa et son évolution*, Toulouse, 1942

426

FUNAN

MALLERET, L.   *L'archéologie du delta du Mékong*, Paris, 1960
PARMENTIER, H.   *L'art présumé du Fou-Nan*, Paris, 1932

The Thai Kingdoms

THAILAND

BLANCHARD, W.   *Thailand*, New Haven, 1958
BORIBAL, B. L.   *History of Buddhism in Thailand*, Bangkok, 1955
————.   *Thai Images of the Buddha*, Bangkok, n.d.
BOWIE, T. R.   *The Arts of Thailand*, Bloomington, 1960
CHAND, M. C. and
 YIMSIRI, K.   *Thai Monumental Bronzes*, Bangkok, 1956
COEDES, G.   *L'art Siamois de Sukhôdaya*, Paris, 1934
DISKUL, S.   *Ayudhya Art*, Bangkok, 1956
LE MAY, R.   *A Concise History of Buddhist Art in Siam*, Cambridge (England), 1938

LAOS

BOULANGER, P. LE *Histoire du Laos français*, Paris, 1930
COLANI, M.   *Les mégalithes du Haut-Laos*, Paris, 1935
FRANCE-ASIE.   *Présence du royaume Lao*, Saigon, 1956
LAFONT, P. B.   *Aperçus sur le Laos*, Vientiane, 1959
PARMENTIER, H.   *L'art du Laos*, Paris, Hanoi, 1954
SASORITH, K. D.   *Le Laos*, Paris, 1953

GLOSSARY

Name	*Language*	*Definition*
AMALAKA	*Skr.*	Ribbed stone cushion; part of a stupa (*see* stupa)
AMRITA	*Skr.*	Dew of Immortality
ANDA	*Skr.*	Hemispherical dome of a stupa (*see* stupa)
ANGKOR	*Kh.*	From the Sanskrit "nagara," meaning "city." A royal Khmer city (*see* vat *and* thom)
APSARA	*Skr.*	Celestial dancer; represented mainly in Khmer art
AVATAR	*Skr.*	Incarnation of a divinity; either zoomorphic or anthropomorphic
BANTEAY	*Kh.*	From the Sanskrit "pandaya," meaning "citadel." Fortified Khmer temple
BARAY	*Kh.*	Artificial Khmer lake or spillway reservoir
BARONG	*Bal.*	Balinese divinity symbolizing the forces of good. A kind of dragon opposed to the Balinese witch, Rangda (*see* Rangda) Earth
BHUMI	*Skr.*	
BODHISATTVA	*Skr.*	Buddhist divinity who has reached the ultimate state previous to the final liberation of existence (at which point he attains Buddhahood)
BOT	*Th.*	Hall used for the ordination ceremonies of Thai monks (*see* uposatha)
CHAITYA	*Skr.*	Buddhist sanctuary-hall
CHAKRA	*Skr.*	Solar disk or Wheel of Rebirth. One of Vishnu's attributes
CHATTRA	*Skr.*	One of the series of parasols topping a stupa (*see* stupa)
CHEDI	*Th.*	From the Sanskrit "chaitya." A Thai stupa (*see* stupa)
CHINTHE	*Bur.*	Fabulous Burmese lion, similar to its Chinese counterpart
CHORTEN	*Tib.*	A variety of votive stupa found in Tibet (*see* stupa)
CLEC	*Mon*	Typically Burmese decorative arch
DAGOBA	*Pal.*	From the Sanskrit "dhatu-garbha," a reliquary sanctuary. A Sinhalese stupa (*see* stupa)
DEVA	*Skr.*	Male divinity
DEVATA	*Skr.*	Female divinity
DVARAPALA	*Skr.*	Divine or demonic door guardian of a sanctuary
GARBA	*Pal.*	Hemispherical dome of a Sinhalese stupa (*see* stupa)
GARBA-GRIHA	*Skr.*	Inner sanctuary
GARUDA	*Skr.*	Mythical bird, traditionally inimical to serpents, ridden by Vishnu
GOPURA	*Skr.*	Entrance gate to a sanctuary

Name	Language	Definition
GU	*Bur.*	Sacred cave
HTI	*Bur.*	Multiple ironwork crown replacing parasols on the tips of Burmese zedis (*see* zedi)
JATAKA	*Skr.*	Story of Buddha's lives
JAYA	*Skr.*	Victory
KALA	*Skr.*	Mythical demon-headed monster lacking a lower jaw
KINNARA	*Skr.*	Celestial being with a human head and a bird's body. Generally a musician
KINNARI	*Skr.*	Female kinnara
KUDU	*Skr.*	Decorative niche, generally circular or horseshoe shaped
LAT	*Skr.*	Pillar topped by a sculpted symbol
LINGAM	*Skr.*	Phalliform symbol of the god Shiva; often associated with its feminine counterpart, the yoni (*see* yoni)
MAHA	*Skr.*	Great
MAKARA	*Skr.*	Mythical monster with the body of a crocodile and an elephant's head; used as a decorative motif
MANDAPA	*Skr.*	Columned building or entire sanctuary complex
MERU	*Skr.*	Balinese temple with multiple stories meant to symbolize Mount Meru
MERU, MOUNT	*Skr.*	Mythical, multipeaked mountain, the center of the Hindu universe
MONDOP	*Th.*	From the Sanskrit "mandapa." A square Thai edifice with superimposed roofs
MUDRA	*Skr.*	Position of the hands having special Buddhist significance
MUKUTA	*Th.*	Diadem-like headdress with sharp, pointed corners
NAGA	*Skr.*	Seven- (or five-) headed serpent; an underworld divinity. Represented with human heads in Indian art
NAGARI	*Skr.*	Writing of the Sanskrit language
NAKHON	*Th.*	From the Sanskrit "nagara," meaning "city." A Thai city
NANDI	*Skr.*	Bull ridden by Shiva
NAT	*Skr.*	Burmese beneficent nature spirit
NOKOR	*Kh.*	From the Sanskrit "nagara," meaning "city." A Khmer city
PHNOM	*Kh.*	Cambodian hill
PRADAKSHINA	*Skr.*	Circumambulatory rite around a sanctuary
PRAH, PREAH	*Kh.*, *Th.*	Holy, sacred
PRANG	*Th.*	Thai sanctuary-tower derived from the Khmer prasat
PRASAT	*Kh.*	Khmer sanctuary-tower
RAHU	*Skr.*	Demon of eclipses
RAKSASHA	*Skr.*	Guardian demon of a temple
RANGDA	*Bal.*	Balinese witch symbolizing the forces of evil; opposed to Barong (*see* Barong)
RISHI	*Skr.*	Ascetic or hermit
SHAKTI	*Skr.*	Feminine counterpart or passive energy of a god
SI, SRI, SREI	*Th.*, *Skr.*, *Kh.*	Lord, woman
SIKHARA	*Skr.*	Tower surmounting a sanctuary, typical of north India
SINGHA, SIMHA	*Skr.*	Lion
STUPA	*Skr.*	Buddhist commemorative monument
TANTRIC, TANTRISM	*Skr.*	Lamaist form of Mahayana Buddhism having magical tendencies

Name	Language	Definition
TARA	*Skr.*	Buddhist equivalent of a shakti (*see* shakti)
TEPANOM	*Th.*	From the Sanskrit "devata." A Thai divinity represented with crossed hands (*see* devata)
TEVODA	*Kh.*	From the Sanskrit "devata." A Cambodian divinity (*see* devata)
THAT	*Th.*	Thai or Laotian stupa
THOM	*Kh.*	From the Sanskrit "maha." Great, large (*see* maha)
TJANDI	*Jav.*	Javanese sanctuary
UPOSATHA	*Th.*	A Thai ordination hall. Equivalent of bot (*see* bot)
USHINISHA	*Skr.*	Topknot of Buddha's hair
VAHALKADA	*Pal.*	Reliquary chamber in Sinhalese stupas (*see* stupa)
VAHAN	*Skr.*	Animal ridden by a divinity
VARMAN	*Kh.*	Title assumed by Khmer kings meaning "protected by"
VAT	*Th., Kh., Lao.*	Monastery. In Laos, a monks' assembly hall
VIHARA	*Skr.*	Monastery
VIHARN	*Th.*	Monks' assembly hall in Thai vats
WAYANG	*Jav.*	Javanese and Balinese shadow-play puppet
YAKSHA	*Skr.*	Demon
YONI	*Skr.*	Female counterpart of the lingam. A vulva symbol (*see* lingam)
ZEDI	*Bur.*	From the Sanskrit "chaitya." A Burmese stupa (*see* chaitya *and* stupa)

SELECTED INDEX OF SITES, TEMPLES, TRIBES, AND EMPIRES

433